THE ROAD TO CLARITY

CONTEMPORARY ANTHROPOLOGY OF RELIGION
A series published with the Society for the Anthropology of Religion

Robert Hefner, Series Editor
Boston University

Published by Palgrave Macmillan

The Road to Clarity

Seventh-Day Adventism in Madagascar

Eva Keller

palgrave
macmillan

First published in 2005 by
PALGRAVE MACMILLAN™
175 Fifth Avenue, New York, N.Y. 10010 and
Houndmills, Basingstoke, Hampshire, England RG21 6XS
Companies and representatives throughout the world.

PALGRAVE MACMILLAN is the global academic imprint of the Palgrave Macmillan division of St. Martin's Press, LLC and of Palgrave Macmillan Ltd. Macmillan® is a registered trademark in the United States, United Kingdom and other countries. Palgrave is a registered trademark in the European Union and other countries.

ISBN 1–4039–7075–0
ISBN 1–4039–7076–9 (pbk.)

Library of Congress Cataloging-in-Publication Data

Keller, Eva.
    The road to clarity : Seventh-Day Adventism in Madagascar / Eva Keller.
        p. cm.—(Contemporary anthropology of religion)
    Includes bibliographical references (p.) and index.
    ISBN 978-1-4039-7076-3
      1. Seventh Day Adventists—Madagascar. 2. Madagascar—Church history. I. Title. II. Series.

BX6153.4.M34K45 2005
286.7′691—dc22   2005048820

A catalogue record for this book is available from the British Library.

Design by Newgen Imaging Systems (P) Ltd., Chennai, India.

First edition: November 2005

10 9 8 7 6 5 4 3 2 1

Printed in the United States of America.

Transferred to Digital Printing in 2011

In Memory of Bodo

Contents

Note on the Pronunciation of Malagasy Words

The dialect spoken in Maroantsetra and Sahameloka contains numerous velar nasals. Following other studies of coastal populations of Madagascar, among whom this sound is common, I spell it as /ñ/ (pronounced as in English "long"). Written /o/ is pronounced [u], written /ô/ is pronounced [o]. Written /tr/ is pronounced something like [tchr], thus Maroantsetra is pronounced [Maruantsétchr].

Glossary

andafy	any country other than Madagascar
fady	taboo
fahaizana (see *mahay*)	knowledge/power, potency
finoana (see *mino*)	trust in, acceptance of, belief in
fomban-drazana	ancestral custom
havana	kin (both matri- and patrilateral)
lôhôlo	lay leader of Adventist church
mahay (see *fahaizana*)	to know, to be powerful/capable
mazava	clear, light
mianatra	to study, to learn
mino (see *finoana*)	to trust in, to accept, to believe in
mpiara-mivavaka	members of the same church; here used to refer to fellow Seventh-day Adventists
ray aman-dreny	parent, elder, senior person (literally: "father and mother")
tanindrazana	land of the ancestors, home
vazaha	all (especially White) non-Malagasy people

Examples of Teknonyms

Papan' i Beby	Beby's dad
Maman' i Claude	Claude's mum
Maman-dRakoto	Rakoto's mum

Acknowledgments

Any ethnographic study is made possible, above all, by the local people among whom fieldwork is conducted. I wish to thank first of all, therefore, the people of Maroantsetra and Sahameloka, to whom I feel particularly indebted. Those with whom I lived, as well as many others, knew that I was going to write a book about them, and they felt proud that their names would appear in it. Because of this, it would be inappropriate to disguise people's real identities, or change the names of fieldwork locations, as is often done in anthropology for the sake of privacy and, sometimes, protection.

My host family in Maroantsetra, with whom I have been friends since my first visit to Madagascar in 1987, introduced me to Seventh-day Adventism and looked after me, in every sense, from the beginning to the end of my fieldwork. For this I am deeply grateful. Papan' i Beby (Dimilahy Maurice) was my teacher, Maman' i Beby (Rasoamalala Arlette) my most intimate friend, their children Kiki (Dimilahy Crispin Odilon) and Beby (Razafindratelo Beatrice Adorée) my little brother and sister. The four of them feel like family, and I hope they feel the same about me.

In Maroantsetra, I also wish to thank many other people not all of whom I can mention here by name. In particular I would like to thank Pastor Ranala Isaac who was always extremely helpful, as well as his wife Lalao Alexandrine. Maman' i Ominò (Zandry Marie Laure) took me along on many of her church-related activities in and around town, and became a good friend. And so did Mandina Eleonore Laurent who helped me understand conversations that I had recorded.

In Sahameloka I lived with a family whom I had not previously known. In spite of this they welcomed me into their household and let me take part in their daily lives. For their hospitality and generosity, I am deeply grateful to Papan' i Claude (Dahy Justin), Maman' i Claude (Mahefa Claire), Claude (Mahefa Claudien) and Mazavatiana; for their tolerance toward a bizarre intruder, I must also express thanks to the two little boys of the family, Mezaquei and Ezakela.

The father of Maman' i Claude (Mahefa) and her brother Papan' i Emilie (Bemanively) were also very welcoming.

Many members of the village's Adventist congregation have become not only invaluable informants, but also close friends. Among them, Papan' i Fredel (Bemitompo Christoph), Maman' i Fredel (Soazafy Martine), Papan' and Maman' i Vangé (Joseph and Maritine), Maman' and Papan' i Silivie (Feno Terrine and Vintice), Papan' and Maman' i Filiette (Fulgence and Zoralette) and Maman' and Papan' i Relien (Noline and Aumat). Outside of church circles my research also greatly benefited from the help of many people in Sahameloka, in particular Claudine, who was my companion in non-Adventist spaces. The late Jaonarison and Ranto Felix, as well as Ravelonavy and Jao Robert were my teachers of village history.

It was the open-mindedness and open-heartedness of all the people mentioned by name, along with many others, that made the project of learning about Seventh-day Adventism in Madagascar not only possible, but also enjoyable. I feel deeply indebted to them for this.

In Antananarivo, I wish to acknowledge the help of Matthew Hatchwell from the Wildlife Conservation Society as well as Razafiarivony Michel from the University of Antananarivo (Musée d'Art et d'Archéologie). Michel not only organized my research visa and proof-read my Malagasy transcriptions, he was also an anchor in an unfamiliar city. I would also like to acknowledge the cooperation of the Musée d'Art et d'Archéologie and to thank the Seventh-day Adventist headquarters in Antananarivo for providing useful information.

A first version of my research results was presented as a Ph.D. thesis at the London School of Economics (LSE) (2002). At the LSE, many people, both staff and postgraduate peers, have contributed toward the development of the argument as it is presented in this book, in particular Johnny Parry and Fenella Cannell as well as Luke Freeman. I would also like to thank Bob Hefner whose review of an earlier draft of this book included many helpful suggestions, as well as Joel Robbins for a number of useful comments. I also thank Oliver Woolley, who copy edited the manuscript and has helped to remove non-native speaker clumsiness in my writing.

The research on which this book is based was funded by several institutions and individuals in Europe. In Switzerland, I wish to express my gratitude to the Janggen-Pöhn Stiftung in St. Gallen, which provided generous financial aid, and to my friend Christian Suter who lent me money when I needed it. In Britain, my research was supported by the Overseas Research Student Award Scheme, as well as the Department of Social Anthropology at the LSE

(Alfred Gell Memorial Studentship). I also received a grant from the Central Research Fund of the University of London and the Royal Anthropological Institute (Sutasoma Award). I express my thanks to all these institutions and individuals.

I would also like to thank my family (and many friends in different countries) for their support over many years of study and for having faith in my future as an anthropologist.

Together with the people of Maroantsetra and Sahameloka, my greatest debt is to Maurice Bloch, one of my Ph.D. supervisors at the LSE. When I returned from fieldwork, I carried with me ten kilos of handwritten notes. These represented the seedling out of which the present book grew. While I often failed to envisage what might come out of it, Maurice saw its potential from the very beginning, and he helped me to develop the argument over the course of many years. He shared my enthusiasm for the project from the beginning to the end and provided dedicated advice right up until publication. His input has been an invaluable intellectual inspiration. His deep empathy for people, including the Seventh-day Adventists he got to know when he visited me in Maroantsetra, represents, for me, an anthropologist's most important quality.

I would like to express equal thanks to Rita Astuti. She, too, has not only been a dedicated supervisor, she has also provided continual support in ways that went far beyond the call of duty. I have always admired her ability to never lose sight of the real people anthropologists write about. Rita's particular strengths, her careful examination of ethnographic evidence, and her clear thinking free of empty jargon, have greatly contributed to the quality of my argument.

I am deeply grateful to both Maurice Bloch and Rita Astuti. If there is any merit in this book, it is, I feel, at least partly due to the fact that I have had the very best of teachers.

I dedicate this study to the memory of Bodo Raoseta, with whom I discovered Madagascar on my first visit in 1987. Bodo tragically died at the age of 20, a year after I had left.

Foreword

Certain philosophers have argued that a statement is true if, and only if, words correspond to the actual state of the world. Making true propositions, therefore, involves matching words to world. The Malagasy Adventists, to whom Keller introduces us with such warmth, clarity and sympathy, would probably agree with this general idea, except that, for them, the problem is reversed. They first take for granted that certain words, those in the Bible, are true and that it therefore follows, if the Bible is categorically true, and, if truth is a matter of matching world to word, the word can be used as a tool for discovering what the world is like.

After all, the claim that the Bible is categorically true is taken for granted in Madagascar by all those whom the inhabitants of Maroantsetra and Sahameloka are likely to come into contact with, even those who belong to no church at all, but especially by those who everybody recognizes as educated, be they government officials, church dignitaries, or those self-appointed experts from, and of, the outside world, the missionaries. The claim that the Bible is true is, therefore, nothing unusual. What characterizes the Adventists is their determination to take the implications of the truth of the Bible into their own hands, so to speak, by, first of all, choosing a church different from the ones they would automatically slip into.

There is, however, much more to this determination than merely the initial act of picking a particular sect and then accepting its authority. Keller shows us how the Malagasy Adventists are drawn by their religion into participating in a continuous and exciting scientific inquiry about what things are really like. This is ultimately because such searching will be a help in understanding the Bible, which, for them, already contains an account of the truths they will discover through their own efforts. However, because the Bible is difficult to decipher, it can be decoded with the help of empirical means. This is because, for these Adventists, the world is rather like a crib, to be used by an incompetent schoolboy, as a means of understanding a text that he does not yet fully master. Studying the world is thus studying the Bible by other means. For the Malagasy Adventists, religion and science are two sides of the same coin.

In fact, the implications of such an intellectual attitude are radical and they make this book exceptionally important for understanding what is happening on the religious front in countries such as Madagascar and many other parts of the world. These implications should also make us reconsider one of the major theoretical trends in the anthropology of religion during, at least, the last 50 years.

Anthropology, as an academic subject, developed toward the end of the nineteenth century in the wake of enthusiasm from social scientists for the Darwinian view of man. Within this context, featuring the famous debates between Darwinians such as Thomas Huxley and the representatives of various churches, religion and science were understood to be competitors, or alternatives. This led to numerous attempts by various anthropologists, most notably Tylor and Frazer, and also many others, to want to characterize the epistemological differences between science and religion and, usually, to see the latter as the forerunner of the former. This is hardly surprising. Religion, as it was presented in these debates, and beyond, was a matter of very precise assertions about the origin of the world and of species, among many other propositions concerned with the reality of the world. Darwinian science offered competing claims about those very same facts.

The fight between these two incompatible alternatives could have been a struggle to the death but, partly out of cowardice, and, partly because of expediency, most establishment theologians and scientists in many European countries, especially in Britain, tacitly negotiated a kind of unwritten nonaggression pact, only breached by a few ill-bred and awkward characters. After all, once their little quarrel was over, scientists and bishops coming, as they did, from the same social milieu had to sit side by side and sip their port in such institutions as Oxbridge colleges.

This genteel disengagement had radical implications for both science and religion. On the religious side, it led to a gradual redefinition of what religion is. The religious establishment in the main churches gradually soft pedaled, or abandoned, cosmological claims and, instead, claimed as central to religion, elements that were certainly not new, but had previously been the concern of only a few. As a result of such a mood, religion became more Jansenist, it became represented as a matter of the heart, its scriptures and rituals were seen as metaphorical and allusive and as using symbols, whose significance would ultimately always escape vulgar attempts at definition. Religion was a matter of experience and of inner light.

This shift in the claims of religion is intriguingly also manifest in anthropological theory, especially British anthropological theory, which was to dominate the anthropology of religion in much of the twentieth century. By the 1950s, anthropologists were beginning to be grudgingly accepted into the older academic establishment and they were, for the most part, eager to blend in. Most famously, Evans-Pritchard, newly installed in All Souls Oxford, inspired by what was to become an open commitment to Roman Catholicism, thus denounced what he had called the "intellectualist" character of the work of writers such as Tylor and Frazer, largely because they had mistakenly thought religion was a proto-science. Instead, he, and very soon his followers, produced a number of famous studies of African religions. Thus, he presented Nuer religion as about an undefined and indefinable "divine," which could only be intuitively understood by those, who like himself, had been touched by grace and had read a number of fashionable theologians. Lienhardt told us Dinka religion was a matter of inner experience. Turner explained Ndembu symbols as combining emotions and meaning in beautiful, but forever inexhaustible, mysteries.

Thus, as the Christian churches were retreating from specific claims about what the world is like, anthropologists, with very few notable exceptions, such as Horton, were telling us that religion had never been about this kind of propositions. In other words, the Africans had always been, in spirit at least, post-Darwinian genteel Christians.

What makes this book so exciting is that it offers a fundamental and documented challenge to this understanding by the mainstream churches and by anthropologists of what religion involves. The challenge comes directly from the people Keller makes us understand so well through her ethnographic skill. They seem to be saying to the mainstream churches something along the following lines: "When your missionaries came to Madagascar, you told us about things which we had got wrong or did not know, about God and Jesus, where he was born and the exact date when he was born, about how the world was created, about what would happen to us after death, where Egypt was, who was the father of David and so on. Now, however, you don't seem all that sure about any of these things yourselves and you seem to avoid giving us straight answers when we ask. So, as you don't seem to be able to be clear, we will go somewhere else, to a church, the Adventists in this case, who are as clear as you once were. We want to know what is true and what is not. In other words, we want a church like the one that faced Thomas Huxley. Perhaps all these other things about faith and experience and symbols are all very true, but we also want to know (science)."

The skill of the author of this book not only makes us understand the point of view of the people who are saying these things, but also enables us to have a great deal of intellectual sympathy for them. Furthermore, through this ability to make us espouse their standpoint, if only for a moment, she thereby makes us rethink anthropological theories of religion, especially the contemptuous dismissal, by such anthropologists as Evans-Pritchard, of those whom he called the "intellectualists." He told us that those benighted Victorian writers did not understand that religion, from the believers' point of view, was something quite different from science, that these authors were being grossly ethnocentric in projecting the debates of their time onto people who were concerned with something quite other. But what the Malagasy Adventists are saying is that what *they* see as lacking in the mainstream churches is precisely that these are not scientific enough, and that what *they* like about Adventism is that it is a religion that is clear about what it claims the world to be like. Indeed they go further, and this is what makes this book riveting, they don't just want to know science, they want to be like true scientists, that is, to be given tools with which to investigate empirical reality, whatever the problems and the suffering this might involve. The search for the truth about the world is for them what religion is.

Now, of course, there is no reason to think that in this definition of religion they are any more right than were Evans-Pritchard or Tylor. This is because most anthropologists are, by now, resigned to recognizing that trying to construct an essentialist definition of religion is a futile enterprise. At best, the term religion can, in some way, indicate a loose association of phenomena that only have in common the trivial feature of reminding us of what the English word has come to mean at this point in time. However, the Malagasy of this book are surely perfectly justified in telling us that Adventism resembles what the missionaries had once declared was "religion," that this is what they like, and that what they get from it is similar to the kind of thing, which that equally difficult word "science" evokes for English speakers.

As a result, the bizarre *modus vivendi* reached in twentieth century Europe between the scientific and the religious factions of the intellectual middle classes, which was imported into anthropology by Evans-Pritchard, probably so as not to be thought a vulgarian by his college colleagues, is, simply, not one of the concerns of the Malagasy Adventists. They reject the churches that are influenced by it and, in order to understand what they want, we must follow Tylor, Horton and Keller and recognize their intellectualism as central.

Maurice Bloch

Introduction

In recent years, there has been an astonishing outbreak of new forms of Christianity in many parts of the world, in particular in Latin America, Africa, and Oceania. Millions of people have been leaving the mainline churches to join one of the numerous "evangelical," "fundamentalist" or "Pentecostal" groups that are mushrooming-up all over these areas. This book represents an attempt to understand what it is that people find so attractive about these new churches. It is a case study of Seventh-day Adventism researched in an area of Madagascar where the Adventist church has been outstandingly successful. The analysis is based on fieldwork carried out in the small town of Maroantsetra on Madagascar's northeast coast and in the nearby village of Sahameloka.

Papan' i Loricà

In the course of fieldwork, I spent much time accompanying members of the Adventist church in Maroantsetra on proselytizing weekend trips to various villages. Sometimes on these trips we stayed overnight. On one such occasion, we all slept on the floor of an old nursery school. It had been a tiring day, and by nine o'clock everyone seemed to be asleep—except for Papan' i Loricà, a slim man in his early 30s with a handsome, dark face and short black curly hair. Papan' i Loricà's teeth are bad, and many are missing, but this is so normal in this part of the world that nobody considers it unbecoming. He is sitting on the floor, cross-legged and barefoot. His head is bent and his eyes attentively fixed on the Bible, which he holds open in his hands. The Bible does not look new: its cover and edges are dusty and bleached from the sun, and the pages are dog-eared; some of them might even be missing. Papan' i Loricà has used this Bible often and has carried it around with him for a long time. As today is the Sabbath—the Seventh-day Adventists' holy day—Papan' i Loricà is dressed not in his very best (not his black suit that he reserves for special occasions such as an important church meeting in town), but in his "almost best" clothes. He is wearing his long emerald-green trousers (always neatly ironed) in which I have seen him so many times before and a faded white short-sleeved shirt, which he must have bought at one of the many stalls in town that sell European second-hand clothes. His outfit is appropriate for a Sabbath in the countryside. On his left, on the floor, there is a candle, one of those ordinary white candles the Malagasy use in the evening to light up their homes. The candlelight is only just strong enough to allow Papan' i Loricà to see the letters in front of him. Papan' i Loricà is not a very educated man. Growing up in the village of Ambodiadabo, where we are now, he completed five years at the local primary school and, unlike most other village children, went on to attend a secondary school in town. He never finished secondary school, however. Although primary schooling is compulsory in Madagascar, teachers are often absent during school terms, sometimes for weeks or even months on end, often because they are busy working the rice fields. When teachers are there, class instruction consists mainly of teachers writing words on the blackboard and pupils copying them. Some children are unable to even write their own names when they come to the end of their education. Papan' i Loricà sits there and reads his Bible. I do not know which chapter he is reading, but I can see that he is struggling with the task of getting meaning out of the letters in front of him; his index finger follows the lines and sometimes he mumbles to himself. Some parts of the text he has chosen, however, he seems to read with ease. I have heard him read from the Bible before. Much of the time, his reading is slow and cumbersome, then suddenly he reads fluently, and then again he stumbles over an expression. Generally he reads hesitantly and from time to time, he comes across a word he has to spell out like a primary school child. Papan' i Loricà sits there on a raffia mat among 20 sleeping people. The old nursery school is a wooden construction, one room of ten by ten meters perhaps, with a door opening, but no door. As with all buildings in this rainy environment, the wooden floor is slightly raised from the ground; the roof is made of old corrugated iron sheets that leak in various places. Almost the entire floor space is taken up by sleeping people. Mat to mat, with hardly a couple of inches between them, men and women, adults and teenagers, sleep, all fully dressed in their day clothes. The nights get chilly at this time of year, so everyone has brought a sheet or a blanket— both quite valuable items—to cover themselves with during the night. Or else they use a *lambahoany*—a piece of cloth displaying some kind of attractive scene and always bearing a Malagasy saying or proverb, which people often wear wrapped around their hips in order to protect their better clothes underneath. Some of us have brought a raffia mat to lie on the wooden floor as well, but most of these were provided by people from the village as were a couple of plastic buckets for us to store water to cook, drink and wash. A mat and a blanket is all Malagasy people need to sleep when they have a roof over their heads. Some of the people in the room have wrapped their blanket around their head, while some have entirely disappeared beneath them. The only sounds to be heard are the occasional dog barking in the night and some snoring; otherwise it is silent. Papan' i Loricà sits on the edge of the sleeping crowd, his candle carefully placed so as not to be too near other people's heads. To his right, on the floor, lie a biro and a cheap, thin notebook of the type children use in school: grey squared paper with a space provided on the cover to write one's name and the subject under study. Papan' i Loricà sits silently, his head bent in concentration. From time to time, he picks up the biro and notebook and writes down something, probably a verse he finds particularly noteworthy or its biblical reference, so that he can find it again later on and study it more fully. Before Papan' i Loricà became an Adventist eight years ago, he was an active member of the Protestant church. Looking back on that time—he told me another day—there were many things he had heard in church that he had not understood and that nobody, not even the Protestant pastor, could explain to him. Now, when he is at home, he often studies the Bible until late at night, long after his wife and two children have gone to bed. Tonight, he continues to study and to take notes for three-and-a-half hours, until half past midnight when he finally blows out his candle and lies down to sleep. He will get up again at six o'clock the following morning.

The nursery school where we all sleep is in the middle of a village of palm-thatched single-room houses. It is a narrow, but stretched-out village with a central path dividing it into two halves. Rice fields extend from the edge of the village to the beginning of the dense tropical forest. Most villages in this area of Madagascar are very difficult to reach because, except for those in the immediate vicinity of the district capital Maroantsetra, there are no roads, but only footpaths and rivers, linking the countryside to the town. Given the high amount of rainfall there is here, walking along these footpaths is often very difficult. One not only continuously sinks into deep mud, one also has to cross endless rice fields, streams and thigh deep ponds. The village of Ambodiadabo, where we sleep tonight, is, however, easily accessible. Most of the way to the village one can travel along a paved road, the only one in the district of Maroantsetra, linking the town center with the small domestic airport. So, off we had gone in the morning on our proselytizing trip to the countryside, in high spirits, all of us packed tightly into the back of a four-wheel drive. When the paved road came to an end, we continued on foot for an hour or so after which time we arrived at a big river. We were carried across to our destination in a dug-out canoe. This was the third Saturday in succession that an Adventist troupe had come to Ambodiadabo. We had entered the village all singing and clapping, parading triumphantly along the central path, and inviting people to join us. Then, following Malagasy custom, we proceeded to present ourselves to the village president, asking permission to conduct the Sabbath and to spend the night in his village. This we were granted. However, unlike the previous Saturdays, we were not put up in the school, but in the old nursery. There had apparently been complaints from people unsympathetic to proselytizing endeavors of this sort about the Adventists using the school.

This is the village where Papan' i Loricà grew up and where his parents still live. Although he now lives with his own family at the edge of Maroantsetra town, where he has a job, he comes here very regularly, often daily, in order to help his parents work the rice fields. He is the only child of his mother; his father has one other son. Papan' i Loricà and his wife are the only Seventh-day Adventists among their kin. Today, he was in his village, but he spent the whole day proselytizing and conducting the Adventist Sabbath in public so that the villagers could see what it was all about. After sunset, the end of the Sabbath, Papan' i Loricà ate with us, and, like everyone else, he prepared his mat and blanket on the floor of the old nursery school where perhaps he had once been taught as a child. But, unlike everyone else, he did not go to sleep at nine o'clock, but spent three-and-a-half hours, until after midnight, sitting cross-legged on his sleeping mat, the Bible opened up in front of him, his head bent in concentration, notebook and pen ready, reading and studying, by candlelight.

Beyond Conversion

My goal in this book is to understand what motivates someone like Papan' i Loricà to devote so much of his time to Seventh-day Adventist religious practice, and to get an idea of what it is exactly that he gets out of it. What do he, and others, see in this religion? What do they find attractive about Adventist religious activity? What is the subjective value of the Adventist religion for those who are engaged in it?

A person's motivation to be involved in a particular religious movement is never a static feature in their lives, but inevitably changes over the course of time. Maman' and Papan' i Claude of my host family in the village of Sahameloka, for example, were very clear that they originally joined the Adventist church because Claude, their eldest son, recovered from severe illness immediately after they had, for the first time, attended a Seventh-day Adventist church service. They had done so on someone else's advice—after having consulted the ancestors and having done everything else they could think of—as a final attempt to save Claude's life. And it had worked. However, living with the family nine years later, it would have been extremely misleading to explain their continuing involvement with Adventism by simply pointing to Claude's recovery, even though the family has obviously not forgotten about it. The conversion story of Maman' i Ominò, involving her joining and leaving several Christian denominations in succession prior to becoming an Adventist, seems largely guided by chance. One time, for example, she simply mistook one church for another, which is how she came to spend three months with a Pentecostal church she had never had any intention of joining. Eventually, Maman' i Ominò tried out the Seventh-day Adventist church. She could not tell me what exactly, at first, had made her remain in this church rather than move on to the next, except that she thought that the choir sounded beautiful and that she had always loved to sing. But when I met her, 15 years after her initial conversion, she was one of the most committed and active members of the church in Maroantsetra, and her involvement clearly went way beyond singing in the choir that, it has to be acknowledged, still sounded beautiful. Papan' i Fredel from Sahameloka had been an alcoholic before joining the Adventist church. He had slowly, but steadily, drunk his family into ruin and had repeatedly beaten his wife under the influence of alcohol. After conversion to Seventh-day Adventism, he was able to master his alcoholism. However, when I came to know Papan' i Fredel several years later, his problem with alcohol had become a distant memory, and what he had discovered in Seventh-day Adventism in the meantime was something quite different. What I am most of all concerned with in this book is to understand what that "something quite different" is, what Maman' i Ominò discovered besides the choir, what the nature of Maman' and Papan' i Claude's commitment was, years after Claude's recovery.

The simple fact of the changing nature of people's commitment to a religious movement seems to be an entirely obvious point. Yet it has tended to be neglected in the social-scientific literature on Christianity, with studies focusing primarily on the question of successful or failed conversion among different peoples at different times (cf. Wood 1993). At the risk of over-simplification, these studies can be roughly grouped, as many other analysts have done (see, e.g., Hefner 1993a: 20–25,

1993b: 118–122; Robbins 2004: 84–87), into two basic approaches: the "utilitarian" approach, which emphasizes the expectation of worldly advantages through conversion, and the "intellectualist" approach, which emphasizes converts' search for meaning in a changing world.[1] Although they are clearly different in their basic claims—one emphasizing pragmatic, the other existential aspirations—the principal goal of both these approaches is to understand why people come to *convert*, or not, as the case may be (see Barker (ed.) 1990, Hefner (ed.) 1993). It has long been recognized that conversion is the product of a process, which can last a long time, rather than a single event (e.g., Rambo 1993). It has also been demonstrated that conversion may present people with unanticipated social entailments that, in turn, influence their perception of the new religion. Several authors have also pointed out the need to differentiate between unfolding meanings of conversion on the level of the individual.[2] However, with the exception of Robbins (2004; see also Hefner 1993b), the observation that the motives of converts in joining a particular religion may be very different from what makes them remain committed to it, has not been made the focal point of analysis and has not been given the theoretical import it deserves.

The focus on motives for *conversion* is particularly evident in studies of what, following Gifford (1994), I will call New Churches.[3] New Churches are not necessarily new in the sense of not having existed before; the Seventh-day Adventists, for example, have been present in many African countries since the beginning of the last century. What is new about them is their tremendous popularity among various sections of society, a popularity so great that they have become a serious challenge and threat to the mainline, or historical, churches. Among these New Churches figure prominently Pentecostal groups, and various types of churches usually labeled "evangelical" or "fundamentalist." The Seventh-day Adventist is a typical example of such a New Church.

The last decade of the twentieth century has seen not only the worldwide mushrooming of New Churches, but also a boom of studies about them.[4] Because the interest in such churches seems to have been mainly triggered by their enormous numerical success, a great majority of studies have approached New Churches with the aim of establishing the reasons that cause so many people to convert. This focus on the causes of conversion is accompanied by the assumption that the people who convert are motivated to do so by an expectation, or at least a hope, that their lives will, in some way or another, improve as a result of conversion to one of the New Churches. The converts' hope of improving their lives, in turn, makes it key for researchers to ask in what ways people perceive their present situation to be less than satisfactory. The answers to this question very often highlight converts' hope to facilitate some kind of upward social or economic mobility through conversion to a New Church. Or else they emphasize the fact that such churches offer orientation and integration during turbulent times, a new anchor of identity allowing people at the margins of modernity to relocate themselves at a time of rapid social change. Thus emerges a focus in many studies on New Churches on converts' discontent with their circumstances prior to, or at the moment of, conversion, and the hopes and expectations attached to the new religion.

In contrast, this study is not an attempt to establish why certain people in Maroantsetra and Sahameloka, where I conducted field work, convert to Seventh-day Adventism at a particular time in their life, or to identify the particular circumstances that may make people susceptible to conversion to the New Churches. Rather, it is an attempt to understand what being a practicing Seventh-day Adventist *comes to mean* to people once they have joined the church, to understand what people *come to see* in the religion that they have embraced as time goes on. I suggest that we pay as much attention to the process of religious commitment as to the events or circumstances that culminate in conversion, because, when trying to fully understand the attraction of a particular religion, it seems problematic to privilege people's motives for initially converting. Indeed, I see conversion as merely the beginning of a long story, and not even necessarily the most interesting part of that story. What I want to do in this book, therefore, is to look at how the story continues, and to find out what Seventh-day Adventism means to practitioners in Maroantsetra and Sahameloka years after they have joined the church, whatever the reason for their original conversion. In this sense, this is not a study of religious conversion, but of the nature of long-term religious commitment.

As such, it is one of very few. The most important of these few is Joel Robbins's recent, beautifully written ethnography about the Urapmin in Papua New Guinea, who have all converted to a Charismatic form of Baptist Christianity (Robbins 2004). Robbins's overall analysis of Urapmin Christianity is based on the recognition of the need to distinguish between the reasons for initial conversion and subsequent religious commitment. In order to make this distinction, he develops a new model of conversion, whose aim it is to synthesize the utilitarian and the intellectualist approaches. According to Robbins's "two-stage model of conversion" (p. 87), people initially convert to a religion, one that is new to them, because by doing so they hope to access something they consider valuable, something that they presently lack or have lost. Utilitarian explanations (understood in a broad, not merely materialistic, sense) are thus best suited to explain the first stage of conversion. But then as time goes on, and the second stage of conversion comes into play, the new religion becomes convincing on its own terms, so that people adopt it as their new framework for thinking about and making sense of their lives.[5]

Ordinary Church Members

If one is primarily interested in establishing the causes of conversion, as most analysts of New Churches are, and if conversion is motivated by converts' hopes of improving their present situation in life, one will have to ask why people think that membership of church X will facilitate such an improvement, or why they expect church Y to fulfill their hopes. In order to understand this, one has to ask oneself what it is that is *promised* to potential converts, with this, in turn, shifting one's attention to religious leaders and the doctrine they promote. Analyzing religious leaders' rhetoric not only involves looking at *what* leaders promise, but also *to whom* they make their promises. This promotes a notable tendency in the anthropological and other social science literature on New Churches to focus on leaders and their public rhetoric, and on defining the profile of those who might be particularly susceptible to listening to them.[6] It seems, however, that this tends to happen at the expense of ethnographic inquiry among the ordinary members of such New Churches, who, in many studies, remain strangely in the shadows, and whose experience as engaged practitioners of particular religions we know rather little about.[7]

The focus of this study is a different one. Neither am I much concerned with official Seventh-day Adventist doctrine, nor with how leaders recruit particular types of followers. Rather, I am interested in the nature of the religious commitment of the ordinary members of the Adventist church in Maroantsetra and Sahameloka in the context of their everyday lives.

*   *   *

The argument I am presenting in this book is based on a detailed analysis of two Seventh-day Adventist congregations in the area of Maroantsetra, which is located on the northeast coast of Madagascar. Fieldwork was conducted between September 1998 and May 2000. I also returned for a short visit in 2004. During the first 14 months of fieldwork, I lived with a Seventh-day Adventist family in Maroantsetra town. I already knew this family from a previous visit to Madagascar in 1987, and I had kept in touch with them ever since. Partly because they had no room to put me up in their rather "unweatherproof" house, I rented a small Malagasy "bungalow" (a one-room palm-thatched hut) in their neighborhood to sleep in and to write notes. However, I always ate and spent most of the day and every evening with them. It was, in fact, our long-term acquaintance and friendship that made me choose this particular area of Madagascar as my field-site, and that made me study Seventh-day Adventism, a religion I had previously not had any contact with and about which I knew absolutely nothing. As will undoubtedly become clear in the course of the book, I owe a great deal of the insight I was able to gain into Seventh-day Adventism to my host family, and in particular to Papan' i Beby, who was my first and, in a sense, my most important teacher during the time I lived with him and his family. During the last six months of fieldwork I lived for the most part in the village of Sahameloka, which is located some 25 km upriver to the north of Maroantsetra, and which can be reached only on foot or by canoe. In Sahameloka I lived in the household of another Seventh-day Adventist family, unrelated to the one in town. I did not know these people before arriving in the village, but they had often seen me at district meetings of the Adventist church in Maroantsetra and knew exactly who I was before we ever met properly. Apart from sharing my host families' daily lives as rice farmers and town dwellers respectively, I participated in all their religious activities both at home and in church. Both families, and everyone else with whom I had contact, knew that I was not an Adventist myself and that I had not come to be converted, but rather to study Adventism. People tended to like this, because they assumed that what they had to say to the rest of the world would become more widespread by my writing a book about them. Although I remain a non-Adventist, living in Maroantsetra and Sahameloka has given me much respect for people one might too quickly, and rather ignorantly, write off as narrow-minded fundamentalists. I sincerely hope that this book will contribute to a more subtle understanding of what so many people around the world love about Seventh-day Adventism, and, perhaps, other "fundamentalist" churches.

For obvious reasons, there is a clear difference between the level of ethnographic detail a single researcher is able to gather with respect to a town and a village, even if the town in question, as is the case with Maroantsetra, is a small, semi-rural place. However, it should be borne in mind that this book is not an ethnography of either Maroantsetra or Sahameloka, but a study of the Seventh-day Adventist communities in both places.

The Seventh-day Adventists, at least in this area of Madagascar, do not live in isolation from the rest of society (a topic that I will discuss fully in part 3 of this book). Because of this and because of the need to contextualize Adventist practice, I also spent a considerable amount of time with local people who had nothing to do with the Adventist church. Moving in and out of the Seventh-day Adventist community, though not entirely unproblematic, proved to be much less difficult than I had anticipated.

*   *   *

Only very few studies concerning New Churches are based on the kind of long-term participant observation among ordinary church members that I conducted in Maroantsetra and Sahameloka. The most important of these is Joel Robbins's rich and sensitive ethnography of Urapmin Baptist Christianity, which resulted from his long-term fieldwork among the Urapmin people of Papua New Guinea, and to which I have already referred (2004, also 2001a, b, c). Another study, which must be mentioned because of its author's exceptional closeness to the ordinary members of the churches discussed, is Birgit Meyer's outstanding analysis of Pentecostalism among the Ewe of Ghana (1999); I will come back to her work in chapter 9.[8] Simpson's recent monograph about a Catholic mission school in Zambia (2003, also 1998)—where the majority of the students are, in fact, not Catholics, but belong to various New Churches, including the Seventh-day Adventist church—is based on his own long career as a teacher at the school as well as on participant observation among the students. However, the analysis hardly moves beyond an account of "fundamentalist" doctrine and rhetoric.[9]

In most studies of New Churches, then, the concerns of the authors are quite different to mine. Ordinary church members can seem distant and, indeed, often absent from these analyses, so much so that one gets little sense of what these church members' daily experience as religious practitioners is, or what they themselves value about their involvement in a particular church. The present study is a contribution to an anthropology of Christianity, whose aim it is to fill this gap.

It might be a banal observation for those familiar with anthropology, but I think it is still worth noting that if one wants to understand what motivates a man like Papan' i Loricà to stay up until after midnight reading the Bible, while everyone around him is asleep after a tiring day of religious activity, if one wants to understand the ordinary church members' experience as religious practitioners, one has to actually live among them. Because it is only when one shares people's daily lives over a long period of time that one chances to witness situations such as the one described at the start of this introduction. Indeed, it was only because I was still present *after* the formal end of the Sabbath that day that I saw Papan' i Loricà reading the Bible and taking notes by himself in the semi-darkness. Studies of Christianity cannot limit themselves to analyses of what happens during church services and of people's conversion stories, however valuable these clearly are. They must also involve observing in what ways religious practice and religious thought are part of, and shape, or do not shape, the day-to-day life of people who live in neighborhoods and villages and who are embedded in networks of kin and friends. They must look at how religious practice and religious thought affect children and teenagers who go to school with peers who may or may not belong to the same church, or who perhaps belong to no church at all.

To say that we need to bring the ordinary members of New Churches closer to our analyses, is not simply to advocate a kind of ethnography that considers its primary, or even only, task "to give people a voice" and "to let them speak for themselves," a kind of ethnography that would amount to little more than long citations of informants' statements. In what follows, I attempt to go beyond the explicit and beyond mere observations of what people do, while nonetheless offering interpretations that the members of the Adventist church in Maroantsetra and Sahameloka could relate to and would recognize as meaningful.

Outline of Book

To sum up: this book is an attempt to understand the nature of the religious commitment beyond initial conversion of ordinary members of the Seventh-day Adventist church in Madagascar, and to understand the role and meaning of religious activity in the context of their everyday lives. It consists of three parts.

Part I introduces the reader to the region in which this study is located and provides background information on Christianity and Seventh-day Adventism in Madagascar as well as in the local context. It also discusses how the local church is organized.

Part II is dedicated to describing and analyzing the nature of people's commitment to the Adventist church. This part looks very closely at daily religious practice both in- and outside of church services, in order to establish the subjective value Adventism holds for its adherents in Maroantsetra and Sahameloka. This part of the book examines how, through daily religious practice, people come to see the world through Adventist spectacles, and how through these spectacles, the world looks amazingly clear. Both the road to, and the nature of, the clarity the Adventist vision provides are discussed in detail.

The members of the local Adventist church are, however, not only committed church members, they are also sons and daughters, parents and grandchildren, and they live in a wider world that is not governed by Adventist principles. Part III draws attention to the difficulties this situation creates both for the members of the church and for their kin who, for the most part, are not Adventists themselves. As a result of the fact that the local Adventists simultaneously live in two worlds, they find themselves confronted with considerable uncertainties as to how to lead their lives. The final part of this book discusses these uncertainties and what it means to be a Malagasy person and to be a committed Seventh-day Adventist at the same time.

Part I

The Setting

Chapter 1

People in Search of a Living

This chapter serves two purposes. First, it introduces the places where the two Adventist congregations, with which this study is concerned, are located: the town of Maroantsetra, which is the center of a remote district in Madagascar, and Sahameloka, a village located some 25 km upriver to the north of the town, which can only be reached on foot or by canoe. Second, it gives a sense of the social context in which the members of the Adventist church live, which is important because, as I mentioned in the introduction, church members do not live in isolation from the rest of society, but are for much of everyday life firmly embedded in it.

Let me start by briefly sketching out the history of the region, a history that is involved to a significant extent with slavery. Indeed, the issue of slave descent will come up at various points in the book and will be relevant in my analysis of the appeal of Seventh-day Adventism.

Maroantsetra: People on the Move

The District of Maroantsetra: Historical Outline

In contrast to some of the populations living in other parts of Madagascar, the Betsimisaraka—the people living along much of the east coast including the area of Maroantsetra—never had a centralized political organization. Rather, the precolonial history of the region is characterized by the existence of many independent "chiefdoms," which were in continuous dispute with one another over the control of the coast and, in particular, its ports (Cole 2001: 36–40; Larson, P. M. 2000a: 141–144[1]). Only at the beginning of the eighteenth century did a "Betsimisaraka Confederation" emerge.[2] This was a short-lived polity which, with the death of its leader, fell apart just 40 years after its creation. In any case, the Betsimisaraka Confederation never included all those who now understand themselves to be Betsimisaraka, and who are generally referred to as such. Rather, it represented a federation between some of the groups within today's Betsimisaraka region who united against other groups from within that same region. The extension of the name Betsimisaraka to its present usage emerged in the nineteenth and twentieth centuries under the influence of outside rule.

The area of Maroantsetra lies within today's Betsimisaraka region, on the island's northeast coast. It is located at the mouth of Madagascar's largest and best natural harbor: Antongil Bay. Because of where it is sited, the region has been at the crossroads of people's movements across the Indian Ocean for centuries, and its history is, therefore, comparatively well documented.

The earliest prolonged contacts with European traders are recorded as taking place during the first half of the seventeenth century, when the Dutch entered into an agreement with the local "king," giving them the monopoly over trade in slaves and goods in the area in return for the "protection" from other outside forces.[3] Antongil Bay continued to be a point of anchorage for cross-continental slave traders until the nineteenth century.[4] Local chiefs, however, did not just sell Malagasy slaves to foreign traders. The people of the east coast are also reported to have gone on regular slave capturing raids to the Comoro islands situated to the northwest of Madagascar as well as the east African coast in the late eighteenth and early nineteenth century.[5]

There is not only a long history of the involvement of different Malagasy groups in the cross-continental slave trade, as slaves as well as slave traders,[6] however, but also of *internal* systems of slavery in many parts of Madagascar (Ellis, W. 1848: 144). Nevertheless, it is important to note that the nature of what has been called "slavery" in Madagascar at different times and in different Malagasy societies is very heterogeneous; the loss of one's freedom could imply very different degrees of hardship as well as a variety of types of non-free status.[7]

Internal slavery also played a significant role in the region of Maroantsetra. Sometime between 1700 and 1730, a group from western Madagascar, called the Zafindrabay,[8] conquered the present district of Maroantsetra, taking control of it for the next 100 years.[9] The legacy of Zafindrabay rule remains important to this day and I therefore recount what is known about this aspect of the region's history in some detail. Within a relatively short time, the Zafindrabay established their rule in both of the region's major valleys with a center of power positioned at the entrance to each one. They demanded tributes from the more powerful local ancestries they encountered, while they simply enslaved the weaker ones. Some people chose the option of flight into the thick forest (cf. Vérin 1986: 115, citing Froberville 1845: 122). Zafindrabay rule still constitutes a powerful memory for the local population. People in the area, both young and old, "remember" them for their cruelty, alleging that they fed their slaves to crocodiles regularly on ritual occasions.[10] Local memory of Zafindrabay rule might be particularly focused on its cruel nature, but this memory is not untypical of people's general perception of their own history. For many local people, their history consists of a string of highly unpleasant experiences with outside rulers. After the Zafindrabay came the Merina.[11]

During the first two decades of the nineteenth century, the Merina of the Malagasy highlands conquered approximately two-thirds of Madagascar including the area around Maroantsetra. With the arrival of the conquering Merina in the early 1820s, the Zafindrabay lost their status as rulers, 100 years after they had arrived in the region. This does not seem, however, to have initiated significant change for the bulk of the local population as the Merina used existing power structures and collaborated with the Zafindrabay in ruling the rest of the population. The social stratification thus remained essentially the same.[12]

In 1896, Madagascar became a French colony and the same year, a colonial residence was established in Maroantsetra town.[13] However, both the Zafindrabay and the Merina remained powerful local actors during colonial rule. Slavery had been officially abolished by the French, but, as during Merina rule over much of the nineteenth century, the Zafindrabay were once again privileged by being integrated into the new administrative system (compare Cole 2001: 45). The colonial report of 1901 notes that a man of Zafindrabay descent had been entrusted with "des fonctions de gouverneur." The French not only respected the Zafindrabay's property, but also, according to local oral history, registered them as the legal owners of the land they had previously taken from local ancestries. Hence the freed slaves remained as landless and poor as they had been before manumission, and many ex-slaves continued to work as sharecroppers for their old owners (Petit 1967: 37). This was not, however, the fate of all the ex-slaves. Many of them left to clear forest for cultivation and founded their own villages, in particular along the middle and upper parts of the Andranofotsy River. Sahameloka is one such village. The first three decades of the twentieth century were characterized by activities of ex-slaves or descendants of slaves to open up new land. However, the only land they could make their own was the land that the Zafindrabay had not yet claimed, and this was basically the land that was poor or difficult to cultivate. Up to the present day, the descendants of the Zafindrabay are said to have the best land in the area and they continue to occupy many of the most important positions in Maroantsetra town.

One of the main aims of the French administration in Madagascar was to break the power of the Merina. In order to achieve this, the Merina were to be removed from their positions of power around the country (Ellis, S. 1985: 112–114). However, in the Maroantsetra region, as elsewhere in Madagascar, this very quickly proved to be completely impractical, because "among the Betsimisaraka, French officials found it almost impossible to find competent, literate officials" (Ellis, S. 1985: 144). Complaints of this sort are frequent in the colonial reports concerning Maroantsetra during the first decade of the French occupation. In 1908, the local administrator asked the central government to send Merina officials to Maroantsetra, thought to be "un peu plus énergique et de mentalité supérieure à celle des betsimisaraka." This request was agreed to, and already by 1913, most indigenous officials were Merina from the highlands. Little changed with regard to local power structures in the next few decades.

As elsewhere in Madagascar, the French imposed many kinds of taxes on the local population right from the very beginning of colonial rule. These taxes included, among others: a poll tax, a cattle tax, a tax for brewing local beer and a tax for selling one's produce at the local market. In 1915, even a tax for owning a dog was introduced in Maroantsetra! Obviously, most local people could not afford to pay all these taxes. But the failure to pay any of them was interpreted as an offence against the colonial laws and offenders were fined an amount of money too high, once again, for ordinary people to pay. Being unable to pay, they were imprisoned and had to earn back their freedom by laboring for one or two weeks on one of various kinds of public works introduced by the French, in particular road building. The same vicious circle was at work with regard to other offences such as drunkenness or the failure to register with the administration in order to be issued a kind of identity card. The need to have such a *livret*, and the punishments not having one entailed, remain among the liveliest memories of colonial rule for the district's older generation. It is not surprising that under these circumstances, vast numbers of people fled to the nearby forest in order to avoid taxation and to escape possibly worse things to come. The colonial reports make no secret out of the fact that between 1902 and 1906, many villages and rice fields were deserted.

On top of extracting unpaid labor from people by way of introducing impossibly high taxes on everything, the colonial administration imposed *corvée* labor—euphemistically termed "regular services" (*prestations régulières*)—in the district of Maroantsetra from 1908 onward. At first, this was four days per year for each person, but this figure had doubled by 1913 and is likely to have increased even further over the course of the following years. Fines paid off through labor and *corvée* together are likely to have used up a significant amount of people's time and energy. Indeed, the effects of taxation and *corvée* are reported to have been backbreaking in all the regions where the French were exerting their power (Cole 2001: 164; Ellis, S. 1985: 134).

The Malagasy uprising against French colonial rule in 1947 did not break out in the area, although one of its leaders, Jacques Rabemananjara, originated from a village very close to Maroantsetra.[14] Rabemananjara came to Maroantsetra just one month prior to the outbreak of the insurrection, on a tour around the district giving speeches that caused much concern to the administration. Any nascent flames of rebellion were, however, immediately extinguished by the administration "incarcérant les individus les plus dangereux," 153 in number.

Since independence in 1960, the district of Maroantsetra has become one of many remote areas of Madagascar that have essentially been forgotten by the central administration. Roads that were perfectly passable during colonial times, are now a nightmare to travel on. Bridges are often on the edge of collapse. State-run schools are underequipped and understaffed. Like many other areas of the country, Maroantsetra suffered the effects of former president Ratsiraka's mismanagement of public resources, and the alienation of these resources for his private benefit, a state of affairs sadly typical of many postcolonial Third World countries.

But let me now turn to a description of Maroantsetra town as it is now, because this is the place where the local Seventh-day Adventists live their daily lives, not only as members of the Adventist church, but also as members of local kin groups and neighborhoods.

Maroantsetra Town

The district of Maroantsetra is largely made up of, and surrounded by, thick tropical forest. This has led to a significant degree of isolation in terms of access and transport, an isolation that represents the district's main problem, hindering its economic development. The relative inaccessibility of the region has been the concern of precolonial agents investigating the possibilities for exploiting the area's natural resources, French colonial administrators and subsequent Malagasy governments alike.[15] Northward, eastward and westward from town one can only travel either on foot or by canoe. A very poor road, only passable in a four-wheel drive during the so-called dry season between October and April—which, in fact, is not dry at all—links Maroantsetra with Toamasina (Tamatave in French), Madagascar's second largest town and international port, to the south. The "dry" season is sometimes jokingly referred to as *la saison des pluies* (the season of the rains) as opposed to *la saison pluvieuse* (the rainy season). This is because both seasons are in fact wet, the only difference being that during "the season of the rains" the water comes down in sudden tropical rainstorms and the days and nights are hot, while in "the rainy season" it drizzles all day long and is often unpleasantly cold, with blankets and clothing remaining damp all day long (the area receives an average of 4 m annual rainfall). But even in the "dry" (hot) season, the journey along the "Route Nationale no. 5," linking Maroantsetra and Toamasina, is extremely bumpy and strenuous, and it takes at least three days to travel the 400 kms. Matters are not helped by the fact that the coast is crisscrossed by over a hundred small rivers between Maroantsetra and Toamasina, and by the fact that on the journey one is likely to find several bridges half-collapsed. There is a small airport just outside Maroantsetra town with almost daily domestic flights, but this method of travel is beyond the economic means of the great majority of the population. The most important means to transport goods is by sea, but as a means for personal travel, boat trips to and from Toamasina are infrequent and expensive and not regarded as particularly safe. So most travelers patiently bump along the "Route Nationale no. 5," or simply walk.

In 1997, the population of Maroantsetra, including adjacent villages, arrived at about 20,000 inhabitants, 40 percent of whom were children under the age of 15.[16] Despite its size, Maroantsetra does not have a clearly urban feel to it. Much of it looks like a very big village. Looking more closely though, life in Maroantsetra is clearly different from life in a village such as Sahameloka. This is a direct result of its history, and present role, as an administrative center.

Maroantsetra stretches about one kilometer from west to east and the same distance from north to south. Its streets are arranged in a chequer-board pattern, part of the heritage of French colonial administration. Apart from one paved road, which begins at the local airport and ends in the center of town (this is the only paved road within a radius of several hundred kilometers), the town's different neighborhoods and compounds are connected by wide sand-streets lined with lychee, coconut and other trees. Behind these are hidden people's small, slightly raised houses that are made of *ravenala* palm and split bamboo. The paved road runs right through the center of town and divides the administrative area from the market and the bulk of the residential area.

The administrative area consists of old colonial buildings, which now house the district administration and local ministries of the Malagasy state—the Ministry of Finance, the Ministry of Population, the police station and the customs office. There is also a prison and a fairly large hospital on this side of the road. The conditions in the hospital, however, testify to the district's desperate economic situation: many beds have no mattress; what mattresses there are, are old and often blood-stained; in most rooms there is no running water and the toilets do not work so that patients' relatives have to provide and empty buckets. More importantly, there is a shortage of trained personnel and many basic medical facilities are simply not available. Also on this side of the paved road, there is a football pitch where matches are played quite regularly and where the annual celebration of Malagasy Independence Day takes place.

When we move along the main road, we encounter many shops run by Karany—Malagasy-Indians who migrated to Madagascar a few generations ago, but who, apart from very few exceptions, do not intermarry with other Malagasy. About one hundred Karany live in the district, most of them in Maroantsetra town. All sorts of goods (mostly imported) such as cloth, plastic buckets, bags, toilet paper, torches, batteries, along with more expensive items like bicycles and tape recorders, are sold in their shops. Apart from these shops, there is a bank, a pharmacy, an Air Madagascar office, the local radio station and the town's large Community Hall (*tranom-pokonolona*). Further out along the road are a couple of French-owned cash crop exporting firms. Cash crops, in particular cloves, are one of the main economic resources of the district.

On the other side of the main road lies the daily market, which is always very lively. People, mostly women, come from near and far to sell their produce or their catch: rice, fish, shrimps, crustaceans, many different kinds of leaves and some tropical fruit according to the season. Some people sell vegetables such as tomatoes, runner beans, garlic and onions. These do not grow in the area due to its extremely wet climate, but are brought in by air or shipped from Toamasina, which makes them extremely expensive by local standards. Honey, milk, oil, bread and snacks such as fried dough balls are also sold at the market. Until shortly before I left, when the town's mayor decided that people had to have a market *stand*, most women sold their produce on sheets of plastic spread out on the sand, sitting on the ground and nursing their babies, occasionally splashing their leaves with water or chasing away the flies from their meat or fish with a leaf-frond. There is also an open market-hall where men sell meat from concrete counters. Parts of animal carcasses covered in flies hang from hooks behind these counters, and there is a strong smell in the hall along with the continuous sound of butchers chopping up meat.

But not only food is sold at the market. There are long lines of stands where people sell cheap goods such as plastic slippers, buttons and thread, pens and soap. And there is a special area for products such as baskets, hats and sitting mats that are made locally out of different natural fibers. Leading away from the market into the residential areas, there are also long lines of semi-permanently built shelters where people (mostly from the more affluent highlands of Madagascar) sell second-hand European clothes. Adjacent to the market, there is an area where *taxi-brousses* (pick-ups) assemble waiting for people wanting to travel southward along the district's "Route Nationale no. 5."

On this side of the paved road, there are very few administrative buildings: the district court, the Town Hall (*Commune Urbaine*) and the post office, which houses surprisingly efficient national and international telephone facilities. Located centrally as well are the massive Catholic and, somewhat smaller, Protestant and Adventist churches, as well as a small, wooden mosque for the local Karany (Malagasy-Indians) who are all Muslims. Public and church-run schools are spread across town.

Behind all the activity in and around the market lies the vast residential area of Maroantsetra. As I have mentioned, it consists of small palm-thatched houses and wide, crisscrossing sandy streets partly overshadowed by massive trees. People tend to live in kin-based settlements, so Maroantsetra is generally made up of small compounds consisting of related households, often centered on a shared well.

Scattered across town, but concentrated in the central area, are dozens of little stalls where women, girls and boys sell homemade snacks and fruit, holding up umbrellas to protect their produce from both sun and rain. Little "corner shops" sell daily necessities and luxuries such as washing powder, soap and biscuits.

On the outskirts of town, by the harbor, is a mini-industrial area. Enterprises that operate here are either engaged in boat building and maintenance (along with associated activities such as producing lumber) or else in shipping cargo to the port of Toamasina. One yard used to be a processing site for ebony, but the ebony market has now almost disappeared.

Still further out, on the way to the beach, one reaches two hotel complexes, one of which is an American-owned three-star hotel, which has only recently opened. Renting one of its picturesque bungalows for a night costs as much as a local teacher earns in a month. In the town center, there are a number of much simpler hotels for budget tourists and Malagasy travelers. Maroantsetra is located at the edge of the Masoala peninsula, which is the largest patch of tropical forest in Madagascar. The bulk of the peninsula was declared a National Park in 1997. Consisting of 230,000 ha, Masoala National Park is the largest "protected area" in Madagascar. An American NGO (Wildlife Conservation Society), in cooperation with the Malagasy "Association Nationale pour la Gestion des Aires Protégées" (ANGAP), manages the park. Tourists can enter the park on guided tours. A tiny, offshore island close to Maroantsetra (Nosy Mangabe) has long been a nature reserve, its only inhabitants being teams of researchers during certain months of the year. The area principally attracts "eco-tourists" interested in hiking across the forest or observing lemurs in the wild. Whale-watching has become the most recent attraction. However, not many tourists come to Maroantsetra, and those staying at the big hotels, which are quite far from the center, hardly venture into town except in order to organize a trip to one of the nature reserves. Indeed, it is rare to see tourists strolling around town.

One feature of Maroantsetra town, which gives it an urban touch is its leisure time entertainment facilities. There are several simple restaurants (*hotely*) and bars as well as video clubs showing films (mostly action movies) at weekends. There is also a disco owned by a Frenchman who has lived in Maroantsetra for many years. A public TV set outside the Town Hall attracts a crowd almost every evening. There is also a local radio station, which many people in the countryside listen to as well. Radio and television represent the channels through which people can receive news of the outside world; there are no newspapers or internet connection available in town or anywhere else in the district.

The urban character of Maroantsetra becomes particularly visible on a Sunday when there is a distinctive European-style Sunday atmosphere. Groups of young women and men, dressed in their smartest clothes, stroll up and down the main road and down to the beach, buying snacks here and there, chatting and standing around. This is a popular pastime after church services in the morning and its purpose is quite obviously to see and to be seen.

In contrast to people who live in villages and largely rely on subsistence farming, people who live in town need quite substantial amounts of money. Most of Maroantsetra's residents live on land they own themselves or on land belonging to their kin and thus do not have to pay rent. But only a relatively small minority of the town dwellers are full-time farmers, these living on the outskirts of town close to their fields. All the rest have to buy at least part of their daily rice intake as well as other food and goods such as sitting mats that people in villages often make for themselves. If a house in town needs repairing, material must be bought instead of being collected for free from the forest. And of course, town life creates the need for money. For example, it creates the need to buy the appropriate clothes to go strolling around on Sunday afternoons.

Migration

Despite its geographical isolation, Maroantsetra is a district capital and administrative center, and has been one for some time. As both, it has attracted migrants from near and far.

> There aren't many children of the land (*zanatany*) here.
> People come from other places to walk around, to settle down, to look for work.

These are the words of one of Feeley-Harnik's informants speaking about "Analalava and such places" (Feeley-Harnik 1991: 231). Maroantsetra town is one such place. Indeed in many respects, it is very similar to Analalava, a town in western Madagascar of similar size and makeup to Maroantsetra (see Feeley-Harnik 1991: chapter 5). As in Analalava, "people moved from rural villages into the post [an administrative center], because they had to supplement subsistence farming with some form of wage labor" (1991: 261). The great majority of residents in Maroantsetra town are people whose family originate from one of the district's rural communities.[17] This is reflected by the small number of burial grounds in Maroantsetra town, a state of affairs resulting from the fact that most inhabitants are taken back to the village of their patrilineal ancestry after they die. The biggest burial ground is in fact that of the "migrants/guests" (*vahiny*). People with roots in the countryside remain in close contact with their places of origin. Many of them still own rice fields and forest land there and they regularly return, sometimes for several months at a time, in order to help their kin with agricultural work. At the same time, their presence in town makes it easier for their kin, based in the countryside, to come to Maroantsetra for a visit or in order to look for some kind of cash income. Support from kin is also vital in other situations such as hospitalization; the hospital provides neither food and sheets, nor a nurse to wash the patients. Relatives take on such tasks, and they watch over the patient day and night.

But migrants to Maroantsetra town have not only come from the nearby countryside, they have also come from many other areas of

Madagascar, and even beyond. Some of them came generations ago, some of them more recently. Together, they make up about 4.5 percent of the district's current population,[18] and probably considerably more in Maroantsetra town. And people continue to come and go, some of them, such as policemen and other government employees, because they are allocated to work in Maroantsetra for a limited period of time only. Others move on because they see a brighter future elsewhere. But many of the residents firmly rooted in Maroantsetra town also move about quite a bit, going away to other places for months, and even years, sometimes for study, sometimes to visit relatives. Others leave town for a month or two to do business, purchasing cheap goods such as Western second-hand clothes from the big cities, in order to sell these for a profit in Maroantsetra where, because of its remote location, such goods are not easily available.

Although people with origins in the district of Maroantsetra make up the great majority of its population, the impact of migrants from elsewhere is not negligible, especially since they contribute to the urban touch of Maroantsetra where all sorts of people meet, interact and live with each other and where the population is in constant flux. Both temporary and settled migrants also link the town to the outside world.

Some migrant groups—in particular the Karany (Malagasy-Indians) and the Merina and Betsileo from the highlands—remain distinct groups because they do not intermarry with local people, while others, such as the Tsimihety from the west of Maroantsetra, have blended in with the local population through intermarriage over generations and have "disappeared" as a distinct group.

Elites

There are hundreds of ways in which people who live in Maroantsetra town make a living. And there are obvious and undeniable disparities between different socioeconomic classes. Some of the migrant groups— that is the Malagasy-Indians, the Malagasy-Chinese and to a lesser extent the Merina, as well as the French residents and absent enterprise owners—although numerically insignificant are economically very powerful.[19] Their economic power is based on their control of trade with the world beyond Maroantsetra. They control both the export of cash crops (mainly cloves and lychees, and also vanilla and coffee) and the import of goods from Europe and Asia. The relative wealth of these groups is perfectly visible: they can be seen in the local bank; some of them have cars; they have large houses that are built of cement or solid wood (rather than palm tree material) and that are equipped with electricity and running water. Only very few other households have electric light and none I have seen have running water.

The economic power of these groups—with the exception of the Malagasy-Chinese—is not, however, linked to political power. But there is another economic elite in town, which is closely linked to local politics, namely the descendants of the Zafindrabay, who conquered the area in the early eighteenth century and who have remained powerful regional actors ever since. Their economic strength is not so much founded on business in town, but on landholdings across the district. They also hold considerable political power, especially one particular family of Zafindrabay descent. Political power, however, does not lie entirely in their hands, but is shared with the Malagasy-Chinese. It was from among the ranks of the latter that the town's mayor came at the time of my fieldwork. The Karany, the Merina and the French stay away from local politics.

Making a Living

A substantial number of Maroantsetra's residents, many more than those involved in the import-export trade, have jobs in the local administration. But although they have the advantage of receiving a regular salary, it is often insufficient to pay for a family's needs and is thus supplemented by many different kinds of income-generating activities such as women sewing or weaving baskets. A large number of people also make a living either by selling products at the market, or by selling snacks at one of the many little stalls scattered along the streets. Others work as carpenters or builders or have jobs in the boat- or tourist-industry. Some young girls and boys act as employees for the Karany families working both as domestic help and shop assistants.

While in 1999 a civil servant's monthly salary was between £30–40 (the exchange rate was roughly 10,000 Fmg to £1), a woman selling fish at the market could make as much as £5 on an exceptionally good day, and on an average day probably half that amount. A woman selling snacks or leaves at the market earned around £1 a day. A girl working for a Karany family, in contrast, received as little as £2,50 per *month* plus board and lodging. While unspectacular food for a family of four or five could be covered with 50 p on an average day, a meter of cloth cost something between £1–2, a pair of imported trainers £6–8, and medicine from the pharmacy cost almost exactly the same as in Europe. Antibiotics were therefore sold over the counter not by packet, but by pill, with the disastrous effect that people only took as many tablets as they could afford to buy.

Opportunities as well as difficulties characteristic of life in town distinguish Maroantsetra from any other place in the district. However, I am wary of overemphasizing the difference between the circumstances people find themselves in, in rural and urban settings. The great majority of residents in town are people who do some kind of job, or a number of jobs, for cash while remaining linked to subsistence farming in the country. And although there is a bank and a disco in Maroantsetra town, only few of its residents have ever set foot in either.

The remainder of this chapter will provide an introduction to the history and the social context of the village of Sahameloka. Perhaps even more so than in Maroantsetra town, the members of the Adventist church in Sahameloka share their daily lives with their close kin, most of whom are not themselves members of the church. This is important in particular with regard to certain rituals relating to the ancestors that are highly important social events but that the Adventists, for reasons I will explain later, cannot take part in. The local church members' predicament resulting from the fact that they are Adventists living in a predominantly non-Adventist society, will be discussed in detail in part III of the book. This chapter outlines the setting that frames their religious commitment.

Sahameloka: People Becoming Rooted

If one looks at a map of the district of Maroantsetra, it is almost entirely forested. Tiny villages are scattered throughout the tropical rain forest, but larger settlements are located either along the coast or along the two big river valleys. It is in these two wide valleys stretching out into the forest that the bulk of the area's rice is produced. One of the villages, where people live as rice farmers, is Sahameloka.

One can reach Sahameloka from Maroantsetra either on foot along a muddy path that follows the course of the Andranofotsy River (this takes four to five hours for a good walker) or else paddle upstream in a dugout canoe, which actually takes longer. Alternatively one can pay a fare and be taken in one of the few motorized *canottes*, which travel up and down the river a couple of times a week carrying goods and passengers (against the current this also takes around five hours). The river is lined with thick tropical vegetation making the journey from Maroantsetra to Sahameloka an extremely beautiful one. As one travels upriver, one sees the densely forested hills in the background beyond the valley, and occasionally one gets a glimpse of bright green rice fields. The whole way one passes people washing clothes or dishes in the river, men crossing with cattle and children having a nice, cool swim in the heat of the day.

The village of Sahameloka does not lie on the shore of the big river itself, unlike most other villages in the valley, but by a much smaller river called Sahameloka—which means "the meander valley" reflecting its winding course—that gives the village its name. Like other settlements in the area, the village of Sahameloka is surrounded by hundreds of rice fields, large and small, covering all the space between the village itself and the forest. Most of people's time is taken up by work in the fields for the production of rice, the major source of subsistence. Also on an almost daily basis, people walk across the valley to their piece of forest in order to harvest, or check on, their other crops. Most of these—various kinds of leaves, bananas, manioc, avocado and oranges according to the season—are for household consumption. But people in Sahameloka also have some cash crops, mainly cloves, with a little vanilla and coffee. The amount of money they make by selling these cash crops can vary dramatically from year to year depending on the world commodity market and the international price of cloves in particular. At one point during the two years I lived in the area, the price for a kilo of cloves rose to five times its normal value. The whole district suddenly seemed to flourish. Lots of people made lots of money and immediately spent it on tape recorders and other "luxury" items. Soon after this boom, however, a devastating cyclone hit the area destroying most of its clove trees. And so, just as quickly as people had made a fortune compared to the kind of money they normally dispose of, the future was destroyed overnight. These events also affected the life of town dwellers. But rural people were much more vulnerable, because their cash income depends entirely on agriculture.

As I have already pointed out, I am wary of exaggerating the differences between living in Maroantsetra town as opposed to living in a village like Sahameloka. The housing conditions, for instance, are essentially the same for most people in both places. In the villages as well as in town, the majority of households share a very small space among many people. A single space is continually being converted from bedroom to living room to working space, as need demands. In Sahameloka, only the village president had electricity—or, rather, a single light bulb—which was powered by a generator behind his house. But in Maroantsetra as well, only a small minority of houses in, or close to, the center of town were supplied with electricity.

However, the contrast between the rural and urban setting does make a significant difference to people's daily lives in a number of ways. On the one hand, as noted, the generation of cash income is much more insecure for the inhabitants of Sahameloka than it is for people in Maroantsetra. Not only is cash income insecure, but it is limited to one short agricultural period of the year, namely the time of the clove harvest, which lasts no longer than two months. Thus it is often difficult for people to pay for things they might suddenly be in need of at any time of the year, such as medicine from the pharmacy. On the other hand, under normal circumstances, the inhabitants of Sahameloka are to a large degree independent of cash. Not only do they produce almost all of their food themselves, they also produce items such as ropes and mats. Some cash, however, is needed to buy daily necessities like soap, kerosene, sugar, a little cooking oil perhaps, matches and the occasional notebook for school. These things are sold in the village in a couple of tiny shops, called *boutiques*. Of course, the shortage of cash also means that people in Sahameloka have few material belongings, other than what they produce themselves.

But perhaps more importantly, living in Maroantsetra or in Sahameloka makes a noticeable difference to people's diet, not so much in terms of quantity—of which, under normal circumstances, both town and village dwellers have plenty—but in terms of quality and variety. Only very few crops actually grow in the area due to its wet climate, and imported food is not available in Sahameloka, nor would people have the money to buy it if it was. The few cattle people own are kept for ploughing the rice fields and are slaughtered for ritual occasions only. And for reasons I never fully understood, people in Sahameloka hardly ever go fishing and do not raise many chickens. Pigs are not raised either in this part of Madagascar. Thus the diet in Sahameloka consists almost entirely of large amounts of rice, leaf broth (leaves boiled in salt water), and ripe and raw bananas in many different forms, while people in Maroantsetra often eat fish, shrimps or meat and fruit, although not necessarily daily. The lack of facilities such as a hospital, a pharmacy or a post office also has obvious impacts on life in Sahameloka.

There are many reasons that bring people from Sahameloka to Maroantsetra. Sometimes people go just for an afternoon in spite of the long trip involved, but mostly people go for a day or two if work at home allows. Most people who live in the district of Maroantsetra have never been outside it. The likelihood of a town dweller having been to other places in Madagascar is, however, significantly greater than that of a person from Sahameloka. For people from the village, contact with the outside world beyond Maroantsetra is largely limited to two kinds of journey, one to Mandritsara and the other to Antalaha. Local men walk to Mandritsara, a town a couple of hundred miles to the southwest of Maroantsetra, in order to trade cattle. While they themselves are incredibly fast walkers, the cattle are not, and thus such an expedition can take up to two weeks. Young men also walk the other

direction northeast right across the thick forest to the comparatively
rich town of Antalaha on the east coast—a two-day walk one way—in
order to buy new clothes for New Year if, that is, the clove harvest has
brought in enough cash.

Sahameloka is situated on a little hill slightly raised above the level
of the valley, which saved it from being flooded in the aforementioned
cyclone. Its overall population comprises roughly 1,000 inhabitants,
half of whom are children below the age of 15. As in every other
village of the area and much of Maroantsetra town, most houses are
built from different parts of local palm trees with floors of split bamboo. A few houses are more solid structures made of hard wood and
covered with mostly rusty corrugated-iron roof sheets. Due to the wet
weather conditions throughout the year, the reddish soil and the paths
crisscrossing the village are muddy and slippery most days. This is one
reason why old people move in with relatives in town, where the sand
absorbs most of the water and hence it is easier to walk.

Sahameloka is divided into two main parts, called "At the foot
of the *varôtro* tree" (Ambodivarôtro) and "The new settlement"
(Antanambao). The distinction between the two parts results from
the settlement history and is not physically visible today. The village is
made up of seven ancestries.[20] With the exception of one ancestry,
each of these occupies a particular part of the village,[21] and all members of the Adventist church live within the bounds of their respective
ancestry's settlement area. Three parallel streets cut through the
village and partly define the borders of the different neighborhoods
within it. Within the compound of a particular ancestry, its members
and their spouses (the prevailing pattern is virilocality) live and work
as nuclear families. However, neighboring kin are in daily contact and
often support each other in little ways such as helping to pound rice
or snap cloves. Moreover, kin often join up to perform work that
is better done in big groups, for example collecting palm leaves
in the forest for house building. The members of the local Seventh-
day Adventist church are fully integrated into these patterns of
everyday life.

Every ancestry has its own burial ground not far from the village
where its members are buried before being later exhumed and finally,
wrapped in several layers of cloth and sometimes clothes, put to rest in
mostly individual sarcophagi (*hazovato*). Ultimately, as is the case with
other Betsimisaraka, a person belongs to his or her patrilineal ancestry.
This is because although kinship and rules of exogamy are reckoned
cognatically,[22] the "father's side is really strong" (*tena mahery ny ilan'
ny ray*[23]). And it is with that side that one's bones are laid to rest after
exhumation.

In fact, the history of the village's burial grounds is a little more complicated than I have indicated and illustrates nicely how, in the course of the past century, people have gone through a "process of implantation" (Cole 2001: 155), becoming rooted in Sahameloka. The last section of this chapter tells the story of the village's burial grounds and of how people have made Sahameloka their "land of the ancestors" (*tanindrazana*). Of particular importance in this context is the issue of slave descent which is discussed below. The question of whether or not it relates to the attraction of Seventh-day Adventism, will be taken up again in chapter 4.

The History of Sahameloka and the Issue of Slave Descent

Local oral history offers two different versions of the foundation of the village. The version presented here is a synthesis of both and goes like this. Before slavery was abolished in Madagascar by the French in 1896, the Zafindrabay—the group from western Madagascar who had conquered the area of Maroantsetra around 1720, ruled it until the arrival of the Merina a hundred years later, and who continued, under Merina rule during the nineteenth century, to hold great influence in the area—had a temporary settlement where, or close to where, Sahameloka is now located. They probably went there sporadically, bringing some of their slaves along, in order to work in the fields and the forestland they owned in the vicinity, staying for a couple of weeks or possibly months at a time. As a permanent village though, Sahameloka is likely to have been founded by ex-slaves of the Zafindrabay about one hundred years ago, at a time when many ex-slaves established new settlements in the region's two major valleys.[24]

Whatever the settlement history, the fact is that today both descendants of the Zafindrabay and descendants of their slaves live in Sahameloka, together with a number of other ancestries. Moreover, they are linked by numerous marriage ties. Indeed, one of the seven ancestries of Sahameloka results from a mixed marriage between a male descendant of the Zafindrabay and a female descendant of their slaves (see later). The intermarriage between descendents of slaves and of free people is remarkable when compared with the situation to be found in certain other areas of Madagascar, in particular the high-lands, where such intermarriage is strongly tabooed (see Evers 2002). But the situation we find today in Sahameloka is not unusual for the region. Margaret Brown (2004) reports a similar pattern of inter-marriage with regard to the eastern shore of the nearby Masoala peninsula.

Every ancestry in Sahameloka has a different history, and it is not easy to reconstruct these. However, for present purposes it suffices to summarize the situation in the village as follows. Out of the seven local ancestries, four are very likely of slave descent, two are not, and one is of mixed slave-free origin. In more detail: one ancestry descends directly from the Zafindrabay. The other ancestry of free descent is a recent immigrant group from Farafangana, a small town several hundred kilometers to the south, who arrived in Sahameloka just 25 years ago "in search of money" (*nandeha nitady vôla*). Of the four ancestries who are most probably of slave origin, two descend from ex-slaves of the Zafindrabay, one from slaves captured in the Comoro islands, and one appears to be linked to the slave trade between Madagascar and the Mascarenes (Mauritius, La Réunion). This means that the majority of the inhabitants of Sahameloka are, as far as I could establish, of slave descent. When exactly the founders of their ancestries arrived and settled in the village is difficult to know. But it seems that apart from the most recent immigrant group from the south of the country, the ancestors of the people of Sahameloka settled in the village in the course of the first three decades of the twentieth century. In other words: Sahameloka is one of the villages that were founded by ex-slaves after the manumission of slavery in 1896.

However, what is perhaps more important than people's exact origins is the fact that there is a strong sense of historical uprootedness among Sahameloka's population. Except for the descendants of the Zafindrabay, who are generally acknowledged as the "masters of the land" (*tompontany*) in the region, all the other ancestries, ultimately, originate from elsewhere, though where exactly this "elsewhere" is remains unclear. "We are all migrants" (*mpivahiny izahay sintry jiaby*) people often said. Indeed, this was the first piece of information about Sahameloka and its inhabitants I was offered by numerous people soon after my arrival in the village. There was no disagreement about the fact that the ancestors of the village's inhabitants, ultimately, had come from elsewhere, and that they had come to Sahameloka in order to "look for land to cultivate" (*nandeha nitady tany malalaka*[25]), in search of a living. But *where* their ancestors had come from and what their situation had been like before they migrated, nobody knew.

Internal migration in search of a better living elsewhere is, and has been in the past, extremely common in Madagascar (see Deschamps 1959). However, migration by itself does not produce the sense of historical uprootedness that the people of Sahameloka feel. Their awareness of their families having been uprooted in the past is directly linked to the fact that the ancestors of most villagers were slaves. With enslavement, kinship ties were cut and people were deprived of the most crucial source of social worth in Madagascar: one's ancestors' blessing. People deprived of ancestral blessing are like branches cut off a tree, without roots and without history (Bloch 1994b; Cole 1998: 622; Evers 2002; Feeley-Harnik 1982: 37; 1991: 57–58; Graeber 1997: 374). The crucial difference between migrants in general and people of slave descent who migrated to new places in order to create a new future for themselves and their descendants, is that the latter are aware of the shallowness of their ancestral history, while the descendants of the former see in their mind's eye a long line of ancestors reaching back much further than anybody can actually remember. Even the best-informed members of those ancestries in Sahameloka, which are of slave descent, cannot trace their history further back than three or four generations, because there *is* no history beyond that point. But it is not simply the memory of actual ancestors that is the crucial point. Rather what makes all the difference is the knowledge that behind oneself in time there extends an almost endless line of ancestors reaching further and further back into the past, and that this line of ancestors is uninterrupted. Or, in contrast, the awareness that one's long line of ancestors has been cut and that much of one's history has been irretrievably lost. It is the awareness that the time before active memory is a black box that gives most of Sahameloka's inhabitants a marked sense of historical uprootedness. Listen to the words of an old man:

> In the old days, there were people who stole children, they stole them and then sold them to people elsewhere. According to what I have heard, our great ancestors were stolen by people, and they were sold in Nandrasana [the village from where the generation of the speaker's father later moved from as freed slaves in search of land]. That's how it came about that they lived there [in Nandrasana], and then they stayed and had children and made a living there, they got used to being there. But I don't know where they came from originally. From far away. [. . .] They were sold in Nandrasana, people from there bought them.[26]

The fact that the slaves were cut off from their ancestors meant that once they were freed, they not only had to look for new land to cultivate, but they also had to restart their history from scratch.

In other parts of Madagascar, the issue of slavery is a highly sensitive one. I was therefore taken by surprise at how openly some people in Sahameloka spoke to me about their own slave descent. I set foot in Sahameloka for the very first time on December 12. Four days later, I visited Papan' i Fredel and his family, members of the Seventh-day

Adventist church who I was eager to get to know. I asked Papan' i Fredel a seemingly innocent question regarding his family background. To my surprise, he told me straight out that both his matrilateral and his patrilateral ancestors had been slaves. He used the word *andevo* (slave), which in many parts of Madagascar is a word that is simply not uttered, or if used only spoken as a whisper. He added that they were, therefore, "a lost kind" (*very karazana izahay*).[27] Papan' i Fredel was to become a close friend and important informant for me, but at this point, he hardly knew me.[28]

But people like Papan' i Fredel or the old man whom I quoted earlier were exceptions. They were exceptions with regard to their actual knowledge of the history of their ancestries, and they were exceptional in how openly they talked about slave descent, sometimes explicitly, sometimes less so. In fact, in the course of my stay in Sahameloka, I became increasingly uncertain as to whether people who I knew were almost certainly of slave descent—thanks to Papan' i Fredel and a few others who made no secret of it—were actually *aware* of this part of their history. If it was socially possible for Papan' i Fredel to tell me that he belonged to a "lost kind" the first time we had a proper conversation, why would it not be possible for others to do the same, even if perhaps more implicitly? But most people did not, even as I got to know them well. What they did tell me, very often, was that their ancestors had migrated to Sahameloka from elsewhere in search of a living (*nandeha nitady, nandeha nitady tany malalaka, nandeha nitady vôla*), and that that was all they knew. I have no reason to suspect that they knew more than they admitted. Young people sent me to ask the old people, and the older people sent me to ask the "village historians" (people like Papan' i Fredel who were renowned for their knowledge of village history). I remain uncertain about the degree of most people's awareness of their own slave ancestry.

What is clear, however, is that the inhabitants of Sahameloka (with the exception of the descendants of the Zafindrabay) are perfectly aware that they all share a history of uprootedness, and they often volunteer this information. Yet time has passed and many generations have come and gone since the ancestors left from wherever they came and settled in Sahameloka (or, in the case of most local women's ancestors, in a village nearby). And the people of Sahameloka have, in the course of the past generations, managed to root themselves where they now live. Despite their awareness of the shallowness of their known history, they have come to regard Sahameloka as their "ancestral land" (*tanindrazana*).

The finalization of this process of becoming rooted in the new land perhaps took place a few years before my fieldwork. Up to 1992, or thereabouts, the dead relatives of the people of Sahameloka were buried in one of two massive graveyards close to the sea, many hours' walk away from the village; and the sarcophagi containing the ancestors' remains after they had been exhumed were kept there, too. I was told by people in Sahameloka, that they were not allowed to bring the sarcophagi back to the village for reasons of hygiene. In 1992, however, things changed, and the ancestors, lying weightily in their sarcophagi, were carried to Sahameloka on their descendents' shoulders.[29] "They have all come upstream" (*efa noriky sintry*), people explained. Every ancestry then founded its own burial ground on the outskirts of what is now people's *tanindrazana* (land of the ancestors).

A hundred years after the abolition of slavery in Madagascar, the social consequences of being of slave descent have not disappeared.[30] But being of slave descent does not matter to the same extent everywhere in Madagascar. In the Malagasy highlands, descendants of slaves often continue to be socially stigmatized and economically dependent on the descendants of their owners to this day. Among the southern Betsileo (Evers 1999, 2002), descendants of slaves are considered "dirty/impure people" (Evers 2002: 43–53), and they do not belong to any named descent group or have any tombs. These people bury their dead quickly and secretly under cover of night, digging a hole in any convenient spot where nobody will ever return to thereafter (Evers 2002: 167–175). Slave descent among the Betsileo is literally visible in terms of ex-slaves' housing situation, their appearance and their behavior. These people are painfully reminded of their non-status every day.[31] The situation is completely different in the Maroantsetra region, and it seems the east coast more generally (cf. Brown 2004, Cole 2001: 73). In Sahameloka, slave descent is "invisible" today. Descendants of free people and descendants of slaves do the same kind of work, they live in the same kind of houses and have similar belongings inside them. In fact, the three families in Sahameloka who are said to be rich belong to ancestries of slave descent. People of slave descent belong to named ancestries and have their own tombs, where they go to ask for the blessing of their ancestors. And they do not differ from descendants of the Zafindrabay with regard to ritual practices such as exhumation or cattle sacrifice.[32] What appears to make the difference between a situation such as that found among the Betsileo and a situation such as that found in the area of Maroantsetra are, on the one hand, marriage rules, and, on the other, access to land (see Bloch 1971; 1980, Brown 2004). Among the Betsileo, intermarriage between "clean" and "dirty" people is strictly tabooed (Evers 2002; Freeman 2001: 27–29, 128–129; Kottak 1980: 103–105), and as a consequence, descendants of slaves remain outside society and have no access to land. In Sahameloka, in contrast, all ancestries have intermarried for generations and everyone has their own land. In Madagascar, land not only gives people economic freedom and security, but something else as well. Without land, there is no *tanindrazana* (land of the ancestors), that is, no home, no soil to cultivate, and no ground to bury one's dead or build a tomb on. And without a tomb there is no ancestral blessing—ancestral blessing, which is vitally important for social reproduction. The people of Sahameloka, whose ancestors were "stolen and sold" and who came to Sahameloka, as free people, in search of unclaimed land to make a living on, have been able to root their ancestors and themselves in new soil. Thus, despite a pronounced awareness of Sahameloka not being their historical homeland, the people of Sahameloka now consider the village their home and that of their short line of ancestors. These ancestors now rest in their sarcophagi on the soil their descendants have made their own.

I have detailed the history of Maroantsetra and Sahameloka, including the issue of slave ancestry, for two reasons. First, the local Seventh-day Adventists are firmly embedded in the fabric of the society in which they live. It is therefore useful to provide an image of that society before starting the detailed analysis of Adventism. Second, as the issue of slave descent makes clear, having a relationship to one's ancestors and receiving their blessing is of vital importance in the local society. The lack of such blessing is considered a serious threat to someone's status as a socially meaningful person. However, the Adventists, for reasons I will come back to in later chapters, cannot participate in important rituals relating to the ancestors, and their whole attitude to the notion of ancestral blessing is highly ambivalent. As we will see in the course of the analysis, this fact plays a significant role in how they live their lives as Malagasy Seventh-day Adventists.

Chapter 2

Christianity and Seventh-Day Adventism in Madagascar

The Importance of Christianity in Madagascar

Christianity has played an important role in Madagascar for almost two centuries now. Indeed, it has been pointed out that the extent of the success of the Christian missions in Madagascar *prior* to European colonialization is quite unparalleled in continental Africa (Gow [n.d.]; also see Engelke 2003: 301). The first Christian missionaries of recent times, Protestants of the London Missionary Society (LMS), arrived in Madagascar in the 1820s. During the first few decades after their arrival, their relationship with the indigenous Malagasy rulers—the Merina monarchy, which was based in the central highlands, but which had brought under its control more than half of the island's territory—was highly ambiguous. On the one hand, the Merina monarchy was keen on the technical expertise, and especially the literacy that the missionaries were introducing to the country; on the other hand, the monarchy was deeply suspicious, and even hostile, toward their missionary work. This ambiguity in the relationship between the Christian mission and the indigenous kingdom resulted in alternating waves of pro- and anti-Christian politics under different Merina rulers. By 1869, Christianity had become such an important influence in Madagascar that the Merina queen decided to channel its power into supporting her own reign. She was baptized and Protestantism was adopted as the official religion of the Merina kingdom. Hundreds of thousands of people soon followed her example.[1]

The relationship between Christianity and power from then until the present day is complex—with the various churches being, at different times, both in support of, and in opposition to, those in power.

Discussing this in detail would take us too far away from the topic of this book.[2] Here I seek only to emphasize that Christianity has for a long time now played a central role in Malagasy society and politics. The following examples illustrate the point.

Between 1895 and 1899—that is at the time of the French annexation of Madagascar—a popular movement called the *Menalamba*, the Red Shawls, emerged and developed into what its best analyst, Stephen Ellis, describes as "a war of national resistance" (Ellis, S. 1985: 148). The aim of the Red Shawls was to expel the French and to restore ancestral custom. In pursuit of this aim, the movement was not only anti-European, but also violently anti-Christian. The Red Shawls, however, failed to achieve either of their aims. Madagascar remained a French colony until 1960, and the influence of Christianity continued to increase.

With time, Christianity became so much a part of the culture and identity of the people in many parts of the island—though by no means all—that defending that culture and identity often implicated Christian institutions (Raison-Jourde 1995: 294–295). Thus in the 1930s, some churches (by now, many different denominations were present in Madagascar) lent a certain amount of support to nationalist aspirations (Esoavelomandroso 1993: 361–364). This was also the case during the insurrection of 1947, a movement that was partly modeled on the *Menalamba* (Ellis, S. 1985: 160–161). The 1947 uprising against colonial rule was suppressed with extreme brutality by the French and cost the lives of an estimated 100,000 Malagasy people (Tronchon 1986: 72). The aim of the insurrection was to restore Madagascar's independence after half a century of foreign domination. The relationship between the insurgents and the Christian churches was an ambiguous one. On the one hand, since Catholicism was associated with France, the insurrection was to some extent anti-Catholic, and there were numerous attacks on Catholic buildings. On the other hand, many Christians fought on the side of the rebels. It was mainly Protestants who were actively involved in the uprising, but some Catholic priests and other individuals too, lent a certain degree of support to the rebels. The Catholic church also publicly condemned the atrocities committed by the French (Rabearimanana 1993: 371–376; Tronchon 1986: 165–168).

The ambiguity of the situation resulted from the long-standing Christian presence in those areas where the insurrection took place— the central and eastern parts of the country—which meant that many of the actors involved in nationalist politics were Christians themselves. Christianity had become an integral aspect of their culture and thus part and parcel of what had to be defended against foreign oppression. Indeed, the struggle for national independence was paralleled by a hesitant desire within the churches themselves to become more independent from Europe, a tendency that ultimately resulted in their increasing *malgachisation* (see Rabearimanana 1993).

With the gradual taking over of the running of the churches by the Malagasy after independence in 1960 came a further reinforcement of the Christian influence on the island (Urfer 1993). During the political crisis of the early 1970s, the churches sometimes spoke-up on behalf of the students who demonstrated against the neocolonial regime (Jacquier Dubourdieu 1997; Urfer 1993: 460–462). In 1992, after almost two decades of Ratsiraka's corrupt socialist regime, the churches formed the core of the opposition forces (Raison-Jourde 1995). They had always been against Ratsiraka and his nationalization program and were particularly against his attempts to replace church-run schools—which played a central role in the spreading of literacy in Madagascar since the introduction of Christianity at the beginning of the nineteenth century—with state schools. Ratsiraka was removed from office for a few years, but regained power in 1997. In 2001, he was once again challenged by the then mayor of the capital, Marc Ravalomanana, who defeated him after six months of nationwide conflict over the disputed results of the elections. Ravalomanana, the new president of Madagascar—who personifies a "rags to riches" story—was educated by missionaries in his home village close to the capital and later went to Sweden for secondary education in a strict Protestant school.[3] At the time of his election, he was the vice president of the Protestant church of Madagascar (FJKM), and he still holds this office, now that he is president of the republic (Jacquier Dubourdieu 2002: 71). His election campaign, for which the Protestant and other churches provided strong support, was full of explicit references to the virtues of Christianity, and his election motto—"Be not afraid, only believe"—was taken from St. Mark's Gospel.[4]

Neglecting Christianity

The long-standing significance of Christianity in Madagascar is undisputed. It is, however, important to note the regional differences with regard to this. In the nineteenth century, Christianity was very much a religion of the highlands—the home of the Merina monarchs who had adopted Protestantism as their state religion in 1869—and, in particular, of the urban upper class.[5] But with the onset of colonial rule in 1896, numerous Protestant, Catholic and Anglican denominations entered the country and, in their struggle for souls and territory, also began to work in areas other than the highlands. It took several decades, however, for Christianity, which was associated by many with the much hated Merina rule, to establish a firm footing.[6] The LMS, which dominated the scene in the nineteenth century, had concentrated its efforts so much on the highlands that the coastal regions were left far behind in terms of literacy and schooling, something that proved a big obstacle to the latter's Christianization. Moreover, on the east coast, with its wet, tropical climate, the missionaries' efforts were hampered by the effects of malaria.[7] In spite of these difficulties though, significant numbers of people converted to the Christian religion in the course of the twentieth century. The process of Christianization on the east coast began later and was much slower than in the highlands, but it did take place nonetheless. Today, the highlands, and especially the capital city, are almost entirely Christianized. The proportion of Christians in the coastal areas is much lower, while the deep south remains all but untouched by the Christian influence.[8] Of the total population of Madagascar, roughly 50 percent are now official members of a Christian church.[9] This means that Christianity plays a significant role in the lives of millions of Malagasy people, even if it has not pushed aside these people's closeness to, and reliance on, their ancestors. In many areas of Madagascar, we find a coexistence between Christianity and what has been called "traditional religion." In the area of Maroantsetra for example, which this study focuses on, Catholics and Protestants (who make up some 50 percent of the population) continue, besides attending church, to engage in non-Christian ritual activities.

Despite the incontestably important presence of Christianity in different parts of the island, the Christian religion as experienced in people's daily lives has received relatively little attention from social anthropologists, even though its overall significance is recognized. In the work of some authors (especially Bloch 1994a [1971], 1986), the issue of Christianity is present in the background of the analysis, but no social anthropologist of Madagascar has made the Christian religion his or her main focus of research. This is especially surprising with regard to the highlands, where, as Bloch states, "The most important feature of the religious life of present-day Merina is that they are Christians" (1986: 39). It seems that Christianity is mainly mentioned in anthropological studies in order to point out how it has not pushed aside ancestral traditions, but has rather entered into a relationship of coexistence or syncretism with the latter.[10]

Among anthropologists in Madagascar generally, there seems to be a certain reluctance to seriously study Christianity. Field researchers tend to either study non-Christianized groups, or else to focus their attention on "traditional" practices to do with the ancestors, which Christianized communities continue to be involved in. In 1997, the *Journal of Religion in Africa* published two special issues on "Religion in Madagascar" (vol. 27, numbers 3 and 4), but not a single contribution concerned Christianity. Since the presence of Islam among Malagasy communities has been given considerably more attention by anthropologists (especially Lambek on Malagasy speakers in Mayotte: Lambek 1981, 1993, 1995),[11] the neglect of Christianity cannot be explained by a lack of interest in world religions in general. I would venture to suggest that the reluctance to approach Christianity as an anthropological subject has, among other reasons, to do with European and North American anthropologists feeling unattracted by, and uncomfortable with, the idea of spending much of their time in the field participating in Christian practices. These feelings perhaps stem from an uneasy relationship with their own Christian backgrounds, along with concerns about the history of the discipline (cf. Barker 1990a: 23; Robbins 2003a). Having said this, however, it is important to stress that I myself am not a member of either the Seventh-day Adventist or any other church. Thus I am not writing about Adventism from the perspective of a fellow Christian. I have simply attempted to look at Christianity as a "truly Malagasy" subject matter, which is as relevant to our understanding of contemporary Malagasy societies as "traditional" practices relating to the ancestors. Indeed, as Barker (1990a) has noted for Oceania and Hastings (1990) for continental Africa, Christianity has become such an integral part of life for millions of people that it no longer makes sense to talk of an opposition between Christianity and indigenous tradition. This is also true for much of Madagascar.

New Churches are, for many scholars, probably even less attractive as a subject of anthropological research than the mainline Christian churches. The term "fundamentalist" conjures up memories of Jehovah's Witnesses pestering us on the street or pushing their way in at our door. Images of American tele-evangelists come to mind, with their index fingers raised to admonish us for our sinful lives. Associations with the political far Right are never far away. We tend to assume that these must be people whom it would be highly unpleasant to spend any considerable amount of time with. I must admit that, I, too, had such worries. However, the opposite turned out to be true: the members of the Adventist church in Maroantsetra and Sahameloka are among the most pleasant and also among the most open-minded people I have ever met.

Historians, unlike anthropologists, have been more willing to address the subject of Christianity in Madagascar, partly because the early history of Malagasy Christianity is particularly interesting, and perhaps also partly because historical work does not usually involve intense participation in the daily lives of one's informants.

Mission Churches, African Independent Churches and New Churches

The neglect of Christianity as a subject of anthropological inquiry in Madagascar is perhaps also due to the relative absence of African Independent Churches (AICs). Inspired by Sundkler's pioneering study of Bantu Independent Churches in South Africa (1961 [1948]), AICs have been, at least until rather recently (Hastings 2000), the main focus of analysis on the African continent since the beginning of the 1960s. AICs—which already numbered some 800 in Sundkler's time and which were estimated by one Catholic source at 10,000 at the beginning of the 1980s (MAC 1993: 28)—are independent offshoots from mission churches, or offshoots from other AICs, whose outstanding characteristic is the mixing of Christianity with elements of traditional African forms of religiosity. Traditional ritual drums, sacred dances and rhythms form part of church services in AICs, as do divination and witch-finding. These latter are practically identical to traditional forms, except for the fact that, of course, the preacher—the diviner and witch-finder—is not inspired by an ancestral spirit, but by the Holy Spirit (Sundkler 1961: 255–259). Many AICs developed under colonial rule and they are sometimes understood as an expression of resistance against it (e.g., in Comaroff 1985). The syncretic nature of AICs—symbols of authentic forms of African Christianity—has fascinated many anthropologists, and other scholars. The mission churches, in contrast, assumed not to be "truly African" and strongly associated with colonial and foreign domination, have been unable to compete in the discipline with the exoticism of the AICs (Hastings 1990: 201–204, 2000: 36).[12] Indeed, I wonder whether the recent academic interest in New Churches has not, to a certain extent, been triggered by the predominance of Christianities in the *Pentecostal* tradition among these churches (see below) and especially by certain deliciously exotic features of Pentecostalism like "speaking in tongues," which is reminiscent of spirit possession. More sober types of Christianities, like Seventh-day Adventism, fascinate less and seem to attract little attention.

In contrast to continental Africa, Malagasy Christianity has, until recently, remained very largely attached to, and part of, the historical mission churches. Only very few movements have developed that could be regarded as similar to the AICs found in abundance on the continent. Instead of AIC-style syncretism, what we generally find in Madagascar is the coexistence of Christianity with forms of "ancestor worship," which are of central importance to all Malagasy communities. There are, to be sure, syncretic moments—when Jesus Christ and the ancestors are addressed in one and the same ritual speech for example— but this is not comparable to the institutionalized syncretism characteristic of AICs (see, e.g., Bloch 1994b, 1995b).

Since the mid-1980s, however, a new phenomenon has occurred, both in Madagascar and continental Africa: the sudden, and rapid growth and spread of New Churches (Gifford 1994, 1998; MAC 1993). The New Churches cannot be easily grouped with either AICs or mission churches. This has led Birgit Meyer, who has conducted perhaps the most thorough study of African Pentecostalism, to urge us to move beyond this dichotomy (1999: xviii). The New Churches are not linked to any of the historical mission churches, but some of them, such as Jehovah's Witnesses or Seventh-day Adventists, do belong to international organizations. Others, especially many in the Pentecostal tradition, were founded by African spiritual leaders. But the New Churches are not simply a continuation of AICs, as many researchers at first tended to assume (Gifford 1994: 515). The main evidence for this—apart from their lack of formal independence in many cases—is the fact that they are categorically against the Africanization of Christianity so typical of AICs (Gifford 1998: 334–337). While we can read in Sundkler of a Zionist angel urging a childless woman to sacrifice a bull to her ancestors to appease them and make her conceive (1961: 250), such a thing is unthinkable in most of the New Churches where ancestral manifestations are thought to be the work of the devil.[13]

However, the New Churches' attitude toward "traditional African religion" is ambiguous. Although they are emphatically against the Africanization of Christianity that occurred in the AICs and to some extent even within the historical mission churches,[14] it is precisely because, according to the analyses of some writers at least, the New Churches take "typical African concerns" such as witchcraft seriously that they have become more successful than the mission churches, which tend to deny or, worse, ignore such concerns (MAC 1993; Meyer 1999).

A New Wave of Christianity

Although reliable overall statistics are hard to get, it is clear that the success of the New Churches in continental Africa and Madagascar is such that it cannot be ignored or overlooked. In Madagascar many—ordinary people, pastors and priests, radio presenters, academics and theologians—have commented on their growth. And, although the number of Malagasy converts is still relatively small—amounting in total to no more than a few percent of the national population—the phenomenon of the New Churches has become important enough to cause much concern to the mainline churches. These churches are becoming increasingly worried about losing members. In 1997, the Catholic church organized a week-long conference in Madagascar's capital to discuss the relationship between the historical churches and *Nouveaux Groupements Religieux*. One of the key issues addressed during this conference[15] concerned the challenge and potential threat posed by the "new religious groups" and the measures that could be taken to mitigate this threat. The fact that the Catholic church felt the need to hold such a conference testifies to the visible and increasing significance of New Churches in contemporary Madagascar. Gifford reports similar alarm among the mainline churches in continental Africa (1994: 521, 1998: 95; also see MAC 1993). There, Catholic and Protestant churches as well as AICs are now threatened by the "Pentecostal explosion" (Gifford 1994, 517).

Although there is a growing body of literature on Pentecostalism in Africa,[16] given the size of the continent and the enormous variety of African societies, we still know little about this new wave of Christianity (Gifford 1994: 514, 526, 1998: 34; Hastings 2000: 41). And we know next to nothing about New Churches *not* in the Pentecostal tradition. In Madagascar, information on the New Churches is particularly thin. To my knowledge, the available social science literature is, in fact, limited to three articles (Jacquier Dubourdieu 1997 [unpublished], 2002; Walsh 2002).

As the term "Pentecostal explosion" indicates, and the literature reflects, in continental Africa, the new Christian wave is dominated by groups following the Pentecostal tradition, be they branches of international, largely U.S.-based, Pentecostal churches, or be they independent African creations. In Madagascar, the situation is less clear. Here we find other types of New Churches that, at least in certain districts of the country, are just as visible as the Pentecostal churches or more so. One of these New Churches is the Seventh-day Adventist church, which is the subject of this book.

Seventh-Day Adventism: A Global Movement

The Seventh-day Adventist church grew out of an apocalyptic-millenarian movement in the 1840s in the United States led by William Miller.[17]

This was one of many religious revivalist movements of the time (Vance 1999: 1, 13). Miller's prophecies—which were based on years of intense Bible study (Hoekema 1963: 89–90, Knight 1993: 35–41)—predicted the Second Coming of Christ in 1844.[18] As the date passed uneventfully, resulting in what has become known as "The Great Disappointment," many of Miller's followers lost hope and the movement split into numerous factions. One of these factions revolved around a young woman, the 17-year old Ellen G. White (1827–1915) who, as a result of an accident at the age of 9, was a partial invalid. Ellen White's spiritual leadership of what later became the Seventh-day Adventist church was based on dramatic visions, which she had been experiencing ever since the Great Disappointment. White became recognized as the contemporary medium of the Holy Spirit and thus as a true prophetess.[19] Her numerous books are perhaps the most important source of knowledge, apart from the Bible of course, for Seventh-day Adventists worldwide. Some of her books are regularly read in church in Maroantsetra town and also, to a lesser extent, in the village of Sahameloka. Some of the more literate members of the local church have one or several of her books at home.

In 1860, the Seventh-day Adventist church adopted its present name and set itself up as a legal organization (Vance 1999: 32). The name Seventh-day Adventist refers to the church's stress on the importance of keeping the Holy Sabbath on the *seventh* day of Creation (considered to be Saturday)[20] and to the certainty of Christ's Second Coming (*advent*).

Seventh-day Adventism grew "from the ashes of the Great Disappointment" (Vance 1999: 25) and soon spread all over the globe, its missionary program focusing on education and health. The tremendous expansion was well under way by 1903, by which time Adventist missionaries had arrived in every continent and world membership already amounted to almost 80,000 (Pfeiffer 1985: 18). By 1961, 195 of the 220 recognized countries in the world had been reached by the Seventh-day Adventist church, and its publications appeared in over 200 languages. World membership had reached one million, and even then, three quarters of all Adventists lived outside the United States (Hoekema 1963: 99–100). At present, some 13 million people worldwide are baptized members of the Seventh-day Adventist church, the vast majority of them living in countries in the Third World.[21] The Adventist church also runs an immense system of schools, colleges, universities, and hospitals. It is important to recognize that the success of the church varies significantly around the globe. Although the church is present in most countries of the world, it has very different degrees of influence in different places.

The percentage of Adventists is particularly high in the Pacific islands. This geographic concentration is reflected in the literature on Adventism in the social sciences, which concerns almost exclusively the Pacific region.[22] There, embracing Adventism has primarily been seen as an attempt to access Western power and goods, as a road toward modernity or as a way of dealing with the problems of globalization.[23]

Four out of 13 million church members live in Africa. There the church experiences enormous growth at the moment,[24] particularly in some areas of eastern Africa.[25] In the majority of sub-Saharan African countries, including Madagascar, between 0.5 and 1 percent of the overall population have converted to Seventh-day Adventism. Social science literature on Adventism in Africa is extremely scarce and geographically limited. Indeed, to the best of my knowledge, all the information we have concerns Zambia (Dixon-Fyle 1978; Poewe 1978; Simpson 1998, 2003).[26]

Adventist Doctrine in Madagascar and Beyond

Before going on to summarize the history of the Adventist church in Madagascar, it is important to explain some key elements of the Seventh-day Adventist doctrine. The Seventh-day Adventist Church Manual and other related publications list 27 "fundamental biblical truths" that church members must accept. Here I present only a few of these, namely those that are generally reasonably well known among church members in Maroantsetra and Sahameloka and that I therefore understand to be, for them, the most significant doctrinal aspects.

The basis of Seventh-day Adventist doctrine is what Ellen White called "The Great Controversy." This refers to the fight between the forces of Good and Evil that has been going on ever since Lucifer's fall. World history, from its very beginning to its very end, is thus understood with reference to the ongoing battle between God and Satan.

Equally important, in the eyes of Seventh-day Adventists, is the fact that Christ's return to earth is not a hope, but a *certainty*. He will return and take all righteous people with Him to heaven. There they will stay for a thousand years, the purpose of the millennium being the eradication of all possible doubt as to the justice of God's judgment. At the end of the millennium, all evil will be annihilated, paradise on earth will be reestablished and the just will live there forever together with God Himself. The start of this sequence of events is thought to lie in the near future and to be foreshadowed by the physical persecution of all people who worship God on Saturday rather than on Sunday.

Seventh-day Adventist doctrine, much of it elaborated in the writings of Ellen White, not only contains eschatology, but also instructions as to what one must, and must not, do. Among these instructions are the following: first, one must keep the Sabbath and neither do any work nor handle money on this day, except when necessary in order to help another human being in need.[27] Second, one must study the Bible in order to understand God's wisdom. Third, one must adhere to the dietary instructions as specified in Leviticus. Fourth, baptism must be by full immersion.

These, and many other, instructions apply worldwide. In Madagascar, the church also demands of its members that they do not communicate with dead people. This is of tremendous significance and I will return to this issue at various points. For the moment, suffice to say that the relationship between living people and their ancestors is of paramount importance in all Malagasy societies. Given this fact, the requirement to *not* relate to one's ancestors, and to *not* communicate with them through ritual work, challenges the very foundation of Malagasy society and is thus particularly difficult for people to follow. Because of this, the members of the Adventist church are continually reminded of the importance of not participating in ritual practices that involve communication with the dead. The Adventist pastor who worked in Maroantsetra at the time of my field-work made the commitment not to participate in practices such as exhumation and cattle sacrifice—locally the most important forms of communication between people and their ancestors—part of the creed that church members have to vow to abide by before being baptized. Reading out the Malagasy translation of the global Seventh-day Adventist creed, the pastor always added a few words of explanation to the effect that to "renounce the sinful ways of the world" (Seventh-day Adventist vow, point three) meant not attending any exhumation or cattle sacrifice or giving money or rice toward either.

The History of Seventh-Day Adventism in Madagascar

The Seventh-day Adventists were the first "evangelical" or, if you like, "fundamentalist" group to set foot in Madagascar. That was in 1926, a few years prior to the arrival of the Baptists.[28] The first Adventist missionary couple, Americans probably of French origin,[29] arrived in the capital Antananarivo, and immediately set up a press and started publishing.[30] One year later, in 1927, the first gathering of all new members was organized and the first Seventh-day Adventist church on Malagasy soil was inaugurated. Other missionaries from Europe and the United States followed, soon working together with Malagasy assistants. The first Adventist mission school was opened in the capital in 1934, and within a decade or so 700 pupils were being taught there (Gerber 1950).[31]

Historical evidence of the early significance of the Adventist church in Madagascar can be found in the French colonial archives in Aix-en-Provence (CAOM). There, various confidential communications, dating from between 1927 and 1933, between the head of the "Sûreté Générale," the "Gouverneur Générale de Madagascar et Dépendences" and other administrators show that the French were clearly worried about the presence of the Adventists in the country. Despite emphatic reassurance to the contrary by the Adventist missionaries, the colonial administration was concerned that the "culte" might be politically subversive.[32]

In 1939, the French conducted a countrywide survey concerning the spread of different missions during the first four decades of colonial rule (Statistiques relatives aux missions religieuses, 1896–1939).[33] There are separate statistics concerning the LMS, the French Protestants, the Catholics, Anglicans, Lutherans, Quakers, Muslims, and, interestingly, also the Seventh-day Adventist church. This was the case even though the number of converts to Adventism was tiny in comparison with the other denominations, probably amounting to no more than a few hundred persons.[34] In addition, statistics on the Adventist church are included in several reports from the coastal provinces, with the church being particularly successful in the eastern province of Toamasina, within which lies Maroantsetra.

By 1947 the Seventh-day Adventist mission in Madagascar had spread to many parts of the island and had built 25 churches (Gerber 1950). In Tronchon's analysis of the insurrection of 1947, we find an interesting footnote reproducing one of the rebels' slogans (p. 164, annex pp. 353–354, emphasis added):

A bas Rome! A bas la maçonnerie!
A bas le protestantisme!
A bas l'anglicanisme!
A bas l'adventisme!
Vive Rakelimalaza![35] Vive Madagascar!

This shows that by 1947, the Seventh-day Adventist church was sufficiently prominent so as to be included in the rebels' list of foreign influences to be thrown out of Madagascar. The impact of the church continued to grow, and by 2003, 73,000 Malagasy people had become Adventists, which is almost 0.5 percent of the overall population of

Madagascar.[36] As is the case for other churches in Madagascar, relatively few Adventists live in the southern parts of the island.[37]

It is beyond doubt that the Adventist church is now much more successful in Madagascar than it was in the 1930s and 40s. A note of caution, however, should be sounded here. Many analysts of New Churches in the Third World use as a starting point the observation of the recent outstanding success of such churches and develop their theories on the basis of such success being a phenomenon of our modern times. However, if we take the example of the Adventists in Madagascar and look at the historical evidence concerning their presence on the island, the conclusion that their success is unparalleled in history has to be qualified. As the archival sources make clear, Adventism was already of significance in the first half of the twentieth century, and we should thus be wary of exaggerating the uniqueness of the present times.

Christianity and Seventh-Day Adventism in Maroantsetra and Sahameloka: A Historical Outline

Before we turn to Seventh-day Adventism in the area, let us briefly review the history of the mainstream churches in Maroantsetra and Sahameloka. In the area of Maroantsetra, Christianity arrived comparatively late. This was probably due to the relative inaccessibility of the region coupled with its tropical disease-prone climate. According to a booklet available at the Catholic church in Maroantsetra,[38] the first missionary, a French Jesuit, arrived in 1897, that is one year after Madagascar had become a French colony. He only stayed two days during which time, however, he managed to baptize ten children. Other French Jesuit missionaries turned up sporadically in subsequent years, each visit resulting in a few more baptisms. But it was only in 1913, that is 16 years after the colonial administration had arrived in Maroantsetra, that one of them actually settled in Maroantsetra town and began the task of building a Catholic community and a Catholic church. Before that time, the colonial administrators reported that "la population est absolument indifférente en matière de religion."[39] The Protestants, too, made tentative attempts to missionize the area during the early twentieth century.[40]

The process of Christianization in the region seems to have been slow. By the early 1970s, a decade after independence, 20 percent of the population had been baptized as Christians: half of them as Catholics, the other half as Protestants.[41] At the time of my fieldwork, roughly half the population were registered as Christians with a slight majority of Catholics (22 percent Protestants, 26 percent Catholics).[42] Besides the massive Catholic church in Maroantsetra, there are at present a somewhat smaller, but for local standards still impressively big, Protestant church and two unobtrusive houses of worship for the small groups of local Anglicans[43] and Lutherans. All the clergy of the different churches in Maroantsetra are Malagasy.

When we look at the village of Sahameloka—the information on the arrival and impact of Christianity is rather nebulous. The old people remember both the Catholic and the Protestant church having been there "already for a long time" (*efa ela*). I did not manage to find out more. However, at the time of my fieldwork, while only a few people in the village would not call themselves Christians, no more than roughly 100 out of the 500 strong adult population attended services on an average Sunday morning. Many more people went to the Catholic as opposed to the Protestant church. As for other villages in the district, there was neither a Catholic priest, nor a Protestant pastor in Sahameloka, and the congregations depended on church elders to perform the necessary tasks. For marriage or baptism services, the priest/pastor either traveled up, or people from the village, down, the river.

The Seventh-Day Adventist Church in Maroantsetra and Sahameloka

There are five different New Churches in the district of Maroantsetra, but the Seventh-day Adventists are by far the most numerous group. The other New Churches present are the Jehovah's Witnesses and three churches in the Pentecostal tradition.[44] While in Maroantsetra these groups have small churches constructed in typical local fashion out of perishable material, the Adventist church is a solid cement structure not much smaller than the Protestant one. It is big enough to accommodate several hundred people. Like the Catholic and the Protestant churches, it is located in the center of town, in the middle of a large courtyard, flanked by the pastor's home and a couple of other small buildings associated with the Adventist church. Outside, above the main entrance of the church, hangs a massive wooden cross, to the left of which one can read the words "eglise adventiste du 7e jour." Two rows of windows, one on either side of this long building, allow the breeze to circulate. As one walks into the church, the first thing one sees is a Bible verse from the Book of Revelation, painted in large letters behind the altar at the other end of the room. This verse reads "*Indro Izy avy amin' ny rahona, Apok. 1:7*" (Behold, he cometh with clouds, Revelation 1:7 [King James Bible version]). Bright red curtains hanging underneath cover two openings that lead to the back of the church. One of these openings is a door to be used by the numerous church members who lead Sabbath church services. The other opening is a glass panel infront of the font revealed only during baptism. Because Seventh-day Adventists practice adult baptism by full immersion, the font is a type of pool, in which both the pastor and the person to be baptized stand in chest-deep water. Apart from the altar and a table in front of it, there is nothing in the church but rows of long wooden benches and a number of school desks at the back. The decoration is limited to the Bible verse painted behind the altar, a white embroidered cloth covering the table and a vase with plastic flowers.

The Adventist church is by far not only the most popular New Church in the district, its local history also begins decades before that of the other groups.[45] As is to be expected, little is known about the history of the Adventist church in remote areas such as Maroantsetra. However, as the colonial survey makes clear the region seems to have been among those where the church was particularly successful from the beginning of its missionizing work in Madagascar, counting as many as 177 Adventists is 1939. This was a high numbers also in comparison to other Christian denominations present (equivalent to 7 percent of the Catholics, 11 percent of the Protestants and 27 percent of the Anglicans). And whereas in the Toamasina region the converts were very largely Merina from the highlands, in Maroantsetra, the vast majority were local Betsimisaraka.[46] There were two places of religious reunion in Maroantsetra and one indigenous *ministre de culte*.

This first wave of success in the 1930s seems to have been interrupted at some point, for the oldest local church members remember 1966 as the year when the Adventist church began to work in Maroantsetra, and in 2004, the church was celebrating its thirty-fifth anniversary. So in the following account, the Adventist history starts anew.

According to oral history, *Pastera* Charles was the first of ten Adventist pastors to arrive and work in the region between 1966 and the year 2004, when I last visited Maroantsetra. Most of these pastors originated from the Malagasy highlands; none of them was of local origin. In 1966, *Pastera* Charles organized a *conférence* in the town's Community Hall, which lasted for two weeks. As a result, 20 people converted and helped to build a church. The first actual baptisms followed two years later. In 1970, when the Seventh-day Adventist mission was first mentioned in the *Monografie de la Sous-Préfécture de Maroantsetra*, it numbered 146 adult converts.

By that year, the Adventist church was also running an elementary school in town teaching 120 pupils, 72 boys and 47 girls. In the same year, the Catholics had 450 children at their mission schools and the Protestants 240, although the number of their converts put together had by now risen to almost 16,000. The number of children taught at the Adventist school is remarkably high and testifies to the church's emphasis on education. Nonetheless, the Seventh-day Adventist school was closed in 1978, for reasons unknown to me. In 1999, the wife of the pastor of the district reopened the Adventist school, teaching two elementary classes in the same building as before. Unfortunately, this building was destroyed by a cyclone a few months later. However, a new one was built after I had left Maroantsetra, and when I visited again in 2004, a number of classrooms had been constructed on the church's premises. Several church members had been employed to teach a total of seven class levels (all five primary classes and the first two secondary ones) totaling 300 pupils, most, but not all of them, children of Adventists.

By the end of 1999, 1,250 people had been baptized as Seventh-day Adventists in the district—that is about nine times more than 30 year earlier and slightly less than 1 percent of the overall population. The Adventist community in the area consists of many small congregations. Despite their comparatively small numbers, they run 47 local churches scattered all over the district, while the Protestants run 66 churches and the Catholics just over 100. Moreover, while about 300 people are annually baptized as Catholics, the number of converts to the Seventh-day Adventist church has, in recent years, been remarkably close to this. This is especially significant when we consider that in contrast to the Catholics, the Adventists practice *adult* baptism. 200 new church members were baptized in a mass ceremony in May 1999 alone.[47] In recognition of the remarkable recent spread of Adventism in the region, Maroantsetra was named "district of the year 1999" by the central Adventist administration in Madagascar's capital.[48] However, not all of these newly baptized people have remained, or are likely to remain, active members of the church. Quite a few of those baptized in May 1999 had already "gone cold" (*lasa mangatsiaka*), as the process of apostasy is described, when I left a year later. The dropout rate is extremely difficult to estimate because the boundary between being in, or out of, the church is fluid. Only very few of those who "have gone cold" officially abandon the church, and they may come back at any time.

In the district of Maroantsetra, Seventh-day Adventism is predominantly a rural phenomenon. Out of the 1,250 baptized church members at the end of 1999, only eight percent (104) were residents of Maroantsetra town. The rest were people from the countryside.

Sahameloka is one of the almost fifty villages where Adventism has taken root.

*   *   *

The history of Adventism in the village of Sahameloka is much more recent than that of Maroantsetra town and only begins in the 1990s. The very first converts to Seventh-day Adventism in the village were Maman' and Papan' i Claude of my host family. They had joined the church, so their conversion story went, because their eldest son had recovered from severe illness after they had attended an Adventist church service. For the first six months after they became interested in Adventism (they were not yet baptized at that time), they regularly went to another village an hour's walk away where there was already an Adventist congregation, in order to attend the Sabbath service. In the course of the same year, 1993, several other people from Sahameloka joined them as converts and soon they decided to build their own church in the village.

At first, the church was a very small building similar to the houses people live in. By the time of my fieldwork though, the Adventist church was, after the Catholic and the Protestant ones, the third largest building in Sahameloka, with enough capacity to accommodate more people than the church actually had members. Its roof and walls are made from parts of various local trees and its floor is formed by the hill on which it stands. At the opposite end to the entrance, there is a table, covered with a white cloth and decorated with a colorful bunch of plastic flowers, which functions as an altar. On special occasions, the walls on the inside of the church are adorned with palm leaves. The two rows of church benches are made from crudely cut wooden planks that have been laid across massive pieces of bamboo.

In 1994, the first four people were baptized. In 1995, however, the Adventist religion really started to become popular in the village. That year, as many as 12 people were baptized in one day in the river, which gives the village its name. The high point of conversion rates to Seventh-day Adventism in Sahameloka occurred, so people told me, between 1995 and 1997. Since then, the church's sudden, impressive growth has subsided somewhat and the numbers have remained more or less steady. With the exception of four people, all those who were baptized have remained actively engaged in church affairs. In the year 2000, when I lived in Sahameloka, it was one of the villages in the district with, proportionately, a very high number of Adventists. Almost 10 percent of the adult population of the village had become church members, compared to an average of roughly 1 percent in the district as a whole. This is obviously an issue that demands explanation. I will return to this question later on in the book.

All of this, however, seems to be the *beginning* of a movement. It remains to be seen how Adventism in Sahameloka develops over the course of the years, and possibly decades, to come. At the moment, I can only state that when I revisited in 2004, all the couples forming the nucleus of the church, with the exception of one, were still actively engaged with Adventism. A number of young, unmarried members had left during the course of the previous years, because, I was told, they found Adventist sexual morals too difficult to abide by.

The Wider Context

The success of the Seventh-day Adventist church in Maroantsetra and Sahameloka forms part of a new wave of Christianity that might well change the religious landscape in Madagascar.

We should not ignore the differences between the various movements I have referred to as New Churches. For example, Pentecostal church services are much more ecstatic than Adventist ones, involving, among other practices, Speaking in Tongues and the dramatic exorcism of demons from people's bodies (Jacquier Dubourdieu 1997). In contrast to Pentecostal services, glossolalia is not present at all, and exorcism rare, in Adventist practice (but see chapter 8). Indeed, the Adventists in Maroantsetra and Sahameloka talk with a degree of contempt about the Pentecostals' "loud" behavior ("They make too much noise!" *Mitabataba loatra zare!*).

Nevertheless, there are some striking similarities between the various movements, such as Seventh-day Adventism and Pentecostalism, which make up this new wave of Christianity. Among these similarities, two are particularly noteworthy.

The first is the New Churches' categorical rejection of those Malagasy practices that they consider to be "devil worship," in particular ritual communication with the ancestors. The claim that the ancestors are categorically "false" is a radical one in the Malagasy context where the relationship between living and dead kin is of such importance, and where the mainline churches have learnt to coexist with ancestor worship. Such coexistence is emphatically rejected by the New Churches and their converts are continually reminded of this.

The second feature most New Churches seem to share is an emphasis on the Bible. The Catholic church picked up on this issue and made the following statement in a publication concerning

New Churches in Africa and Madagascar:

> These new Christian groups claim that the Bible is their centre and
> foundation. Pastors preach with the Bible in their hands, and constantly
> turn to particular texts. Ordinary members take their Bible to services,
> and underline texts during sermons. Most Churches insist on Bible
> study sessions during the week. [...] Members of these new groups
> describe themselves as biblical Christians to distinguish themselves
> from other Christians—especially Catholics. By contrast, many
> Catholics appear to give little importance to the Bible. [...] In
> Catholic discourse, all too often other authorities appear far more
> important. The [Catholic] Church will have to make the Bible more
> central . . . (MAC 1993: 35)

. . . or it will continue to lose members to the New Churches. The
Catholic church seems to be more aware of this than many social scientists. Although these often note the key role of the Bible in New
Churches, they do not seem to take the issue very seriously and hence
move on quickly to other concerns (on Madagascar see Jacquier
Dubourdieu 1997; Walsh 2002: 375–376; on Africa see Gifford
1998: 78, 169; Meyer 1999: 135–136). Yet, when we recall Papan' i
Loricà reading his Bible for three-and-a-half hours, we ought to
recognize that Bible study may indeed be of great significance in
this new wave of Christianity.

In Madagascar, the two features I have highlighted—the rejection
of the ancestors and the emphasis on the Bible—are not just shared by
many of the New Churches that are entirely independent from the
Catholic and Protestant mainline churches. They are also shared by a
movement that has, very recently, gained tremendous significance in
the national political arena: the Revival movement (or *Fifohazana* in
Malagasy) within the Lutheran and Protestant churches of Madagascar
(see Jacquier Dubourdieu 2002). The Revival movement is comparable
to Pentecostalism insofar as it shares some basic characteristics with
the latter, namely glossolalia and the integration of a therapeutic
dimension into church services, in particular spiritual healing through
the exorcism of demons (see Jacquier Dubourdieu 1997; Rakotozafy
1997; Sharp 1993: 255–275).

Within the Lutheran church of Madagascar, the Revival movement
has a long history going back to the late nineteenth century. However
it is specifically since the 1970s, that this movement has begun to
flourish (Jacquier Dubourdieu 2002: 72–74). In response to the
Lutherans, the Protestant church of Madagascar (FJKM)—of which
the incumbent President of Madagascar, Marc Ravalomanana, later

became vice president—opened its own, internal *Département Fifohazana* (Revival department) in 1982. By the time of the first serious political challenge to the regime of former president Ratsiraka in the early 1990s, the Revival groups had developed into important political entities. The election of Marc Ravalomanana, a publicly devout Christian, as president of Madagascar in 2002, was not only a victory for all churches, but also a triumph for *Fifohazana*. The personal religiosity of Ravalomanana is incontestably of revivalist *couleur*, and the public rhetoric he employed against his adversary during the election campaign came straight from the evangelical repertoire: in order to "heal" the nation, Ratsiraka, as the anti-Christ, needed to be "expelled" from political power just as demons need to be exorcised from people's bodies (Jacquier Dubourdieu 2002). Consecrated preacher-healers of the Revival movement—called "sheperds" (*Mpiandry*), who are easily discernable by their long white robes— were not only prominently present during the new president's inauguration ceremony (Jacquier Dubourdieu 2002: 70), they also played a leading role in the transition of power. Here is an account by an eye witness:[49]

> A most amazing process occurred this past week: the installation of President Ravalomanana's new ministers in their office buildings. Each time, the process began with prayers and speeches at 13 May Plaza in downtown Antananarivo [the capital]. Afterwards, the peaceful crowd of over 100,000 [Ravalomanana's supporters] escorted the new ministers to their offices. The whole procession was led by "*Mpiandry*" or "Shepherds" in the revival movement of the FJKM [Protestant] and Lutheran churches. The marching crowd sang hymns. Upon reaching each ministry, the *Mpiandry* led the crowd in prayer and singing. The *Mpiandry* then exorcised the evil that had been conducted in the offices and dedicated them to a new just use. After this ceremony, the new minister entered the office building. This scene was repeated 16 times, culminating with the installation of the minister of defense on Friday.

Not only does the new president of Madagascar openly move toward an "evangelical republic," he has also introduced compulsory worship in all ministries (Jacquier Dubourdieu, personal communication). There is no doubt that the churches in general, and in particular the Revival movement, represent Ravalomanana's principal power base.

Fifohazana and Seventh-day Adventism are two of many different, yet to some extent similar, manifestations of the new Christian wave in Madagascar. Because new forms of Christianity have become so important in the lives of tens of thousands of Malagasy people, it is important to understand what motivates these people's religious commitment. Much research is needed. This book makes a start by attempting to grasp the meaning of Adventism for local practitioners in Maroantsetra and Sahameloka.

Chapter 3

International and Local Structure of the Adventist Church

Organization

Globally, the Seventh-day Adventist church is organized along several hierarchically related levels from, at the top, the General Conference, with headquarters in Silver Spring, Maryland (USA), to, at the bottom, any local church anywhere in the world.[1] Sahameloka and Silver Spring, for example, are linked by a string of ever larger geographical and organizational units. So we have (1) the local church in Sahameloka, which is part of (2) the Adventist community of Antakotako (which includes Sahameloka as well as a handful of other nearby villages), which in turn is part of (3) the Adventist district of Maroantsetra, which forms part of (4) the *Fédération du Centre* of Madagascar which, together with two other federations in the north and south of the country, form (5) the Adventist church of Madagascar, which beyond the boundaries of Madagascar is part of (6) the Southern Africa Indian Ocean Division, which is finally part of (7) the World Church.

The degree to which people in Madagascar are aware of their membership in these organizational units varies significantly and largely depends on their knowledge of the geography of the world, which in a place such as Sahameloka is generally extremely hazy. However, church members are routinely reminded of the fact that they are part of a globally organized church in various ways. In particular, they are regularly sent the Malagasy translation of a booklet produced in the United States, which is meant to help Adventists all around the world to study the Bible, and which is distributed to Adventist communities across the globe. Also, about every three months—during meetings of the Adventist district of Maroantsetra—testimonies of how God helps, as told by Adventists from around the world, are read to the congregation. However, to most people present at such district meetings, names like Brazil or China mean very little, if anything at all. This is because many people in Sahameloka, for example, imagine the world to consist of Madagascar along with many other islands the names of only a few, like France or America, they have heard before.

On the local level in Madagascar, not every Adventist congregation has the same official status. A group of people interested in Adventism who meet informally on Saturdays to pray and read the Bible is not officially recognized as a Seventh-day Adventist congregation. Such groups nevertheless appear in the church statistics[2] and the local pastor and other baptized members may spend considerable time with them in an attempt to solidify their commitment. When a group's numbers reach five to ten baptized members, they select a *Directeur d'Eglise* from among their ranks, which enables them to become recognized as a *Groupe organisé*. This move needs no specific authorization except for the consent of the local pastor. To become an *Eglise organisée* however— that is, an officially recognized Adventist congregation—requires the authorization of the local pastor based on three criteria: first, spiritual maturity, second, at least 20 baptized members with named persons willing to take on particular offices, and third, financial independence. The local pastor's decision to accept a new *Eglise organisée* is subject to approval by the Adventist headquarters in Madagascar's capital.

On the structural level then, the Seventh-day Adventist church in Madagascar and elsewhere is organized along clearly hierarchical lines, with the consequence that disregarding regulations may entail reprimand. One day during fieldwork, a large group of Adventists from a town further north (Andapa) turned up in Maroantsetra in order to proselytize in the area. This they had decided to do without the authorization of either their own pastor or of the pastor working in Maroantsetra, and nobody in Maroantsetra had heard anything about their intensions before they arrived. Moreover, the town where they came from belonged to a different Adventist federation than Maroantsetra, which meant that they needed a specific authorization from the center in the capital to embark on their mission work. They had not bothered to obtain any of this and hence they had clearly breached a number of rules. So when they suddenly turned up in Maroantsetra out of the blue, they were simply ignored by the local pastor who denied them access to the church.

Participation

The rather rigid administrative and organizational structure of the church is, however, counterbalanced by the active participation of all baptized members in important decision-making processes. In every *Eglise organisée*, there are a number of offices, such as that of lay leader, deacon and treasurer. The people holding such offices are democratically elected on an annual basis in a process that involves several stages in which the congregation is actively involved. During this process, every baptized member of the local church may speak up against a particular candidate who they consider morally or otherwise unfit for the office in question (the same is the case with candidates for baptism).[3] The people elected to specific offices in this way together form a committee (*comité*) that deals with the affairs of, or problems within, the local congregation.

This formal participation of all baptized members in the affairs of their own church is mirrored by the fact that everyone who wishes to do so—including people who are not yet baptized, or "guests" such as myself—can actively participate in any church service. Indeed, such participation is always strongly encouraged. The first time I walked into the Adventist church in Maroantsetra and sat through a service, I was astonished by the number of people taking an active role in it. I kept asking Maman' i Beby, next to whom I was sitting, who all the people performing some task or other were. "They are just ordinary people (*ôlo tsotra fô*)." At that time, the answer surprised me. As I came to learn, however, an Adventist church service is not at all dominated by the pastor, even if he is present. Many lay members play an active role reading from the Bible, explaining biblical texts, giving sermons, announcing songs or leading prayers. Watching the proceedings, I often felt that had I not already known who the pastor was, I would not have been able to identify him. I remember one occasion when his role was limited to musical accompaniment on an electrical keyboard, while seven members of the congregation led the Sabbath service. Since there was only one pastor in the district, he tended to spend many Sabbaths with congregations in the countryside where church members normally rely entirely on themselves to run their church. The service in town was always conducted in the same way with or without the pastor. Organizational matters, such as mission work to be undertaken, were also jointly discussed during church services.[4]

It is possible however for people to be banned from taking on any specific role during church services apart from that of an ordinary participant; and indeed, this seems to happen rather often. Such a ban is usually placed on someone for morally unacceptable behavior, especially extramarital sexual relations. The decision to place a ban on someone and to lift it is taken by the local church committee.

Although some people, in particular lay leaders, play a prominent role during church services much more often than others, active

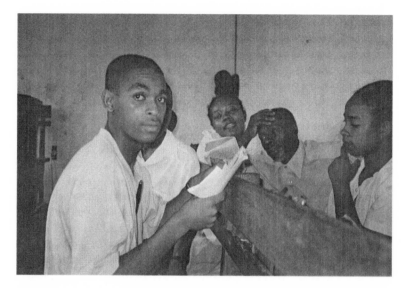

Figure 3.1 A young man chairing a Bible study session in church.

participation is not just limited to a handful of persons.[5] Not only is it not always the same individuals who lead church services, but everyone present, young and old, men and women, can actively participate and tend to do so.

On the whole, Malagasy societies have a comparatively strong tendency toward gender egalitarianism (Bloch 1987, 1992, 1993a, Lambek 1992b). This tradition is maintained by the local Adventists. Although certain offices—in particular that of pastor and lay leader— are only open to men and although Seventh-day Adventist doctrine is patriarchal, local Adventist women are as active and as vocal as men, when engaging in Adventist religious practice both in church and at home. It is worth mentioning that I never observed women's opinions and views being taken in any way less seriously than men's. Gender relations will therefore not play a big role in the course of this book.

Similarly, young and old participate equally. Church services are regularly led by one more experienced person along with a boy or girl, who is assigned an easy task such as announcing songs. And the young are also listened to, when they speak in church.

In fact, the lack of age hierarchy during religious activities is very striking, in church and at home. In Sahameloka, it was often Claude, the eldest son, who taught his parents about biblical matters, simply because he was by far the most literate of the family and thus his Bible expertise was superior to theirs. During church services, older people had no authority over younger ones by virtue of their age. It sometimes happened that a young man, someone like Kiki who was 18 at the time, chaired a Bible discussion among a group of people that included many persons much older than himself, and indeed persons considered elders in Malagasy society (see figure 3.1).

Seniority

This age-blindness practiced by the local Adventists is strikingly different to the every day Malagasy emphasis on seniority as the principal source, and legitimation, of authority. Everywhere in Madagascar, the young learn from the old, and the old learn from the ancestors, and any breach of this seniority principle tends to be strongly reprimanded. As is widely documented in Malagasy ethnography, age—or its social representation—is a crucial aspect of status and informs much social behavior (see e.g., Bloch 1993b, Lambek 1992b: 77–80). Although the norms of daily interaction between younger and older people vary considerably in different parts of Madagascar, everywhere juniors are expected to show deference toward their seniors, in particular to kin. Senior people are approached and treated respectfully, and one does not contradict what they say, but rather seeks their advice and consent.

Maturity measured in terms of age is, however, not a prerequisite for a lay leader of the Adventist church, which is why I translate *lôhôlo* (the local dialect equivalent of *loholona*) as lay leader and not as elder. Many criteria come into play when choosing a lay leader, but particularly important are literacy, biblical expertise, moral integrity and commitment to the church.[6] In Sahameloka, the two *lôhôlo* were both young men while more senior, but less literate, people, were simply ordinary members of the church. In Maroantsetra where there were many more *lôhôlo*, their age ranged from 30 to 60. It is also important to note that Adventists who hold more important positions in society at large are not more likely to be chosen as lay leaders than those of low status. The lay leaders in Maroantsetra and in Sahameloka were not people who were in any way more influential—socially, politically or economically—than other church members. Rakoto, for example, was one of the elected lay leaders in Maroantsetra. Rakoto was young (he was in his early 30s), he did not have any proper job, and he was probably of slave descent.[7] Vice versa, a person does not become more influential socially by virtue of being an Adventist *lôhôlo*.

But let me now return to the issue of seniority. I noted that interaction between Adventists is strikingly age-blind. However, this assertion must be qualified.

First of all, it is important to point out that the concept of an elder in Malagasy society and that of an Adventist lay leader are clearly distinct, and different expressions are used to refer to these positions. While a senior person in Madagascar is referred to as *ray aman-dreny*—which literally means "father and mother"—the term *lôhôlo* means "head of the people." Elders in Malagasy societies are associated with morality and wisdom as revealed by the ancestors (see e.g., Bloch 1993b: 99–100, Cole 2001: 283–284), and therefore what they say is almost unchallengeable. Being a *lôhôlo*, in contrast, does not in any way imply moral authority. For example, when during my stay in Sahameloka one of the elected *lôhôlo* fell out with the rest of the congregation over a money matter, the local committee withdrew his right to act as leader and to perform his duties in that capacity until the issue was resolved.

Second, *inside* the church a young man may, when leading a service, call upon his uncle, or even father, to step forward and perform a particular task such as reading a passage from the Bible. Significantly, the young man would not, in this situation, use teknonyms as is otherwise always done, and he would not address his father as "papa." Rather he would address everyone by their "proper" name. However, the minute the two men step *outside* the church, they slip back into their traditional roles as senior and junior kin. During Bible study at home, Claude acts as teacher of his parents. But other than in this specifically Adventist context, Papan' i Claude has full authority over his son, and Claude would never dream of challenging the authority of his father or that of other church members who are senior to him in ordinary life. I have observed this code switching many times, both in town and in the village, and mostly it happens smoothly and skillfully. In the rare cases when junior members of the church fail to act according to the seniority principle outside the church, they are sharply reprimanded by their seniors, just as anyone else would be, irrespective of their position within the church. Interaction within the church is something out of the ordinary and hence the seniority principle can be temporarily overridden. But this is not allowed to transform social relations beyond that specific context (compare Bloch 1993b). Thus it is clear that, unlike in the case of Pentecostals in Malawi discussed by van Dijk (1998), Adventist practice does not constitute a challenge to, but coexists with, the Malagasy concept of seniority.

Third, the notion of seniority and of elderhood, which is so important in Madagascar, is not entirely excluded even *within* the Adventist church. The clearest indication of this is that the pastor and his wife are considered to be the elders (*ray aman-dreny*) of all church members, rather than *lôhôlo*. This is so regardless of their actual age, because their status as elders is a social representation of seniority. In the case of Maroantsetra the pastor and his wife were indeed much younger than many other church members. The recognition of their status as elders became particularly clear around New Year, when they were paid a visit by a large number of representatives of the local Adventist community and were presented with piles of gifts including rice, coconuts, bananas, eggs and several chickens, as well as money. This is a clear imitation of the local custom of gift-giving between kin, with gifts directed especially to one's *ray aman-dreny*.

Moreover, older members of the church are treated with respect, regardless of whether or not they are *lôhôlo* or hold any particular office within the church organization. Papan' i Claude, for example, could not act as lay leader of the church in Sahameloka due to his insufficient literacy. However, because he was the most senior of all Adventists in the village, he was made an honorary member of the village's church committee.

The fact that the principle of seniority is generally respected by the local Adventists and that it is not categorically excluded from within the church context also came to the fore shortly before I left Sahameloka. In order to thank everyone for the hospitality and generosity they had shown toward me, I stepped forward to speak on the last evening I attended church, accompanied by Papan' i Silivie who at that time was acting as *lôhôlo*. After I had expressed my thanks and handed him an envelope with some money for the village's congregation as a farewell present, he replied in a consummately Malagasy style with more or less these words: "I am but a child (*mbôla zazahely izaho*) and know nothing. Therefore I want to ask the *ray aman-dreny* (elder) among us to respond to what our sister has said and to wish her well on behalf of all of us," thus giving the floor to Papan' i Fredel who was the oldest member of the congregation present that day. When I returned to Sahameloka for a brief visit in 2004, a similar farewell-situation occurred in church. Before starting to speak, Papan' i Vangé, the most senior person present, ascertained that it was indeed he who was supposed to speak by asking the congregation: "Is there someone here who is my senior?" (*Misy zoky?*). Only after this question had been answered in the negative, did he proceed to deliver his speech.

In sum, it is only strictly within the context of religious activities that age stops playing the role it normally does in everyday life in Madagascar. As soon as that specific context is departed from—even if physically, as in the above examples, people are still in church—traditional notions of seniority prevail.

Authority

To end this chapter on the existence—and nonexistence—of hierarchies within the Adventist church, we need to look at church members' attitude toward authority. From the Adventists' point of view, there is one key distinction: God's authority on the one hand, human authority on the other. While Adventists accept the former without qualification, they categorically reject the latter.

From an Adventist perspective, everything that happens on earth is the outcome of a continuous struggle between God and Satan. There is not one inch of neutral ground. Therefore, everybody *must* choose between either serving God or serving Satan as their master (*tompo*). There is a very strong sense among local Adventists, and I suppose Adventists elsewhere, that total freedom from any kind of authority is not possible for human beings. In this respect, the Adventists are very much trusting of authority, as is generally claimed to be the case for "fundamentalists."[8]

However, this is as far as the Adventists' submission to authority goes. It is an acceptance of, and submission to, God's authority, and God's authority alone. But this does not imply, contrary to what many writers suggest, that "fundamentalist movements, because of their insistence on singular truth, are likely to establish leadership structures that are strictly hierarchical in form" (Ammerman 1994: 158). On the contrary, human authority in religious matters is categorically rejected by the Adventists. The alleged date of Christ's birth, as declared by some Pope or other, is valueless for them, since it is based on *human* authority. Nowhere in the Bible does it say that Jesus was born in December, Maman' i Claude explained to me as we were harvesting rice in the summer heat. Hence Seventh-day Adventists do not celebrate Christmas, Easter or Pentecost, since all of these celebrations are based on incorrect human calculations. Papan' i Fredel embarked on a similar line of argument with regard to Sunday as the day of worship:[9]

> When we look in the Bible, [we understand that] it was *people* who invented Sunday as the day of worship, but not God. That's explained in this book [probably a book by the Adventist prophetess Ellen White] . . . there it says that the Sabbath has always been the day of God, but that it was *we* who replaced the Sabbath with Sunday. It was some Catholic priest who signed this in the year 321.[10]

Maman' i Claude's and Papan' i Fredel's explanations are not primarily anti-*Catholic* statements, rather they express their nonacceptance of human authority in religious matters in general. Indeed, the Adventists' skepticism toward human authority does not stop at the doorstep of their own church.

As we have seen, the organizational structure of the Adventist church gives certain people the right to make decisions and to authorize or sanction certain actions. But no position in the church gives anybody *spiritual* or *moral* authority, not even that of the pastor. In the aforementioned story of a group of Adventists suddenly turning up in Maroantsetra to proselytize without having previously informed anybody about their mission, the pastor denied them access to the church. The majority of the church members in Maroantsetra, however, felt that people intent on spreading the gospel were doing "God's work" regardless of whether or not they were breaking church regulations. Thus, against the pastor's explicit wishes, they organized food and shelter for the guests as well as a place for them to hold events. Ironically, as a result of the successful mission work of this group, within a couple of months large numbers of people in the district converted to Adventism. This made Maroantsetra "district of the year," with the largest number of converts in all of Madagascar, for which the *pastor* was rewarded with a trip to Mauritius.

The pastor does, however, have spiritual authority in some ritual contexts. Unless specifically authorized, baptism in particular can only be carried out by a pastor. The Communion is normally led by the pastor, but if he does not happen to be around, elected lay leaders of the church may perform Communion too.

The Adventists' rejection of human authority is also very pronounced with regard to Bible interpretation. For obvious reasons, the pastor knows the Bible much better than most other members of the church who therefore happily accept the pastor's explanations and interpretations most of the time. However, they do this not because a pastor, by virtue of his office, has any claims to better understanding than any other member of the church, but because he has more knowledge of the Bible. Nor is the pastor necessarily right in case of dispute over interpretations of the Bible dictating what proper behavior is. When it happens that different pastors have diverging opinions on a particular matter—one such scenario I witnessed concerned the question of contraception, an issue raised on the occasion of another pastor's visit to Maroantsetra—it is up to every single member of the congregation to make up their mind as to who is right.[11] The Adventists in Maroantsetra and Sahameloka would agree that there is only one truth. But in their view, everyone is equally entitled and qualified to discover for themselves what that truth might be.

This situation is, in fact, not unique, but rather typical of "fundamentalists." Lehmann (1998: 617–621) and Bruce (2000: 98) have both pointed out that although "fundamentalists" are convinced of the inerrancy of their sacred text, "any right-spirited person can discern God's will by reading the scriptures" (Bruce 2000: 98). It follows from this that there is no one authoritative interpretation of the Bible.

However, there are limits to this general interpretative egalitarianism, since it does not apply to the basics of Seventh-day Adventism either in terms of doctrine or behavior. The creation of the world in six days for example or, around Maroantsetra, the interpretation of exhumation as a manifestation of Satan's power, are not negotiable and it is not up to every member of the congregation to form their individual opinion on such fundamental issues. This is a topic to which I will return in chapter 6.

Chapter 4

Profiles

The discussion in chapter 3 of the international and the local structure of the Seventh-day Adventist church has revealed Malagasy Adventists' participatory approach to decision making as well as to the running of their church. The pronounced lack of hierarchy among church members including the pastor, within the confines of church affairs, also became clear.

In this chapter we move closer to the local church's individual members and look at who they are. One question that needs to be considered is whether or not these church members belong to a particular kind of sub-group within the general population of the district. In order to answer this question, I begin with a discussion of church members' religious and ethnic background, their socioeconomic position and also their age. The second part of the chapter provides biographical sketches for a number of selected people. These vignettes offer a first glimpse of different church members' daily lives in- and outside of the Adventist church.

Background

Religious and Ethnic Background

In terms of their religious background, the members of the Adventist church differ only slightly from the general population. While only about half of the district's population are affiliated with any church at all, most Adventists were members of either the Catholic or the Protestant church before they converted to Adventism, with a slight majority of former Protestants over former Catholics. Only a few people without any previous church affiliation become Adventists. Some individuals had tried out other New Churches present in the district before joining the Adventist church. Both in Maroantsetra and

Sahameloka, most of the teenage members of the church were born into families already practicing the Adventist faith, so they did not go through the same process of conversion as their parents or, more rarely, their grandparents.

With regard to church members' origins, we find that the Adventists are entirely representative of the district's population. Most members of the Adventist church in town originate from the nearby countryside, while a few of them are migrants who have come from further away. In Sahameloka, all the church members are either from the village or, in the case of most women, from a village in the vicinity.

Socioeconomic Position

Neither do the members of the Adventist church form a particular sub-group of the general population with regard to their socioeconomic position and their status in society at large. Let us first look at the data concerning the town. Between 1998 and 2000, three church members had jobs in the post office in Maroantsetra, one worked as a civil servant, two worked as teachers, one as a carpenter, and one as a mechanic; several women sold food or clothes at the market; some church members were rice farmers; and many made a living by engaging in a mixture of activities. Like other people in town, church members tended to remain in close contact with both non-Adventist and Adventist kin in their villages of origin. In other words, the Adventists are, on the whole, perfectly average inhabitants, if such a thing exists. Except for one very wealthy family, who runs a shop of the kind run by Malagasy-Indians, church members do not belong to either of the two types of elite that exist in town. Neither are they involved in the lucrative export of cash crops, nor are they part of the elite connected with political power. Generally speaking, they belong to the poorer sections of society without, however, forming any kind of particularly poor minority. Although this is an assertion that is difficult to prove, there are at least some indicators we can follow.

First, again generally speaking, the Catholic church in Maroantsetra tends to attract more affluent sectors of society while poor people are more likely to be Protestants. As we have seen, slightly more Adventists used to be Protestants than Catholics. In some cases, poverty can indeed be an issue. Vavon' i Giselle is an old, extremely poor woman who used to be a Catholic, but who, for many years now, has occasionally attended Adventist church services. She lives by herself in a tiny room in Maroantsetra that serves as her bedroom, living room and kitchen. All her belongings are rolled up in the one corner where the floor is not broken. What she likes about the Adventist church, she explained, is that nobody looks down on her for her shabby clothes and lack of shoes as happened with the Catholics.

A second indication of the relative poverty of church members in town is the sometimes very small contribution given to the collection in church on the Sabbath. Many times I observed people giving less than 500Fmg, which even for a poor person would not have been much (500Fmg was worth about one cup of rice). People were expected to give at least 500Fmg, and those who could not give that much seemed embarrassed when the hat passed by and they only put in a few small coins or nothing. If they could have given more, they certainly would have done so.

But perhaps one of the best indicators of people's financial situation is the way they dress in church or at New Year, because on such occasions, everyone tries to dress as well and as lavishly as possible. While one never sees anybody barefoot in the Catholic or Protestant church in Maroantsetra, I have seen many members of the Adventist church dressed in stained or mended second-hand clothes and not wearing plastic sandals, let alone shoes, even on their day of baptism. The day of baptism is a very important day for Adventists and I am certain they would have put on some footwear for that particular occasion had they had any. One Sabbath, 106 new members were baptized during a district meeting. Half of those to be baptized were barefoot and not one of them wore proper shoes. However, it is important to note that most of these people came from villages in the countryside, where shoes are a great luxury that only few people possess.

The Issue of Slave Descent

The question of whether the Adventists in Sahameloka come from a particular socioeconomic class brings us back to the issue of slave descent. One of the reasons that made me choose Sahameloka as a second fieldsite was the fact that I wanted to investigate a possible link between slave descent and Adventism. Sahameloka has a very high number of Seventh-day Adventists. In the year 2000, almost 10 percent of the adult population were members of the Adventist church, in comparison to only 1 percent in the district as a whole. At the same time, many inhabitants of Sahameloka are of slave descent. It would be tempting to conclude that there is a link between these two facts, and the literature on religious "fundamentalism" and New Churches would clearly suggest such a conclusion. However, the ethnographic evidence is in fact highly ambiguous.

First of all, as we saw in chapter 1, people of slave descent are neither socially stigmatized nor economically marginalized in this area of

Madagascar. Thus one cannot simply assume that this aspect of their background is decisive in their lives.

Second, four of the seven ancestries who live in Sahameloka are almost certainly of slave descent. However, only in two of these are there significant numbers of Seventh-day Adventists; of the other two ancestries one has only one Adventist, and the other none at all. A significant number of Adventists are also found among the ancestry which stems from the marriage between a man of the Zafindrabay lineage (the former rulers and slaveholders) and a female descendant of slaves of the Zafindrabay. There are no Adventists, however, among the descendants of the Zafindrabay, and only one among the recent immigrant group from the south of Madagascar. Thus although it is true that it is precisely the two ancestries who are *not* of slave descent that do *not* have any Adventists, it is also true that there are *no* Adventists in another two ancestries whose ancestors *were* slaves. The following summary may make this information clearer. In the ancestries underlined, there is more than one Adventist.

ancestries of slave descent: <u>One</u>, <u>Two</u>, *Three, Four*
ancestries not of slave descent: Five, Six
ancestry of mixed origin: <u>Seven</u>

The suggestion that there is a link between Adventism and slave descent in Sahameloka is at least questionable also because of the timing of people's conversion. In chapter 1, I told the story of how the people of Sahameloka carried the bones of their ancestors to the village and established their own graveyards. This was around 1992. I interpret this return of the ancestral bones as the finalization of the process of becoming rooted in Sahameloka. Not only have the inhabitants of Sahameloka now established a home for themselves, they have also created a new "land of the ancestors," *tanindrazana*, and the arrival of the ancestral bones completes that creation. In Madagascar, it is the absence of one's own *tanindrazana*, the nonexistence of ancestral history and of ancestral blessing, which marks slave, or quasi-slave, status. Thus by creating a new *tanindrazana* in Sahameloka, the village inhabitants have in fact stopped being of slave descent, except in terms of historical memory. Significantly, it was only a year or two *after* the transferal of the ancestral bones to Sahameloka that the first people joined the Adventist church with many following soon after. If one was claiming that Adventism is attractive to people of slave descent because it offers an alternative route of integration, as much of the literature would suggest, it would seem extremely strange that the members of the church in Sahameloka should have joined the church almost immediately after having overcome their slave descent. It would seem extremely strange that as soon as they became fully rooted in a new *tanindrazana*, they would opt to give up their (newly won) ancestors, as the Adventist church demands of its members. If slave descent were the issue, the timing of people's conversion would make no sense at all. How, then, can one explain the fact that there is such a high number of Adventists in Sahameloka? This is a question we must leave aside for the moment, but to which I will return in chapter 12.

Age

One of the striking features of the Adventist congregation in Sahameloka, but not in Maroantsetra, is the youth of its members.[1] With the exception of three couples and one bachelor in their late 40s, all of the members are young couples in their 20s or early 30s, or people not yet married. There are no very old people in the church except for one woman who occasionally attends a Sabbath service, but who is not baptized. In Maroantsetra town, however, the picture is different. There, many old people who are regarded as elders in Malagasy society are baptized members of the church and regularly attend Adventist church services not only on the Sabbath, but also during the week. While in Sahameloka the church is largely run by young people, it is the more senior members who have a leading role in Maroantsetra, though this does not exclude younger people from actively participating. The reason for this ethnographic difference is not clear to me. In his analysis of Pentecostalism in Malawi, van Dijk suggests that the Born-Again movement is primarily an attempt by young people to liberate themselves from the grip of the traditional gerontocratic society (1998). This interpretation is not supported by my data from Madagascar because, as we saw in chapter 3, the seniority principle is not challenged by young local Adventists outside the context of church services.

We can conclude, then, from the analysis of church members' background that—in all but the last point concerning their age, and that only with regard to Sahameloka but not Maroantsetra—they do not form, or belong to, a particular kind of sub-group of the general population of the district. This picture is confirmed when we look at church members' daily lives and at what role their involvement with Adventism plays within these. I will begin with the families with whom I lived.

Vignettes

In the area of Maroantsetra, it has, up to now, always been individual people or nuclear families who have joined the Adventist church. Consequently, in almost all cases, church members remain a small minority within their kin group. In contrast to cases such as the Urapmin (cf. Robbins 2004) or the Boroi (cf. Josephides 1982) in Papua New Guinea where the whole community converted to Baptism and Adventism respectively, in Madagascar, conversion to Adventism causes significant tensions between Adventist and non-Adventist kin. The Adventists do not take part in important ritual activities through which people in the area communicate with their ancestors. This is because according to Seventh-day Adventist interpretation, what people take to be their ancestors is in fact the devil in disguise. For their non-Adventist kin, however, such ritual communication with one's ancestors provides the basis of the community's future and prosperity. The tensions that result from these contradictory interpretations will be discussed in depth in part III of the book, but they are already foreshadowed in the biographical sketches that follow.

An Urban Family

The members of my host family in Maroantsetra lead a life typical of town dwellers. Papan' i Beby,[2] a man in his early 50s, is a civil servant. He comes from a poor family, but nevertheless managed to train as a hydraulic technician at a college in the capital of Madagascar. He has been working for the local *Service du Génie Rural* (Rural Engineering Department) for a very long time and receives a regular, if low, salary. One of his main jobs is to make maps of different parts of the district, and so he spends a considerable amount of time—weeks and, occasionally, months at a time—in the countryside conducting the necessary surveys. Maman' i Beby is responsible for doing the daily shopping at the market and for the cooking and other household-related activities. They have three children. The oldest, a daughter, moved away from Maroantsetra many years before I arrived for reasons that were not directly spoken about. Contact between her and her parents has been minimal ever since. The other two children, an 18-year old boy called Kiki and a 15-year old girl called Beby, live with their parents. As there is no Adventist school for pupils of their age, both go to a Catholic school. They spend their free time with Adventist and non-Adventist friends alike.

During the course of the many years Papan' i Beby has worked for the Malagasy government, he has been transferred to several towns in

Madagascar. In 1982 he was transferred to Maroantsetra where, since it is a rice-growing area, his specialization as a hydraulic engineer is in great demand. The family has lived in Maroantsetra ever since. However, despite their long-term residence in the region, they continue to feel like strangers there and long to go back to Brickaville, further south along the east coast, where they both originally come from. They feel uprooted and torn away from where they belong.

The family is not well off, partly because neither Papan' i Beby nor Maman' i Beby have kin or land in the district. Therefore they have to pay rent and buy all the rice for family consumption. They live in a small house whose roof leaks in numerous places, and whenever it rains, buckets are quickly distributed around the house. The formal education of Kiki and Beby is their parents' top priority, and they dedicate a large percentage of their income to this end.

The member of the family who "shines the brightest," it seems to me, is Papan' i Beby. Though self-taught he is extraordinarily learned, and not just by local standards. He loves to read and study and always has done, he says. He is an intellectual man who enjoys discussing issues of all kinds, eagerly absorbing any information he comes across. Many times he impressed me with his tremendous knowledge of world history, geography and scientific inventions—which far surpassed my own—not to mention his biblical expertise and his fluency in French. I was amazed, for example, to hear him explain the meaning of the expression *pachyderm*, or the fact that it was the Roman Emperor Vespasian who first introduced public toilets and that therefore men's public toilets are called *vespasienne* in France. On one occasion his daughter Beby asked him what a *mausolée* was. Without a moment's hesitation he explained that there used to be, in antiquity, a ruler called Mausol who had a tomb built for himself in the style of what came to be known as a *mausolée*. Papan' i Beby continued by saying that this was one of the Seven Wonders of the World which, of course, he was able to list with ease. Looking back on his days at school, he recalls having studied by the cooking fire for lack of paraffin and having been in possession of just one pair of trousers and a single shirt until his teacher, noticing both his poverty and his talent for study, gave him a second shirt as a present.

Maman' i Beby's level of literacy is also high by local standards, though not comparable to Papan' i Beby's. She suffers more than her husband does from being far away from home. She often speaks with great affection about her *grandmère* who brought her up, because her own mother was only a teenager when Maman' i Beby was born. Despite the fact that *grandmère* has been a spirit medium all her life, and thinks of church-goers in general as hypocrites, Maman' i Beby has real hopes that *grandmère* might go to heaven, because of her good heart which, after all, is what matters most. Maman' i Beby also has a great-grandmother of Arab origin from southeast Madagascar, a fact that she often mentions rather proudly pointing to her facial features, which bear that heritage. Maman' i Beby is liked by many people in town, and she has friends in many non-Adventist households. She has an especially good relationship with a Malagasy-Indian family that runs a shop in the town center, as well as with the owner of the local pharmacy. In her free time, Maman' i Beby does beautiful embroidery, decorating sheets and pillow cases with *sujets Malgache*— depicting colorfully dressed people planting rice, riding in canoes or carrying babies on their backs. This goes to supplement Papan' i Beby's income.

Maman' and Papan' i Beby joined the Adventist church shortly after they arrived in Maroantsetra in 1982. Both Kiki and Beby grew up with Adventism. When I first met them in 1987, and still when I lived with them a decade later, they were all very committed church members. Everyone had specific duties within the church, and Papan' i Beby had been a lay leader of the local congregation for many years. He was often approached for advice on church-related affairs and other matters. When Maman' and Papan' i Beby walk to church on a Sabbath morning, dressed in smart clothes and polished shoes, one would never think that they had just come out of a house that leans so much that the family jokingly calls it "our Boeing" (*Boeingtsika*).

A Rural Family

Like everyone else in Sahameloka, Maman' and Papan' i Claude spend almost all of their time looking after their rice and their crops in the forest. They have four children. Claude, their first child aged 20, Mazava, his younger sister aged 14, and two considerably younger boys. Two other children died young, probably of malaria. Claude and Mazava are an indispensable help to their parents in managing the daily workload.

Papan' i Claude has lived in Sahameloka all his life, while his wife comes from a village an hour's walk away. Their main ambition and desire is to provide their children with enough land for them to make a living in the future, together with their partners.[3]

Both Maman' and Papan' i Claude went to local primary schools for a few years, but neither of them is fluent in reading or writing. In fact, Papan' i Claude is practically illiterate, but he knows a lot about village history. Maman' i Claude can manage to read fairly long texts, though only slowly and not without stumbling over a word or an expression here and there. Claude, the eldest son, completed primary school in Sahameloka and even began secondary school in Maroantsetra—which is very rare indeed for rural children—while his sister Mazava never took to schooling much and is hardly able to read, let alone write. Mezaquei, the 9-year old boy, finds every possible reason to skip school and is often discovered sneaking up to his mother or brother as they go into the forest. He has repeated the first grade five times already but still cannot read or write any word other than his own name, and even that not with ease. The members of the family only have the vaguest of ideas about the outside world. They were immensely impressed both by my literacy (and especially by how fast I could write) and by my technical equipment that consisted of a simple camera and a tape recorder.

Maman' and Papan' i Claude were the very first members of the Adventist church in Sahameloka. Papan' i Claude at 47 years of age is also the oldest baptized member in the village and is thus respected as an elder (ray aman-dreny) within the congregation. However, neither he nor his wife can play a leading role in the local church because of their lack of literacy and biblical expertise. In spite of this though, they are very committed church members.

Maman' and Papan' i Silivie from Sahameloka

Maman' and Papan' i Silivie are a young couple with two daughters, aged 6 and 1. While Papan' i Silivie was born and raised in Sahameloka, Maman' i Silivie comes from a village further downstream. They are relatively well off rice farmers mainly because Papan' i Silivie only has three siblings, so his parents' land did not have to be split between too many parties. In spite of their economic status, they live in a tiny house, even by local standards. Both attended a few years at primary school, and their reading and writing skills are good. However, despite knowing that he was born in 1966, figuring out his age proved a difficult task for Papan' i Silivie. Giving up on his mental calculations, he concluded: "I may be roughly thirty or so."

Both Maman' and Papan' i Silivie are enthusiastic members of the Adventist church in Sahameloka, and they both have a number of duties within it. They were among the first people of the village to join in 1993 and both were baptized a year later, and now have their baptismal certificates proudly displayed on the wall. Papan' i Silivie in particular is a very vocal member of the congregation. He is always one of the first to detect laxness in religious matters among its members and to remind people of the necessity of studying the Bible every single day, and of trusting in God even in times of hardship.

Papan' i Silivie often chairs Bible discussions in church, while his wife sits outdoors with the young children teaching them a new song.

Christa

Christa is a 17-year old boy from Sahameloka who at the time of my fieldwork lived in Maroantsetra, together with one of his younger brothers, in order to attend school there. When I met him, he had been interested in Adventism for about two months. He was really enthusiastic, and before the day of baptism urged me to take his picture on that occasion. Christa's parents in Sahameloka, however, were extremely hostile to the idea of him joining the church and threatened to disinherit him and bar him from the house if he did so. Christa remained firm, announcing that he was going to be an Adventist regardless of what his family said. He stopped attending exhumations to demonstrate his commitment. As a result, his parents stopped paying his school fees thus forcing him to move back to Sahameloka. Just two months after his baptism, Christa had already left the church never even bothering to pick up the pictures of his baptism that he'd been so keen to have taken. Everyone in the village agreed that he simply could not take the pressure from his family.

Christa is an example of someone intensely, but only briefly, involved with the Adventist church. He is also an example of someone torn between different loyalties, again a common problem for members of the Seventh-day Adventist church certainly in the Maroantsetra area, and probably throughout Madagascar and elsewhere. This was brought home to me when he appeared in church on one of the first Saturdays after I had arrived in Sahameloka. Sitting right at the back with the nails of his little fingers painted pink—a contemporary fashion among young urban men in Maroantsetra, but frowned upon by the Adventists who are not in favor of any kind of makeup—he did not utter a word during the entire morning. I am sure he wanted to give me the impression that he was still with the Adventists as he claimed. However, he only came that one time and I never saw him in church again. After all, Sahameloka was his parents' village, and his parents upon whom he was dependent disapproved strongly of his involvement in the church.

Maman- and Papan-dRakoto from Maroantsetra[4]

Rakoto's mother and father are among the oldest members of the Adventist congregation in Maroantsetra town. They joined the church in 1968 and have been with it ever since. Three of their six children are Seventh-day Adventists as well. Neither Rakoto's father nor his mother originate from the area, both coming from other towns along the east coast. While Maman-dRakoto was brought to Maroantsetra as a child to be looked after by her grandmother, Papan-dRakoto came as a young man in search of land to cultivate. He is said to be of slave descent. Today, the couple have their own rice fields, but they also work as sharecroppers on other people's land. They are very poor people.

While Maman-dRakoto regularly attends church service on the Sabbath, together with her children and in-laws, Papan-dRakoto only turns up occasionally and only when there is no work to be done in the fields. When he does come to church, he seems to sleep most of the time (he is also hard of hearing). Moreover, he holds the ritual office of "the guardian of the tomb" (*mpiambinjiny*) of his ancestry in Maroantsetra.[5] This office necessitates his participation in exhumations and sacrifices which is entirely against Adventist principles. Maman- and Papan-dRakoto are, of course, aware of this but, like Christa, they are torn between different loyalties—toward the church, toward their families and toward the wider community within which they are respected elders (*ólo maventy*). They would "feel ashamed" (*henamaso*), they explained to me, if Papan-dRakoto gave up his ritual office. But, they added, since the church disapproves, they prefer to keep quiet about this (although everyone in church knows anyway).

Maman' i Ominò

Maman' i Ominò lives with three of her four children, aged between 6 and 17, in a tiny place in Maroantsetra that is just big enough, but only just, to accommodate all of them with their few belongings. She also has a 24-year old daughter (from a brief relationship with a French man) who lives in Madagascar's capital city. Throughout my stay in the region, her husband, a teacher, was away training in the capital and only came to visit once a year. Maman' i Ominò, together with her husband, became an Adventist in 1983.

Despite being local people, neither she nor her husband have their own rice fields, for reasons that remain unclear to me. And so Maman' i Ominò has had to find other ways of making a living for herself and her children as best she can. At one point she used to make hats that she sold at the local market. Six years before I got to know her, she had taken up selling books on behalf of the Adventist church, a job several of the local church members have (I will come back to this point later on in the book). However, she neither possessed nor had she read any of the books she sold, as the books were beyond both her financial means and her reading abilities, especially as most were written in French. She also worked on other people's rice fields helping out here and there.

Maman' i Ominò is a well-known walker. Once she decided to go and visit her husband in the capital hundreds of kilometers away. Because she could not afford the entire *taxi-brousse* fare, let alone the cost of an airplane ticket, she walked some 200 km both ways in order to cut down her expenses. From the capital she brought back with her a big bag full of second-hand clothes (transported by a *taxi-brousse*) which she then sold at the market.

Maman' i Ominò had ended up with the Seventh-day Adventist church more by luck than by design and was intrigued at first only by the choir. Nevertheless, when I met her, she was committed more strongly to the Adventist worldview and lifestyle than many other members who had consciously chosen it.

Miry's Grandmother

Miry's grandmother, Dadin' i Miry, as I came to know her, is from the offshore island of St. Marie south of Maroantsetra, which she and her husband left some forty years ago in search of land and work. Dadin' i Miry never went to school and is completely illiterate. She has given birth to 18 children of whom 11 are still alive. The father of her children left her seven years ago for another woman and she now lives with three of her children and five of her grandchildren in a sizeable house in Maroantsetra. They are rice farmers and despite her age, Dadin' i Miry still spends a lot of time working in the fields.

Dadin' i Miry was a spirit medium for over forty years until, at the age of about 65, she joined the Adventist church during my stay in Maroantsetra. Never before had she belonged to any church. As she explicitly stated, she joined the Adventist church because of her disillusionment with being a spirit medium. What had she gained in all these years? The father of her children had left her, and she was still poor. But the spirits who possessed her nevertheless kept demanding more and more expensive things. She had long resisted the attempts made by two of her children, who have been Adventists for many years, to convince her to join the church. But then suddenly—perhaps in anticipation of the year 2000—she changed her mind and got baptized just a few months after having held her last spirit possession *séance*. She expressed the pragmatism of her decision in the following way:

> I will join and see what happens; if things remain the same as before, I will just sit there and do nothing [neither serve the spirits nor go to church].

But if I see that things change for the better, then I will stay with the church.

She was still in it, when I returned in 2004.[6]

The Fredels

The Fredels, as I like to call them, are a family of ten. Maman' and Papan' i Fredel were both born and raised in Sahameloka. They are proud of the fact that neither of them has any children with another partner. Together they have eight children, all sons except for little Raclinette, the last child who is adored and spoilt by everyone. Before they became members of the Adventist church in 1995, during the most pronounced wave of conversions to Adventism in the village, they used to be extremely poor even by Sahameloka standards. This was partly because they did not have much land of their own, and partly because Papan' i Fredel wasted the little money they had on drink. They used to live in misery, their children barely having any clothes to put on, but these days, they are doing alright for themselves. This, they see as the outcome of having joined the Adventist church, and of Papan' i Fredel having stopped drinking as a result. They do have some land, but by no means enough to feed all their hungry mouths. So they also work as sharecroppers for a family of Zafindrabay descent who lives in another village, both parties seeming to be happy with the arrangement. The Fredels say that they were chosen to be the sharecroppers, because Adventists have a reputation for being trustworthy. Strolling past their house, one always finds at least a couple of the younger children pounding rice or Papan' i Fredel sitting out front chatting with his relatives, none of whom are Adventists themselves. The latter are perfectly happy that he and his family have joined the church, because they, too, can see the benefits.

While Maman' i Fredel's parents never went to any church (they live quite a distance away in the middle of the forest), Papan' i Fredel grew up as a Catholic, but stopped attending church services once his parents had died. The couple's three eldest sons, however, joined the Protestant church as teenagers and it was they who became the first converts to Adventism in the family. Their parents and siblings followed soon after.

* * *

This chapter has addressed the question of what kinds of people the Adventists in Maroantsetra and Sahameloka are. We have looked at church members' backgrounds and taken a glimpse at a few biographies. What has emerged from all of this is a picture consisting of variety. My two host families, for example, have little in common: one is a family of town dwellers who are migrants to the region, the other rice farmers in a forest village. The level of their educational achievements is equally different. What they and the other members of the local Seventh-day Adventist church all share, however, is their religious commitment. This is what we now turn to in part II of the book.

Part II

The Road to Clarity

Chapter 5

Bible Study

It is the Sabbath School that is the heart of the church. If the Sabbath School dies, then the church does not progress anymore.

Sekoly Sabata no fon' ny fiangonana. Raha maty ny Sekoly Sabata, dia tsy mandeha ny fiangonana.

(lay leader in Maroantsetra)

The most notable Adventist activity in Maroantsetra and Sahameloka is Bible study. There is a very clear focus on Bible study as part of institutionalized Seventh-day Adventist church services, but the members of the church also study the Bible at home with their families throughout the week.

The Bible Study Guide

Adventists' study activities, whether at home or in church, are based on the Adventist *Bible Study Guide*. This is a quarterly booklet translated from the original English version, which is produced in the United States, into hundreds of languages including Malagasy.[1] For each and every day there is a specific lesson (*lesona* in Malagasy) dealing with topics such as "Death in the animal kingdom," "The Biblical flood and modern geology" or "The healing power of God's creation."[2] These daily lessons are to be read and discussed by all Seventh-day Adventists worldwide. Here is an example of such a lesson in its English version. As always, it includes a combination of Bible verses from both the Old and the New Testament—Seventh-day Adventists do not, in theory, privilege any particular books or chapters of the Bible over others—to be studied alongside the text in the Guide.

"Sunday[3]   *December 19*
CITIZENS OF A NEW COMMUNITY (Phil. 3:20, 21; 2 Cor. 5:1)[4]

What does Paul say about our true citizenship? Phil. 3:20.

This earth, contaminated with sin and wickedness, is not our true home. The Lord has promised us 'new heavens and a new earth in which righteousness dwells' (2 Pet. 3:13). Clearly, the present condition of this world shows us that we are near the end of all human sorrows. The day is coming when everything will become new forever. Even today we see many signs announcing that the 'new earth' is near.

'The Christian needs a constant awareness of the fact that he is a citizen of heaven. Attachment to one's country leads him to be loyal to it. Wherever he may be living he will conduct himself in a way that will honor the good name of this country. Keeping in mind the kind of life we expect to live in heaven, serves to guide us in our life on earth. The purity, humility, gentleness, and love we anticipate experiencing in the life to come may be demonstrated here below. Our actions should disclose that we are citizens of heaven. Our association with others should make heaven attractive to them.'—*SDA Bible Commentary, vol. 7, p. 172.*

Why does Paul compare our earthly body to a tent and the body we will have in heaven to a 'building from God, a house not made with hands, eternal in the heavens'? 2 Cor. 5:1.

Himself a tentmaker, Paul makes an accurate illustration of our earthly body. Just as a tent is made of earthly materials, so is the body. Just as a tent is a temporary dwelling, so is the body. And just as a tent can be easily destroyed, so can the body.

In John 1:14, we read that 'the Word became flesh and dwelt among us' (NKJV). The original word translated 'dwelt' literally means 'tented' among us.

Peter also compares our earthly body to a tent in 2 Peter 1:13, 14: 'Yes, I think it is right as long as I am in this tent, to stir you up by reminding you, knowing that shortly I must put off my tent, just as our Lord Jesus Christ showed me' (NKJV).

As our body grows older or becomes diseased, we become increasingly conscious of how wonderful it will be to have 'a building from God, a house not made with hands . . .' (2 Cor. 5:1, NKJV). What about this 'building' from God will you be most grateful for?"

Every lesson introduces a topic and phrases a number of questions related to it. The approximate answers are in most cases provided, too, but at the same time, the students are encouraged to think through the questions and the suggested answers in view of their own lives and experiences, in order to make sure that they have properly understood what is being suggested to them. Many lessons contain questions, as food for thought and discussion, to which no answers are provided. The lesson of November 1, 1999, for example, dealt with the topic "One in Christ." In the course of the text, the student is asked to reflect upon the meaning of to "be of one mind" (2 Corinthians 13:11). "Does it mean that we all must think and act alike? Why, or why not?" No answer is provided.

A week's seven lessons are organized around a specific topic and together form a chapter. Examples include "Creation in six days," "Was there death before sin?" or, as in the example reprinted above, "The Heavenly Family." At the beginning of every new chapter, there is a "Key Question" to be kept in mind while studying the week's lessons. I quote again from the week discussing the Heavenly Family. "What must the church do to prepare for Christ's second coming? What must we as individuals do? How will the anticipation of the Second Coming motivate our decisions and the way we live?" At the end of every week, there are several "Discussion Questions" and a short "Summary" of the week's main topic. The 13 weekly chapters of one booklet in turn relate to one overall topic, for example: "The Nature of Man," "God Shows and Tells: Studies on Revelation and Inspiration" or "The church in today's world."

It is clear that the daily lessons guide the members of the Adventist church in their intellectual involvement with the Bible: topics are introduced to them, specific questions are addressed, answers are proposed. However, it is equally clear that the point of the Bible Study Guide is not to lecture people on truths that they must learn by heart. Rather, those reading the lessons are encouraged to study the texts provided, and the Bible verses referred to, and to discuss these with other church members. The daily lessons are formulated so as to encourage people to reach an understanding of biblical truth through careful examination of what is being proposed to them.

Because the text of every Study Guide is, in literally translated versions, exactly the same around the world, it is inevitable that some lessons are, at least in part, inappropriate for readers in places like Sahameloka or Maroantsetra. On June 16, 1999, for example, it remained a complete mystery to everyone present in church, what on earth was to be understood by the term "New Age," upon which the day's lesson was based and which it criticized, but which I, being asked to explain this bizarre expression, could only partly succeed in clarifying. Moreover, the Study Guide is obviously not produced for readers with little formal education. Given the fact that most church members today live in countries of the Third World, this is rather surprising. However, the Adventists in Sahameloka and Maroantsetra never failed to make the text meaningful for themselves by concentrating on those passages to which they could relate. Indeed, whenever they received the new Bible Study Guide late, people felt that they were missing out on something important and relevant, and the arrival of their copies of the new Study Guide was awaited with impatient anticipation. While they were left without new lessons to be studied, they improvized, either by repeating old lessons, or by selecting particular Bible passages themselves that they then proceeded to read and discuss.

Bible Study at Home

In both households in which I lived, Bible study formed an integral part of the daily evening routine, with the most literate person in the family "presiding" over affairs. It is, however, important to note that the job of the Bible study chairperson is not to preach to the others, but to offer them help, when needed, so as to enable everyone to participate in the discussion.

In Maroantsetra, it normally fell to Papan' i Beby to guide us through daily Bible study since he was extraordinarily well versed in biblical matters. Almost every evening after dinner we all sat down together on the eating mat in order to study the day's lesson, which, most days, lasted between 15 and 30 minutes. After an initial prayer, often spoken by Maman' i Beby, and sometimes a song chosen by one of the children, Papan' i Beby began to read and explain the text provided in the Study Guide, while we followed his words in our own copies. Maman' i Beby offered her own thoughts and views on the topic for discussion, and occasionally asked for some point or other to be clarified. I asked questions, which both of them answered with interest and patience. While Kiki, being 18 years old, took part in our adult discussions, Beby, who was only 15 at the time, had her own Bible Study Guide specifically written for the younger members of the church. Bible study was taken very seriously in the family, but the children were nevertheless encouraged not to neglect their homework for Bible study's sake, especially since Kiki and Beby often gave preference to studying the Adventist lesson over maths or geography.

Active participation in Bible study was always entirely voluntary, and it could happen that Maman' i Beby felt too tired to take part. This was always accepted by the others. Most days, however, everyone participated. Although it would be an exaggeration to say that everyone always participated with great enthusiasm, most days the daily lesson was studied attentively and with noticeable engagement on the part of the participants. Whatever the intensity of the participation of various family members during daily Bible study, it was clearly undertaken in a spirit of learning, and the focus always lay on discussion and comprehension of the text presented in the Study Guide and accompanying Bible passages. Here is a small extract from one such discussion, which conveys the participatory atmosphere during these sessions.

> Papan' i Beby reads from the lesson: "The day is coming when everything will become new forever. Even today we see many signs announcing that the 'new earth' is near."
>
> *Papan' i Beby.* What signs have we seen lately? Does anybody have any suggestions (*misy soso-kevitra*)?
>
> *Maman' i Beby.* Yes, I have a comment. There has been an unusually high number of deaths since the beginning of the new year. I think this is a sign that Jesus will come back soon, because Satan is working very hard here in Maroantsetra.
>
> *Papan' i Beby.* Thank you. It is true what you say, but I see also that many people here are simply stupid, they get drunk and then get into a fight.
>
> *Maman' i Beby.* Yes, but it is Satan who makes them behave like this.
>
> *Papan' i Beby.* That's true. I agree.
>
> *Kiki:* I agree with what Mum is saying. In other places, too, many people are dying. There is AIDS, criminality everywhere in the world now. All of this is a sign that Jesus will come back soon.

More examples of happenings that are interpreted as signs of the imminent end of this world follow. Maman' i Beby mentions tensions among the members of their own church. Kiki tells us of the introduction of school exams on *Saturdays*, Saturday being the Seventh-day Adventists' Sabbath and holy day during which they are not allowed to do any work. (This explains why holding school exams on Saturday is, for Kiki, a manifestation of devilish forces. In fact, the rules relating to the Sabbath are extremely important for the local church members and for Seventh-day Adventists worldwide, as indeed the name of the church indicates.) Papan' i Beby continues the discussion by applauding Virgin stores' illegal opening on *Sundays* in France—which he has heard about I don't know where—and interprets this as a sign of the coming end, which is preceded by an intensified struggle over the "Sabbath issue." They discuss all of these issues for some time and then continue to read the day's text. Every now and again Papan' i Beby stops to ask whether anybody has any suggestions or comments to make, and new discussions ensue. At all Adventist study sessions, whether at home or in church, one hears continuously the phrase "Are there any comments/suggestions?" (*Misy soso-kevitra?*). And this is not a rhetorical question, but one that often leads to a lively discussion of a particular issue.

Of the members of my host family in Sahameloka, Claude, the eldest son, is the most literate and educated, so he acted as Bible study leader. It was usually he who read the actual text from the

Study Guide, and who offered the most explanations and clarifications for the others' benefit. His mother, and sometimes his father also, made comments and suggestions as to how the text could be understood. On the rare occasions when Claude was not around, his mother took over the leading role since she is the only other person in the family who can read more or less fluently. Because Papan' i Claude was unable to read a text such as the lessons provided in the Study Guide, he was limited to making verbal contributions. Mazava, the 14-year-old girl, and the two younger boys, aged 9 and 4, never took any active part in these discussions and very often fell asleep before they came to an end. Mazava was sometimes asked to read a Bible verse, but she was embarrassed about the inadequacy of her reading skills and usually gave up, giggling and ashamed, after having given it an unsuccessful try.

The family's enthusiasm for studying the lessons was less constant than that of the family in town. Sometimes they neglected Bible study altogether for a week or so, although this was not normally the case. When they went through a good phase, however, they always studied the lesson very thoroughly and without haste—sometimes it took almost an hour—even after a long, tiring day out in the rice fields.

In both families, the goal of Bible study was not to learn doctrine by heart. Neither was it seen as a matter of one person teaching the others, although it was inevitable that Claude and Papan' i Beby acted as teachers to a certain extent. The aim was clearly that everyone should reach an understanding of the issues under question by way of serious study, reflection and discussion with others. Because of this I refer to this way of learning as Socratic.

The Morning Watch

Besides the daily lessons provided in the Bible Study Guide, church members are also meant to read the so-called Morning Watch (*fiambenana*), provided in a supplementary booklet to the Study Guide. It usually consists of a single Bible verse and a reference to an explanatory passage to be found in one of the books by Ellen White, the American Seventh-day Adventist prophetess. Most church members in Maroantsetra and Sahameloka, however, are not in possession of any of Ellen White's books and thus limit themselves to reading the relevant Bible verse. Therefore, quite often, my family in Sahameloka was not clear as to the meaning of the text they read in the mornings. However, in spite of that, and even when they had lots of work waiting for them and were already running late, they never neglected the Morning Watch, which they also supplemented with singing and prayer. My family in town, being in possession of several of Ellen White's books, read the entire text suggested on many days. However, the Morning Watch is regarded more as a thought for the day than as an integral part of Bible study, and there is therefore not the same expectation of discussion and exchange of ideas as with the evening lessons.

Bible Study on the Spur of the Moment

I was often impressed by the eagerness with which the members of the Adventist church conducted Bible study and the genuine engagement with, and discussion of, the presented texts. However, what was perhaps even more remarkable was the way many people in town and in the village engaged in Bible study on the spur of the moment, that is outside the somewhat routinized context of the evening study session. I began this book with the image of Papan' i Loricà engaged in intense Bible study for several hours until late at night, while everyone else around him was sleeping. This was a completely spontaneous studying effort on his part at the end of a long Sabbath spent proselytizing in the countryside that had already involved several hours of Bible study. Papan' i Loricà is, perhaps, a particularly keen member of the Adventist church, but his example is nonetheless indicative of the kind of spontaneous Bible study effort, which numerous local Adventists regularly engage in.

Maman' i Claude, for example, sometimes reads the Bible while waiting for the rice to cook or at any convenient moment. Claude could often be seen sitting on his bed or on the veranda completely absorbed in studying the Bible or the Study Guide, sometimes taking notes on a loose sheet of paper. He also knew a great number of Bible verses by heart, which he took joy and pride in reciting. I especially remember one summer evening when we were all sitting on a mat outside the house, looking at the bright stars above us and enjoying the pleasant warmth of the evening. Nobody was saying anything much, when all of a sudden Claude started to recite Bible verses— always stating their biblical reference—continuing for about half an hour without stopping. In many ways, though, it was Papan' i Claude who impressed, and moved, me most in his effort to learn.

Papan' i Claude is practically illiterate. Writing especially is extremely difficult for him, and he struggles to sign his name. His ability to read is better, but still very limited, so that to read a whole sentence or an entire paragraph demands a lot of concentration and patience on his part. When studying the lesson together with other people—in church or with his family at home—he mostly listens silently to what the others say. Only rarely does he make an active contribution, and when he is encouraged to do so, he timidly remarks that he is not a knowledgeable man ("I don't know much" [*tsy mahay zaho*]). Nevertheless, sometimes, when he was at home on a rainy afternoon, he would pick up the Bible and try to read from it. I do not know which passages he chose on such occasions, because he was very shy about being seen or overheard when studying privately. But whatever he read, he was very much involved in what he was doing, and would continue for half an hour or more. He sat there, by himself, struggling with the particular passage he had chosen, mouthing every word with his lips, muttering to himself. Although he probably only managed to read a couple of Bible verses at a time, the effort he expended was enormous.

Kiki was very eager to study as well. Sometimes I found him sitting at his table bent over a chaotic pile of exercise books, and when I asked him what he was doing, it often turned out that he was revising and writing out a fair copy of the sermon of the previous Sabbath, during the course of which he had taken rough notes. He did this completely of his own accord; nobody told him to do so. At other times, he could be found lying casually on his parents' bed or on a mat on the veranda reading the Bible and underlining—equipped with a ruler and a number of colored pencils I had brought him from Europe—those passages he considered particularly important.

Indeed, the local church members use the Bible very much like a school book, writing references and notes in it, and circling or otherwise marking specific passages. On one occasion, Papan' i Beby glued into his Bible a newspaper clip I had brought him from Europe that concerned the "creation versus evolution" debate in America. The Bible as a book is in itself not treated particularly "respectfully"; it is its content that matters. Bibles in my host families were to be found lying on the floor, in a dusty corner or in a cupboard muddled up with all sorts of other things, and even occasionally used as a pad. The Bible is not regarded as a fetish that has intrinsic power, rather it is thought of as a collection of wise and truthful words that need to be read, analyzed, understood.

Kiki's younger sister, Beby, spent a fair amount of time neatly writing down passages from the Bible to which her attention had been drawn, and decorating the pages with flowers and ornaments. She also continually sang church songs while doing tasks in and around the house. I saw Maman' i Beby less often engaged in spontaneous Bible study, but this might have been because when I was around we tended to chat. However, one time she did read the entire St. Matthew's Gospel while Papan' i Beby was away in the countryside. Papan' i Beby, for his part, often devoted much of his free time to reading the Bible or one of his many Adventist-inspired books.

I witnessed countless examples of church members engaging in Bible study on the spur of the moment. Whenever I strolled around Sahameloka intending to stop for a visit at one of my Adventist friends' house, it was not unusual to find one of them studying the Bible alone or together with another member of the church. On one such occasion I encountered Papan' i Fredel and his nephew Ranary sitting on a bench outside Papan' i Fredel's house. Both men had their heads bent over their Bibles and hardly noticed my arrival. It turned out that they were involved in a discussion of a Bible passage that Papan' i Fredel had asked his nephew, who was well versed in biblical matters, to clarify for him.

Church members' level of literacy in general, and Bible expertise in particular, varies greatly. Papan' i Claude, for example, cannot use the Bible or the Study Guide in the same sophisticated manner as Papan' i Beby whose level of literacy and biblical knowledge is exceptional. However, although there is a vast difference in the levels of education of the two men, and although Papan' i Claude struggles to read just one paragraph while Papan' i Beby can read any book, in Malagasy or French, with complete ease, they are alike in their eagerness for Bible study and in their effort to learn. Whatever church members' individual level of education, literacy and biblical expertise, they are constantly involved in a *process of learning*. And this process appears to give them great joy.

Studying and Learning in Church

Every week, there are several Adventist church services that the members of the church are expected to attend regularly. On every Wednesday and every Friday evening, there is a service lasting for about an hour. However, the main church service is on Saturday, which Seventh-day Adventists consider to be the biblical Holy Sabbath of the week, and during which one ought not to engage in any other than religious activity. The Sabbath service lasts from morning till sunset with a break at lunchtime.[5]

Adventist church services follow a set pattern that specifies when to pray, when to sing, when to say what sort of thing, when to stand up and when to kneel. But during any service, there is always room to discuss things, or to put forward one's opinion or to ask questions on a particular matter if anyone wishes to do so. On the Sabbath, however, there are particular times specially *designated* for learning, studying and discussion.

Sabbath School

In Maroantsetra and Sahameloka, the Sabbath morning service normally lasts for about three hours—in town often a bit longer, in the village a bit shorter—with some variations according to the program; baptism, for example, considerably increases the length of a service. The Sabbath morning service consists of two central parts, with additional features and activities such as praying, singing and "sharing testimony" (sharing personal experiences thought to evidence the presence of God or Satan) taking place before, in between and after these two central parts. The first main element is what Seventh-day Adventists call Sabbath School (*Ecole du Sabbat, Sekoly Sabata*); the second main element is the so-called *Culte*, which I will briefly come back to later in this chapter. Sabbath School represents one of the central pillars of Seventh-day Adventism worldwide and has been of paramount significance since the beginning of the movement in the nineteenth century. In Maroantsetra and Sahameloka, approximately forty-five minutes are dedicated to the *Sekoly Sabata* each Saturday.

The purpose of Sabbath School is to discuss, in small groups, the past week's lessons from the Bible Study Guide—which ideally everyone has already read at home with their family—and to help each other clarify and understand their meaning. It is in particular the questions that have been asked, but left unanswered in the Study Guide, which the members of the church jointly explore during Sabbath School. People exchange, and argue about, divergent interpretations of the week's chapter. They discuss their respective points of view, cite biblical verses as evidence for their opinions and weave their own experiences into their discourse. They listen to each other attentively, and then make new comments, which might support or question the previous speaker's point.

While the congregation in Maroantsetra is, for the purpose of Sabbath School, divided into groups of ten to fifteen persons, no such division is necessary in Sahameloka. In every discussion group one participant, in most cases a man, acts as "class teacher," called *moniteur*.[6] As during Bible study at home with one's family, the job of the class teacher is explicitly, first and foremost, to guide the discussion and to encourage everyone to participate rather than to lecture others about biblical truth. It is also the duty of a class teacher to make sure that the most relevant points of the chapter (previously discussed with the other *moniteurs*) are not missed. When a class teacher delivers a monologue rather than encouraging discussion, this behavior is duly criticized by the participants as not being proper Bible study, which ought to engage everyone present. Bible study is clearly not seen as an activity

where the truth is *taught* by an authority like the pastor, let alone a
moniteur. Neither is "right-answerism" practiced—whereby a teacher
asks questions to which there is only one correct answer that the students have to deliver—as Simpson found to be the case among
Seventh-day Adventists in Zambia (2003: 87, quoting Holt 1969).
Quite to the contrary, the purpose of Sabbath School is for all participants to exchange ideas, opinions and interpretations of what they
have read during the course of the week at home, and to possibly,
though not necessarily, develop through group discussion a common
understanding of the past week's chapter. People often spontaneously
take on and continue the argument of the previous speaker, or else
criticize it and express a different view. Many people have both Bible
and Study Guide in hand, and some take notes of particularly important points, or of biblical references, on a flimsy piece of paper or in a
school exercise book. Or church members may underline a paragraph
in their Bible, which they consider especially significant (figure 5.1).

During Sabbath School, not only people's verbal participation, but
also their body language was very revealing. Often participants would

Figure 5.1   Sabbath School in Maroantsetra.

lean forward when listening to what someone else said, cupping their
chin in their hands. Or they would fix their gaze on a speaker, and
then on another who responded to the first, and then another, without losing concentration, and never noticing that they themselves
were being observed.

The atmosphere during Sabbath School is informal and free of
strict discipline, and everyone present—women and men, young and
old, the literate and the less so—can speak anytime they please.
Indeed, I was often reminded of university seminars while sitting in
Sabbath School, both in town and in the village. Some issues were
hotly debated, and, in these cases, there was no one final answer to
the question in discussion. Once, for example, the participants in a
study group I attended discussed whether or not the Sabbath *pre-
dated* creation. Had God created the Sabbath specifically for the needs
of humans, or was it a divine institution independent of our creation?
The pros and cons of either view were debated at length with people
citing appropriate passages from the Book of Genesis and pointing to
other sources supporting their opinion. When the little bell rang to
indicate the end of discussion time, no final answer had been reached.
This Sabbath School had provided no answers, but it had introduced
a question the answer to which everyone had to, in discussion with
others, establish for themselves.

Perhaps the best way to convey the atmosphere of Sabbath School
is to quote one discussion in detail. It is December 25, 1999, but since
Seventh-day Adventists do not accept the alleged date of birth of Jesus,
it is a Sabbath day like any other. The study group I join consists of ten
participants between the ages of 18 and about 50. By chance they are
all men, except for me. This is only because they happened to sit next
to each other; however, most discussion groups are gender-mixed.
There is no particular seating arrangement in Adventist churches, and
women and men sit wherever they please. Study groups generally form
on the basis of where people happen to be positioned. I am attending
and recording the discussion without actively taking part in it. Eight of
the ten men present make at least one active contribution in the course
of the discussion, and many of the eight, several. One of them acts as
class teacher. The other participants, I have numbered according to the
order in which they were sitting.

Before I reproduce their discussion that morning, however, I need
to briefly explain one aspect of Seventh-day Adventist doctrine, which
is referred to several times. According to Seventh-day Adventist
prophecy, there is a set sequence of events that will eventually lead to
Christ's Second Coming, the millennium and life in paradise thereafter.
One of these events is what Seventh-day Adventists call "The Sunday

law" (*ny lalànan' ny Alahady*). The Sunday law refers to a worldwide prohibition on worshipping God on any day other than Sunday under threat of severe punishment. It is believed that the prohibition will be set in motion by the Pope and will come into force shortly before Christ's return to earth. Hence the Adventists in Maroantsetra and Sahameloka expect to be persecuted in the not too distant future.[7] The introduction of the Sunday law is the fulfillment—Papan' i Beby once explained to me—of the prophecy Daniel made more than 2000 years ago: ". . . And he [the Pope] shall speak great words against the most High, and shall wear out the saints of the most High [the Adventists being persecuted for keeping the Sabbath], and think to change times and laws [the introduction of the Sunday law]. . ." (Daniel 7: 25). It is the time of persecution under the Sunday law that the participants in the discussion below often refer to as "the difficult times" when their faith will be truly tested.

The discussion of December 25, 1999 begins after a brief introduction by the class teacher, a man in his 30s. Before the actual Sabbath School begins, five or ten minutes are reserved for people to "share testimonies" or anything they consider relevant.[8]

Number 10 (a man in his late 20s):
I have noticed that many Adventists are changing these days. Even those who used to do things which were not really acceptable, are now preparing themselves for the difficulties of the last days. For example, many Adventists are getting married these days. We should follow the laws of God as He gave them to the Israelites. He was very strict at that time and He is still the same God. One has to return to worship on the Sabbath, only then can one be sure to go to heaven. God told the Israelites not to cook on the Sabbath, and we should continue to respect that law. Immediately after sunset on Friday [the beginning of the Sabbath], we ought to go to church. We shouldn't wait until a particular time such as 6.30 to meet in church, but we should go immediately after sunset, because that is the beginning of the Sabbath. That is what I plan to do from the beginning of next year [the year 2000].

Number 7 (a teenager on holiday from his studies in the town of Toamasina):
In Toamasina, we go to school on Saturdays, too, and almost all exams are held on Saturdays. And I said to my teacher that I couldn't take exams on Saturday, because I am an Adventist and that I would always, under all circumstances, go to church on the Sabbath. He replied that there were other Adventists at our school who sit exams

on Saturday, which is true. He said I was just a troublemaker and that I
was lazy. I told him that I wasn't trying to cause problems and that I
wasn't lazy, but that I was an Adventist and that I would always go to
church on a Saturday. And I said that I'd prefer to fail the exams
[*mahazo zero*] rather than to sit them on a Sabbath. He said, well then,
you'll fail. That is my testimony which I also shared with my classmates.

Number 8 (a young man):

We all know that Christ's return is imminent. Some church members
have even suggested that we should all leave our homes and hide in
the forest [waiting for the persecution to start]. And I have heard of
some living further north who have sold all their property and who are
now just waiting for Christ's return. But that is wrong, because God
doesn't tell us to sell our things, to prepare materially for Christ's
return, He tells us to prepare spiritually. Those who sell their wealth
are concerned with "matters of the flesh," but one should only be
concerned with "matters of the spirit." We should prepare our spirits,
because during the difficult times, we may die. That's why it is more
important to prepare spiritually.

Number 2 (a man of about 50 who works as a mechanic):

It's like with time: The clock won't turn twelve if it hasn't turned
eleven yet; and it won't turn eleven before it turns ten. Similarly, we
must pass through many stages before the return of Christ. Some
Adventists say that Jesus may return tomorrow, but nobody knows
exactly when He will return. We only know that we have to pass certain stages prior to that. The spirit of prophecy is our *radar*. There are
always clouds prior to the rain. The reason why those Adventists in the
countryside who sell their things are wrong is that they don't understand the spirit of prophecy. We first have to wait for the Sunday law.
At the moment, they [the Pope and his allies] have not become fierce
yet, but they already encourage people to pray on Sunday. The wages
of civil servants working on Saturday, for example, will rise at the
beginning of the new year [thus tempting them not to respect
the Holy Sabbath]. We all have to make decisions and we have to
prepare ourselves for the difficult times.

At this point, the little bell rings to indicate the beginning of
Sabbath School proper. Before we start, we kneel down for a prayer.
Then the class teacher starts with a reminder of the subject of this week's
chapter and calls on everyone present to quote any Bible verse they
may have learnt by heart during the week; several people recite verses.
Then the discussion begins. This week's Sabbath School discussion

concerns "The Heavenly Family" (one day's lesson of which is reproduced at the beginning of this chapter). After every contribution, the leader thanks the speaker for his contribution (an example of Malagasy communication skills[9]).

Leader:
Our new lesson is about the Heavenly Family. We start by discussing the first lesson: "Citizens of a New Community"; what does that mean?

Number 3 (a man in his 40s):
Our community here on earth is already in a really bad state. Because everything is full of sin. But the new community in heaven will be good. There won't be any fights, life will be full of joy. There won't be either illness or death.

Number 8 (second contribution):
Some people think, but that is wrong, that when we are dead, we go to some invisible life and join an invisible community [Seventh-day Adventists reject the idea of a spiritual afterlife]. But nobody has any idea as to what this invisible life is like. One can't say anything about it. But the new community where we will go is completely different. One can know what it will be like. We will see everything with our own eyes just like we see things in the here and now.

Number 10 (second contribution):
We are speaking here about life in paradise. The Bible says that there is no sin there, but here on earth, we still commit many sins. We are used to sinful life here on earth. But it is those who are already used to a devout lifestyle, according to the Bible, who will go to paradise. One should live according to the Bible so that one is already used to the new life in paradise. Because those who become used to this good life here on earth will be those who go to heaven.

Number 9 (a man in his early 30s):
These days there are two kinds of communities; both have their different ways. One is our community here on earth, the other is the community that lives with God. The community that lives with God provides an image of life in heaven. The lesson leads us towards the new life we should already be learning about while on earth. Those who don't get used to the ways of the new life while still on earth, won't be able to live there. For example, if someone is used to drinking alcohol, they won't be able to live there. They will go and look for alcohol and they will suffer [since there won't be any]. But there,

there will be nothing which makes you suffer. This is my view on the new community.

Number 2 (second contribution):

It is as though one of us went to France. If we didn't speak French, we wouldn't be able to live well there. Therefore, we would have to learn French before we went in order to prepare ourselves. And so it is with heaven. Those who want to go to heaven have to learn the language of heaven whilst still on earth. Otherwise, they won't be prepared.

Leader

We don't have to look far. Look at Eva who is with us. Well, she learnt Malagasy before she came here, didn't she? She knew she was going to come to Madagascar and so she learnt our language. When we talk about the new community, we are not talking about other people, but about ourselves. What the lesson teaches us is that we are here on earth only temporarily, just passing by, but that we will go to heaven and live there forever. We are like those people who build their houses of palm tree material rather than cement, because they know that they will soon move. That's why we already study now, learning the ways of the new life so that when we arrive there [in paradise], we won't have any problems.

Number 2 (the mechanic, third contribution):

What one can know for sure is this. It's like with someone who makes a motor. They know what is good for it. A motor that needs diesel may stop working if it is given petrol. Similarly, God knows what is good for us. He tells us in the Bible what is good for us, because He made us and so He knows. Think about the food which it is taboo for us to eat. What is good for our health is written in the Bible. We Adventists are very healthy, because we don't eat the things God tells us not to. All doctors agree that the Adventists are healthier than other people and that they recover very quickly when they fall ill. Why is that? Because we don't eat the things that God tells us not to. That's my contribution [soso-kevitra].

Leader (second contribution):

My wife was hospitalised recently in order to have an operation. The doctor asked us which church we belonged to. When we told him that we were Adventists, he said, before he had operated on her, that she would be coming home in seven days at the latest. Well, she was operated on Wednesday and by Friday she had already left the hospital. [. . .] We are built not on rotten wood, but on good, healthy wood. Let's read Isaiah 35: 5–10. That's where we can read about the truth of the new life. Who would like to read?

Everyone picks up their Bible and Number 4 (a middle-aged man from the countryside) who has up to now been silent, volunteers and reads the verses slowly and with some difficulty. The text tells of the beauty of life in heaven, free of illness, sorrow and pain.

Number 2 *(fourth contribution)*:
One can't enter the house if one isn't clean. And God tells us not to care for dead bodies, because they are dirty. When people die, then their bodies inevitably rot. If we wear clean clothes, but then go somewhere dirty, we get dirty. That's how I see it. And God says that those who are not clean won't be able to enter the new life. The first thing we have to do is to keep the taboos God has given us. And concerning our health, we must not eat tabooed food.

Leader *(third contribution)*:
Health is happiness. When we read the Bible, we see that those who are blind will see [in paradise], the dumb will sing and the weak walk.

Number 3 *(second contribution)*:
My contribution concerns the same issue. There are people whose clothes and shoes may be clean, but whose spirit is dirty. What is necessary is a clean way of living. Do we all understand that? [confirmation by the others]. What really bothers people are illnesses. Whether rich or poor, if they are ill, they cannot be happy. If someone rich is constantly ill, they are less happy than someone poor who is not often ill. The greatest joy in heaven is health. It is we Adventists who have the greatest access to health. We drink a lot of water, we don't eat shrimps or pork, we don't eat dirty animals.

Number 4 *(first contribution)*:
We should learn here on earth the things which are right and the things which are not. For example, I easily get angry. That means that in heaven I will also get angry easily if I don't learn not to. But in heaven there are no fierce lions.

Not everyone seems to be clear as to what he means. Number 9 helps to clarify:

Number 9 *(second contribution)*:
What he means concerning the lions is that in the new life there will be nothing fierce, for example no fierce lions, no fierce animals, and

there will be no violent people either, he says. So if we are used to being fierce, it will be difficult there. We must look at our own lives and if we act in ways which are not according to the Bible, then we must try to change those ways. That is what he means.

Number 4 (second contribution):

Yes, like when one forgets one's watch somewhere, and the person who finds it doesn't return it to its owner. Even within this very house [the church] things are lost [stolen]. And church members still fight over land. And there are even people who come to church on Saturday, but who then in the evening go and do *tromba* [spirit possession].

Several people:
That is true!

Leader (fourth contribution):
I would like to say something. It is like with a competition. If one doesn't know what the first and second prizes are, people will hesitate to take part. But if they know what they can win, they will rush to take part. If people know that the first prize is a bicycle, then everyone will want to take part. You see, it is just like that with us knowing what is waiting for us in paradise, knowing for example that the blind will see, the deaf will hear and that we will see God sitting there. But it is not really the fact that the blind will see and the weak will become strong which is so fantastic about this place [paradise], but that we will *see* God living together with us. [Number 2: Yes, that's exactly right!] What we have long been wondering about is: what is Jesus really like? What are His hands which had the nails in them like? What is God's life like? And what is His name? We will carry His name just as you [pointing to someone wearing a T-shirt which says Ronaldo] carry the name Ronaldo on your shirt now. All of that we will *see* there! Any ideas?

Number 2 (fifth contribution):
Yes, what I would like to say is this. Moses really wanted to see God. God said to him: Nobody who sees my face will be lost. I will show you my glory. Moses was sitting beneath two big rocks, but when God passed by, Moses shone with light. The Israelites couldn't bear to look at him.

Number 8 (third contribution):
Many people were blind at the time of Jesus, but not those who were close to Him. Those who were close to Him, He healed. Here on earth there are still many ill people, because we are not yet physically

close to God. But when we are there [in paradise], nobody will be ill anymore.

Leader (fifth contribution):
We won't see all of this before we get there. Only there will we see it all. None of this will happen before what happens? Before Jesus comes back. When he comes back, everybody will see Him, but not everyone will be happy [those who aren't going to be saved won't be happy].

Number 9 (third contribution):
Those who have no holiness, won't see the Lord. And they should start asking for forgiveness today. They should ask for forgiveness for all their sins and for all the bad things they have done. First of all, one must know God's character. And one can only know His character if one studies His word. Therefore, one must study the Bible, the lessons and the prophecy and act accordingly. And one must proselytize so that other people know what it will be like in heaven, and what you have to do to go there.

Number 8 (fourth contribution):
I would like to make a comment which I have been thinking about because of New Year. I sell clothes in the countryside. As soon as I arrive anywhere, the children's clothes sell out immediately, because the parents want their children to have nice clothes for New Year. But the parents don't get anything for themselves. They only think about their children. But what about themselves? Where are the clothes for them? I think that's wrong. And one must not act this way with regard to religion [fivavahana]. For example, if I only think about Kola [his son], and don't think about my own life and what I have to do in order to go to heaven myself, then what about me? The basis of all our lessons concerning the return of Christ is the story of the ten virgins [Matthew 25: 1–13]. Whenever we talk about Christ's return, we read this story. There are five clever ones, and five stupid ones. And the clever ones look after themselves and don't worry about the stupid ones. Each of them just thinks about herself. That is why I don't think about other people's lives. My own life still needs sorting out, so, should I really care about other people? The preparations you need to make to go to heaven are not like having a party [fety]. Sometimes one loses time thinking about other people.

Several people disagree.

Number 10 to the previous speaker (third contribution):
Don't you remember Cain and Abel? God asked Cain "Where is your brother?", but Cain replied that he wasn't his brother's guardian.

What this meant was that he didn't care about his brother. But that is wrong!

<u>Leader:</u>

"Cain didn't understand."

<u>Number 9</u> (fourth contribution):

No, he didn't understand. God of course already knew that Cain had killed his brother. But He wanted to see whether Cain would repent or not. That is why He asked him. Not because He didn't know.

Someone asks the speaker to repeat his contribution, which he does. Then number 2 makes another contribution.

<u>Number 2</u> (sixth contribution):

The lesson is here to help us to put into practice what we are taught. We know perfectly well that we must follow God in everything. But do we really do so? That is the question which matters. We have learnt many lessons, but will we also apply what we have learnt? That is the crucial question.

<u>Leader:</u>

Does anyone have any ideas on this?

Everyone talks at once.

<u>Number 9</u> (fifth contribution):

That's what our brother meant [Number 8 talking about the ten virgins]. It is because we really need to look closely at our own lives that this is no longer the time to go and convince other people. We have to prepare our own minds for Christ's return, because it is very close. Jesus is already knocking at the door.

<u>Number 3</u> (third contribution):

Let's read Matthew 24: 44. [Everyone finds the passage in their Bible.] "Therefore be ye also ready: for in such an hour as ye think not the Son of man cometh." What can we learn from this? We must not think that Jesus will not come back for a long time yet. If we think that, we won't prepare ourselves properly. And then we won't be ready when He comes, but we will be surprised by His sudden arrival. It's like with a burglar. One doesn't know when a burglar is going to come. So one must be prepared at all times. We don't know the day or the time of Christ's return.[. . .] Daniel prayed three times every day, and we should pray even more often. It all depends on us.

Number 4 (third contribution):
We mustn't be surprised by Christ's return. There is a book written by Ratrema William I think he was called, about a man who had a gardener. His master went away for two years, but the gardener continued doing his work every day. Everyone told him he was crazy, since he was working while his *patron* was away. But he replied that he didn't know when his *patron* would return and so he just continued to do his work. People thought him crazy. But firstly, he was paid to care for the garden, and so he did. And secondly, when his *patron* returned, he was very pleased with the gardener. What we can learn from this story is that we must be prepared for Christ's return at all times.

Leader:
I would like to thank everyone for their contributions to our discussion. What the lesson teaches us is simple. Jesus will come back for certain, but we don't know when, so we must prepare ourselves. We must pray and wait for Him, so that we will be able to go to the new life in heaven. Our government is in heaven. God give us strength, Amen.

Everyone: Amen.

In my experience, the above example is representative of the character and style of Sabbath School discussions in Maroantsetra as well as in Sahameloka. However, it would be misleading to imagine that all discussions are always as lively as the one I have just quoted. Indeed, while listening to the participants, I had the impression that they were spurred on by my taping of the discussion; everyone wanted to "go to Europe," if only on a tape.

The degree to which people actively participate in Sabbath School discussions depends on several factors. Individual participation often depends on literacy. Old women, in particular, are often almost, or entirely, illiterate and they rarely make active contributions during Sabbath School discussions. Hence, if a discussion group has a lot of old women in it, it tends not to be very animated. Similarly, if a teacher speaks in a manner too complicated for most people to understand, or if he is overly keen to display his own expertise, the discussion tends to be less involved. A single enthusiastic participant, in contrast, may trigger a discussion that then gains momentum and ends up involving many people. Other aspects, too, such as the general morale of the congregation, which itself depends on a variety of factors, can have a noticeable effect on the atmosphere, and the enthusiasm with which people engage in Sabbath School discussions. But even if at times the participants of a study group do not succeed in producing a lively discussion, the leitmotif of any Sabbath School is clearly the intention to encourage intellectual engagement with biblical text, not to foster crude indoctrination and a simplistic reproduction of "the truth." Most Saturdays people actively participate in the debate and it is precisely this active participation that church members seem to enjoy most.

On rare occasions, the actual content of what is discussed during Sabbath School is of a distinctly scholarly nature, in the sense that the focus lies on subtle distinctions and definitions of particular terms. In such situations, the atmosphere is slightly different and the study session tends to take more the form of a lecture given by someone with exceptional expertise rather than of a discussion partaken among equals. I witnessed two such instances. Once, different kinds of biblical texts—namely poems, symbols, allegories, parables and types (using the French terms)—were at issue. The point of the week's chapter was to understand the distinction between these different forms of biblical narrative. Papan' i Beby, who on this occasion was the teacher (few others would have been able to explain the differences), explained that rising smoke, for instance, could be a "symbol" of prayer ascending to heaven. The character of a "parable," in contrast, he illustrated by way of the story told in Matthew 13: 3–9 in which "a sower went forth to sow," his seeds falling on ground of variable quality with only those that fell on fertile soil actually producing grain. The most difficult kind of narrative, which, I am quite certain, remained unclear to many of Papan'i Beby's listeners but which fascinated himself, was the "type." A "type" in Adventist discourse is a story or character that foreshadows its own full realization, called its "anti-type." The sacrifice of animals in the Old Testament, for instance, is a "type" of Christ's crucifixion because in both cases, as Papan' i Beby explained, there is an exchange of death for life. Similarly, Abraham's son Isaac, nearly killed by his father at God's command, is a "type" of Jesus Christ, because in both Isaac's and Jesus' case, a father is willing to sacrifice his own son. For Seventh-day Adventists, the Old and the New Testament are equally important, and church members emphasize that one must not neglect one for the other. Biblical narratives using "types" and "anti- types" were seen as proof of the fact that the Bible was one coherent whole. Many more members than understood the definition of what exactly a "type" was, understood this point. The second instance of a Sabbath School discussion of such a scholarly nature that I witnessed concerned the difference between what were referred to in the Bible Study Guide as *âme* (soul) and *esprit* (spirit). Unfortunately, both are translated by the same Malagasy word (*fanahy*) and thus the distinction this particular lesson sought to elaborate on, employing the French expressions *âme* and *esprit*, caused considerable confusion.

So far, I have talked about Sabbath School discussions among adults, that is, people of the age of 16 and above. Those aged 10 to 15—the so-called *Explorateurs* (or *Explos* for short)—have their own Bible Study Guide, specifically written for these younger members, and their own Sabbath School sessions. While the adults hold their Sabbath School inside the church, the *Explos* meet elsewhere to discuss their own text that they, too, are supposed to have studied over the week. I only occasionally attended these *Explos* meetings, but my impression was that the leitmotif of these teenage Sabbath Schools was very much the same as among the adults. Although one or two adult members of the church were present and partly led the sessions, most of the meeting was actually run by the *Explos* themselves and active participation was encouraged as with the adult congregation. While the teenagers and the adults hold Sabbath School, the little *Aventuriers*, aged 6 to 9, learn a new song that they later proudly perform for the whole congregation.

The "Culte"

The second key element of a Sabbath morning is the *Culte*, whose core is the sermon. The sermon is not necessarily delivered by the pastor, even if he is present, and the *Culte* always involves the participation of several church members. Unlike Sabbath School, the sermon is not a time for discussion and the active participation of all church members, rather it is a time for listening to a few people who have prepared speeches and presentations. Nevertheless, for many, it is, like Sabbath School, a time for study. I often observed people taking notes while listening to the sermon and writing down the biblical references mentioned by the speaker, so as to enable them to reflect on the sermon later at home. This is precisely what Claude or Kiki were doing when I sometimes found them absorbed in Bible study.

Theoretically, Seventh-day Adventists do not privilege any book of the Bible, nor any chapter or verse over any other, because the entire Bible, from Genesis 1:1 to the last word in the Book of Revelation, is considered God's word, transmitted through the medium of human prophets. In practice, however, some books are given considerably more attention than others, in particular Genesis, Exodus, Daniel and Revelation. However, the daily lessons in the Bible Study Guide, as well as sermons delivered in church, combine Bible verses from a variety of chapters, so that in the course of one sermon, or one lesson, people jump to and fro between the Old and the New Testament reading passages from, say, Exodus, the Epistles to the Hebrews, the Book of Psalms, St. Mark's Gospel and Job. By doing this, they continually create novel texts. This is, of course, particularly true for those church members who actually write sermons and other speeches. However, everyone who studies in such a way, freely combining any Bible passage with any other, is involved in what Harding succinctly describes as "endlessly generating a third Testament" (1992: 54).

Apart from the sermon that, depending on the speaker, is often rather lengthy, the *Culte* also involves a number of ritualized features such as particular prayers and songs. The end of the *Culte* marks the end of Sabbath morning, the point at which people return home for lunch, shaking hands, on their way out, with all those who have led the proceedings.

Playful Learning on Sabbath Afternoon

Like the morning of the Sabbath, the afternoon service follows a ritualized sequence and consists of two core parts: "the time of the grown ups" and "the time of the young," each of these lasting about one hour. Sabbath afternoon was often a playful time with children, teenagers and adults providing entertainment for each other. Anyone who wishes to can perform a song, or demonstrate their expertise in some area, or make some other kind of contribution. On one occasion, in Maroantsetra, a young man read a poem about beautiful landscape that he had written himself. On another occasion, in Sahameloka, a young woman came forward during "the time of the grown ups" and read two different Bible texts that she had practiced at home. Though she read very slowly and got stuck a couple of times with a particular passage, which she had to spell out, she persevered having obviously made a huge effort practicing reading these texts at home. The audience appreciated her effort and applauded. Sabbath afternoons, as Sabbath mornings, remained distinctly knowledge-oriented.

Sahameloka, January 22, 2000
We are witnessing "the time of the grown ups," time dedicated to improving the biblical expertise of the adult members of the church in Sahameloka.

First, Vangé, an 18-year-old member of the church, steps forward and poses the question, to the assembled congregation, of whether it is proper to do such things as cooking or plaiting hair on the Sabbath. A lively discussion ensues; everyone feels concerned; pros and cons are discussed and Vangé keenly writes down people's arguments and the biblical passages, which support the claims made. The discussion continues for some twenty minutes, but no "right answer" is established in the end. Some people voice the opinion that work on the Sabbath is to be categorically rejected, while others think that there is nothing wrong with plaiting one's hair beautifully to honor the Sabbath (supporters of this more moderate attitude sometimes privately call those embracing a more radical view *fondamentalistes*[10]). Still others recognize the theoretical correctness of not even cooking or plaiting one's hair on the Sabbath, but consider this impracticable.

Then, as on many other Sabbath afternoons both in Maroantsetra and Sahameloka, comes a quiz testing people's Bible expertise. One of the members of the village congregation has prepared a series of questions and everyone is now called to join the quiz. Six people, equipped with their Bibles, line up at the front of the church ready to be challenged. The first question is asked: "How many years did the Israelites live in Egypt prior to their exodus?" The participants, and many people in the audience, quickly and keenly start to leaf through the Bible. They all know that the answer is somewhere in Exodus, and some of them seem to have a clear idea which chapter must contain the information. As though in an exam, they try to cheat a little by glancing to their left and right to see whether one of their co-competitors has already succeeded in finding the relevant passage. Soon enough, one of them indeed finds it, and after whispering the correct answer into the ear of the quiz master, goes back to his place smiling proudly. The other participants are given some more time to find the passage, but since none of them succeed, the correct answer—430 years—is announced, and everyone present is called upon to memorize the information. Then the next question is asked: "At what age was Ellen White [the Seventh-day Adventist prophetess] baptized?" Everyone starts guessing; again, it is a difficult question to which, in the end, the organizer of the game has to give the answer. The quiz continues: "Find a passage in the Bible [state book, chapter and verse] which explicitly speaks of *finoana* (trust/belief)." This time, several people succeed in finding a relevant Bible verse quite quickly. Other questions follow. In the end, all the participants manage to find the correct answer to at least one question despite the difficulty of the afternoon's quiz. And so, "the time of the young" begins.

Sahameloka, December 18, 1999

First, it is the turn of the little *Aventuriers.* Given their young age and limited knowledge of biblical matters, they are asked easy questions such as: "In which book of the Bible is the creation of the world described?" or "What was the name of the person who led the people of Israel out of Egypt?" Those who do not know the answer to any of these questions can sing a song or recite any Bible verse they know by heart instead—often they recite Genesis 1:1 when this happens—and thus win the right to sit back with their friends without being shown up as ignorant.

Then it is the turn of the *Explos* who are given questions just as difficult as those for the adult members of the church. "At what age was Jesus baptized?" Several participants guess, but they need to know the exact age. "How is the Adventist church organized from the international down to the local level?" One 15-year-old boy can, to everyone's surprise and joy, list all levels of the church's organization right from top to bottom (General Conference, divisions, unions, missions, federations, etc.), only confusing two of them. The quiz continues: "Which verses in which chapter of which book describe the Holy Communion?" This belongs to the standard stock of knowledge of many teenage Adventists and so they open their Bibles at 1 Corinthians: 11 without hesitation and quickly find the relevant passage.

Maroantsetra, May 15, 1999

A quiz is organized for the *Explos* in Maroantsetra town. The questions focus on Moses: "What is the name of the river where Moses was abandoned in a basket?" "What does the name Moses mean?" "What was Moses' wife called?" The participants have to find not only the right answers to these questions, but also the exact passages in the Bible that contain the relevant information. There is a lot of whispering and leafing through the Bible in the audience as well as among the participants, and not all the questions can be answered satisfactorily.

On one occasion on a Sabbath in Maroantsetra, two *children* organized the afternoon's quiz. First a 6-year-old boy put biblical questions to a group of adults who had volunteered as participants. Those who failed to come up with the correct answer were made to sing a song by the little boy. Partly because the adults hardly knew anything, and partly because of the peculiar reversal of roles, this quiz generated a lot of laughter.

It is obvious that those involved in these quizzes take great joy in learning and pride in knowing. It might be argued that Sabbath afternoons demonstrate the opposite of what I am claiming to be the case, that is, that Adventist practice is, at least partly, a matter of doctrine being learnt by heart and reproduced. However, this would be to forget that the aim of such quizzes and other forms of knowledge-oriented entertainment is to give people biblical expertise to be used as food for thought. Sabbath afternoons are not geared toward "right-answerism." Rather, the Bible expertise promoted on Sabbath afternoons is designed to allow the members of the church to juggle with ideas and advance them in discussion, much as a professor of anthropology employs her knowledge of Malinowski and Lévi-Strauss to think and argue with.

As with Sabbath School in the morning, the character of learning sessions on Sabbath afternoon can be greatly determined by the contributions of just one or two individuals. The following account provides an example.

Ampoafana, May 13, 2000, during a sector meeting
(A sector represents the organizational level above a single congregation.)

Only about 100 people are present, which is few for such a meeting. After a relatively quiet morning, during which not many people have actively participated, Sabbath afternoon once again takes on a real study session atmosphere when someone asks the following question: "Satan, so the Bible says, will eternally burn in the Great Fire. At the same time though, the Bible says that after the final resurrection, there will be no space for *any suffering* at all in paradise. So, where is there space in paradise for a suffering devil?" "This is a very good question," the church leader in charge of the afternoon's program replies, going on to explain that the expression "eternal" did not mean that Satan will burn forever, but that the *consequences* of the final resurrection will last eternally, that is, that the destruction of evil will be final. The answer satisfies the young man, but several other people are now inspired to ask their own questions regarding points of doctrine they are not clear about and that they seek to have explained to them. Due to the initiative of one person, the atmosphere had completely changed.

However, Adventist practice in Maroantsetra and Sahameloka is not always just a matter of more or less serious Bible study. People have fun, as I have shown in some of the anecdotes used in this chapter. People want to learn, but they also want to enjoy themselves, and so church services are often broken up by "light" parts such as quizzes that, apart from being aimed at improving people's Bible expertise, are also good entertainment and often produce a lot of giggling and laughter. On two occasions when I was present, members of the congregation in Maroantsetra performed a sketch in church on Sabbath afternoon. One sketch imitated the customs of different ethnic groups of Madagascar with the performers dressing up in "ethnic costumes" (Sakalava, Antaimoro, Betsimisaraka, Merina, etc.). The other related to issues of poverty and corruption and also involved people dressing up this time as a doctor, a beggar, a city slicker along with other roles. As everybody could recognize Maman' i Beby underneath the doctor's robe and *Madame Pasteur* as the arrogant lady, it was a lot of fun and the sense of comedy was enhanced by the fact that the acting was not exactly professional.

It is important to recognize the joy and happiness people get from their involvement in the Adventist church. The atmosphere in church often seemed to abound with such emotions when people were singing, which they love to do, and which they do incredibly well. But one occasion on which I went along with a large group of Adventists from Maroantsetra to spend the Sabbath in one of the district's villages is particularly memorable for me. We were transported in the trailer of a tractor and had much fun chugging along the bumpy road, singing church songs loudly and happily all the way there, and all the way back.

The family with whom I lived in Maroantsetra were big fans of the pop group Boney M. because of the Bible-inspired lyrics found in some of their songs. After I had completed the job of transcribing the lyrics to "By the rivers of Babylon," the entire family indulged in practicing this song for weeks while dancing around in the house. We even considered performing it in church, but after careful reflection upon the matter, decided against it.

Times for Learning

During the Sabbath, as we have seen, many times are specifically designated for Bible study, learning and knowledge acquisition. However, there is also always room to discuss things, or to ask questions or to put forward one's opinion on a particular matter during services held on Wednesday and Friday evenings.

Once, for instance, on a Wednesday evening in Maroantsetra, Maman' i Luc, a woman of about 40, stepped forward and asked the congregation whether St. Luke 23: 34—"Father, forgive them; for they know not what they do."—meant that all sins would automatically be forgiven? A discussion ensued that involved several members of the congregation spontaneously expressing their interpretation of the verse under consideration. Maman' i Luc was then asked whether she was satisfied with the explanation. She answered in the affirmative, thanked everybody and sat down. Similarly on another day in church, Hery, a teenage boy, presented the congregation with the question of whether or not God had also created "darkness". If not, where did "darkness" come from? He had become confused about this issue when studying the first chapter of the Book of Genesis at home and was eager to have it clarified. It was then discussed what exactly was meant by "darkness"—was it to be understood metaphorically or did it refer to darkness as opposed to light?—and whether the "darkness" in Genesis 1:2 referred to the earth or the entire universe. Note how a young person such as Hery can speak up in church completely unprompted and, by initiating such a discussion, take on a leading role.

On Wednesday evenings, the service in Maroantsetra town normally included the person in charge reading from one of Ellen White's books and offering some interpretations as to the relevance of the text. One such evening, however, Rakoto, the town's youngest lay leader who was in charge of the program that day, decided to turn the evening's "lecture" into a "workshop-seminar." He split up those present, including the pastor, into four groups of six to ten persons. He then allocated each group a particular passage of the chapter by Ellen White he had chosen, and then asked each group to first read and then discuss the text among themselves. After some twenty minutes of discussion, every group appointed one or two speakers, who summarized what their group had discussed and what conclusions had been reached.

On another occasion, it was the pastor who employed an unusual teaching method. As part of a weekend-long district meeting, which had attracted several hundred Adventists from far-flung villages, he on Friday evening gave a speech on the difficulty of human communication, and the importance of avoiding misunderstandings due to the distortion of information. He referred in particular to the misunderstanding on the part of some members of the Adventist church that Christ would return *in the year 2000* (this was shortly before the turn of the century). To prove his point, he conducted the following experiment. He whispered a sentence into someone's ear and told that person to whisper what they had heard into the next person's ear and so on. He asked the fifth person to repeat aloud the sentence he had heard. And indeed, so the pastor said, the content had changed remarkably. This experiment in Chinese whispers confirmed what the pastor then wrote on the blackboard, namely that only 20 percent of what is said in human communication survives after having been passed on five times.

Conclusion

The fact that people we tend to think of as "fundamentalists" or "evangelicals"—especially since they proclaim the inerrancy of a particular Holy Scripture—emphasize the importance of knowing that text is perhaps not surprising. Indeed, one could argue that intense Bible study is to be *expected* of groups such as the Seventh-day Adventists. However, what the ethnography presented in this chapter shows is not only that local church members engage in intense Bible study, but that Seventh-day Adventist practice in Maroantsetra and Sahameloka is of a distinctly Socratic nature. I choose the expression Socratic, because Bible study is aimed at understanding biblical truth through reflection and dialogue, rather than encouraging the consumption of ready-made doctrine.

More of this chapter has been dedicated to describing Bible study in church than at home. This, however, should neither be taken to indicate that the former context is more relevant than the latter, nor that the Socratic method of Bible study is only employed in church. In fact, these two contexts of Adventist religious practice can only be properly understood jointly. The reason why the church context is more prominent in my description is simply because there is a greater variety of activities in church than at home.

The focus of Sabbath School, like during other times of Bible study, always lies on comprehension and the discussion of particular texts, rather than on memorization and reproduction. Indeed, it is my impression that the purpose of the Sabbath is as much to *study* and *understand* God's word as it is to *worship* Him. I witnessed one Sabbath during which there were only two songs sung and two prayers spoken in the course of an entire day. The rest of the time, that is more than six hours, was spent studying and learning.

In every context I was able to observe, Bible study was of a dialogical, discursive and participatory nature, and involved much intellectual engagement and critical thinking for those taking part. And indeed, it seems to be the very *activity* of studying and learning, which fascinates and interests local church members, and which gives them pleasure, perhaps even more so than the answers they get from studying. Whenever I asked any of them what they liked about the Adventist church, their answers were saturated with the word "to study" (*mianatra*[11]).

Many observers of New Churches in Africa and elsewhere have noted the tremendous significance of Bible study as part of religious practice.[12] And some of these authors describe Bible study scenes that are very reminiscent of what I have observed among Seventh-day

Adventists in Madagascar. Ault, for example, describes Baptist practice in the United States in the following way:

> Both adult Sunday school and Wednesday night service are given over largely to instruction in Bible reading. The pastor leads the congregation in the study of an assigned passage. The result is much like a college seminar, provoking spirited responses and concentrated effort by any academic standard. (Ault 1987: 15–16)

Walsh observes that church services held by Jesus Saves converts in northern Madagascar

> can seem more like lectures than ceremonies. Standing on altars in little-adorned halls, pastors read biblical passages and discuss their relevance to the lives of congregation members who, for their part, listen intently, pens and notebooks in hand, taking note of readings that they might continue to study at home.[. . .] Home-study of the Bible is encouraged, and is in fact *the directive of the movement that is most attractive to some converts.* (Walsh 2002: 376, emphasis added)

Kessler observed "many opportunities for controversy" (1967: 226) during Sabbath School among South American Seventh-day Adventists in the 1960s, while Vance notes, with regard to Adventist practice in the United States in the 1990s, that

> most [Sabbath School meetings] provide a format for discussion [. . .] allowing and even encouraging questioning of doctrine and examination of the parameters of Adventist teachings. . . . (Vance 1999: 61)

And we might also recall the passage from a text in a Catholic publication concerning New Churches in Africa in general, which I quoted in chapter 2:

> These new Christian groups claim that the Bible is their centre and foundation. Pastors preach with the Bible in their hands, and constantly turn to particular texts. Ordinary members take their Bible to services, and underline texts during sermons. Most Churches insist on Bible study sessions during the week. (MAC 1993: 35)

With the exception of the last one, all of these observations are made in passing and their significance is not further elaborated on. However, they lead me to think that it might not only be the Malagasy Adventists whose religious commitment is motivated largely by enthusiasm for study and learning, but that this type of motivation may be relevant for followers of other New Churches and in other parts of the world as well.

I have drawn attention to the Socratic nature of local Adventist practice, which aims at comprehension of biblical truth through engaged study and dialogue. The term "Socratic" is usually employed to refer to a method of learning, which not only emphasizes students' active input in the process of finding answers to particular questions, but which also leaves the *conclusions* thus reached totally *open*. This is true for Adventist practice only to a limited extent, because despite the intellectual nature of Bible study, many of the answers people come to are largely predetermined by Adventist doctrine. This issue will be discussed in the next chapter.

Chapter 6

Knowledge of the Bible and
Scientific Inquiry

Books are the source of all science.

Ny boky no fiandohan' ny siansa rehetra.

One doesn't only learn at school, everyone has to study for themselves.

Ny fianarana dia tsy vita fotsiny any an-tsekoly, fa ianao mihitsy no mampitombo azy.

(Seventh-day Adventist bookseller)

"Adventists are People who Know the Bible"

In chapter 5, I illustrated the eagerness with which the members of the Adventist church in Maroantsetra and Sahameloka engage in Bible study, both in church and at home. However, the Adventists are not only committed to Bible study; they also define what it *means* to be an Adventist in terms of knowledge of the Bible. This was captured in the phrase "Adventists are people who know the Bible" (*ólo mahay baiboly ny Advantista*) that was regularly and emphatically voiced. "Why do we conduct Bible quizzes?" Papan' i Silivie once rhetorically asked the congregation during a service in Sahameloka before immediately providing the answer himself: "Because the Adventists are people who have knowledge of the Bible." This is why they promote the acquisition of such knowledge through various means such as quizzes.

Whenever members of the church went proselytizing in the countryside, they did so not by giving speeches, say, about the glory of God or the necessity to repent, but rather by visiting people in their homes in order to engage them in Bible study. The prototypical procedure went something like this. We would stroll around a village and knock at those doors where somebody appeared to be in. Once the usual words of welcome and thanks had been exchanged and we had been offered something to drink or to eat, my Adventist friend would explain that he or she was a member of the Seventh-day Adventist church and would immediately ask whether whoever they were speaking to had heard of Adventism. The listeners would normally reply politely that, yes, they had heard about it and, following Malagasy custom never to offend a guest, would add that Adventism was surely a good thing. The church member would then point out how important it is to read the Bible and would suggest that they do so together for a short while. By this point, several members of the visited family would normally have gathered and if there was no Bible at hand, a child would be sent to fetch one from a neighbor's house. The Adventist would then choose a particular passage in the Bible, read it and explain its meaning to those present. At the end of a short Bible study session like this—these lasted normally no more than ten minutes—those present would be encouraged to attend the Sabbath service that the Adventists were presently conducting in the village. It was also pointed out that there was much more to be learnt from the Bible. Moreover, those villagers who visited the Adventists' Sabbath service as they were invited to—many of them probably out of politeness or pure curiosity—would see that Adventist practice was all about Bible study. And those proselytizing promised the listeners that, if they joined the Adventist church, they would discover how they had up to now accepted, unknowingly, many things that were actually untrue. In particular they would discover, by reading the Bible, why Saturday, not Sunday, was the proper day of worship. The message thus sent out was a promise of knowledge. It was a message that sounded something like this: "If you become an Adventist, you are going to study the Bible and acquire knowledge of what is written in it, and Bible study will open up your eyes to many things which you have not been able to see up to now."

Knowledge of the Bible is, according to local Adventists, not only what characterizes themselves, but also what distinguishes them from the other Christian denominations that they are familiar with and to which many of them used to belong. Catholics and Protestants are said to simply carry the Bible to church and back without ever opening it, let alone reading and discussing it, and are thus thought to be totally ignorant of its content. On the basis of this interpretation, members of the local Adventist church would sometimes contemptuously remark about other Christians that they "just believe [in Jesus/God]" without understanding why they believe what they believe (*mino fö zare*).[1] Similarly, they would say that "the Catholics don't ask any questions" or that "the Protestants don't explain things clearly." Consider the following statements.

> I used to be a Protestant. But there I didn't really learn anything much about what the Bible says. And I realized that the Adventists really explain things about God. That is what made me join them. With the Adventists, there really is sufficient Bible study! One really studies a lot! When I joined them, I really began to study a lot! Because the point of going to church is to learn about God and His words. (Papan' i Filiette, Sahameloka)[2]

> When I was a Protestant, there were a lot of things which I didn't understand when I read the Bible and which they [the Protestants] couldn't explain to me either. For example, I didn't understand about the Sabbath. I went to ask the Protestant pastor three times, and finally he said to me: "Go and ask the Adventists, they can explain this to you." One day, we [himself and a friend] went to see the Adventist pastor, and we asked him about many things. We asked him 15 questions in total. And he answered them all according to the Bible! (Papan' i Loricà, Maroantsetra)[3]

Thinking back on their time as Catholics, one couple said:

> We used to be Catholics. But with the Catholics, one doesn't study the Bible very enthusiastically. They simply say "The Catholic religion is true." (Papan' and Maman' i Fredel, Sahameloka)[4]

Such statements are not only a criticism of Catholic or Protestant practice. They also, by way of contrast, highlight people's view of what it means to be an Adventist, namely to study the Bible and to be knowledgeable about its content.[5]

One might object that these are retrospective interpretations, and also that what the Adventists say of the Catholics and the Protestants is not necessarily correct. This may be true. However, the question of authenticity is irrelevant here, because irrespective of their truthfulness, these narratives convey church members' subjective understanding of the nature of Seventh-day Adventism and of why it is attractive to them.

Becoming Convinced

The emphasis on knowledge and understanding is also evident in church members' accounts of the process of becoming convinced by Seventh-day Adventism. I often perplexed my Adventist friends. From the beginning to the end of my fieldwork, that is, over the course of

20 months, I lived with members of the Adventist church and took part in all their church-related activities. Moreover, I wandered around Maroantsetra and Sahameloka, visiting various church members and asking them all sorts of questions related to their church membership. Everyone was always more than happy to talk to me about what they thought, felt and knew about their religion. I was therefore inevitably exposed to an intensive introduction to Adventism and everyone was clearly aware of this. With time, I became knowledgeable about the basic facts of Adventist doctrine, and familiar with Adventist practice. And the people who taught me noticed my growing expertise with delight. I knew about the importance of keeping the Sabbath and could easily find the relevant Bible passage in Exodus; I was aware of all the Adventist consumption taboos, and kept them; I had learnt much about the Bible and could now quickly open it at Matthew or Isaiah. In short: I knew enough. In fact some people observed that I knew more about Adventist teachings than many members of the church. However, I did not get baptized, and this puzzled many of my Adventist friends. Some of them sometimes took me aside after a church service, or invited me to their house, in order to give me further instruction and to clarify possible uncertainties on my part. They would inquire: "Is there anything which is not clear to you yet, anything that you haven't understood?" (*Misy mbôla tsy mazava aminao?*) The only reason they could think of for my not getting baptized, despite the fact that I had obviously acquired sufficient knowledge of the Bible, was that something must not be clear to me. It was assumed that the reason that stopped me from deciding to get baptized as an Adventist must be that I did not fully understand what I had learnt. Comprehension, to the local Adventists, was the key prerequisite of religious conviction, the former inevitably leading to the latter, and the lack of the former inevitably hindering the latter. Nothing was as important in the process of becoming convinced by Adventism, and hence of getting baptized, as knowledge of the Bible. Nobody ever asked me whether I perhaps did not accept as true what I had learnt.

Scientific Inquiry

We have seen that local church members conceive of the nature of Adventism as necessarily and fundamentally linked to the study, and hence knowledge, of the Bible. However, from their point of view, biblical knowledge is not isolated from, but, on the contrary, closely connected to other sources of knowledge, in particular scientific findings. Naturally, for an Adventist, the Bible is the ultimate source of truth, and hence science will always remain infinitely inferior to it. However, science can nevertheless help to prove biblical truth. "True things have proof" (*misy porofo ny zavatra marina*), members of the church would sometimes state. To find new proof of what the Bible says is not to establish the Bible's truthfulness, which is beyond question, but merely to add new pieces of knowledge confirming that truth.

In this section, I will demonstrate how ordinary members of the Seventh-day Adventist church in Maroantsetra and Sahameloka make use of the scientific knowledge they encounter.[6] I must begin, however, with one particular scientific theory that Seventh-day Adventists around the world emphatically oppose, namely the theory of evolution. It is obvious why this should be so from the perspective of people who accept the Bible as literally true: the theory of evolution contradicts, and belittles, God's creation as told in the Book of Genesis. In Maroantsetra, and more rarely in Sahameloka, the theory of evolution—although not always called by that name—is often discussed in church. Thus many local church members are aware that there are people, somewhere in the world, who claim that humankind was not created by God as we read in the Bible, but instead developed out of other species, in particular monkeys. As there are no monkeys in Madagascar, the pastor or other more educated members of the local church might explain to those with less formal schooling, that monkeys are similar to lemurs, animals endemic to Madagascar that everyone is familiar with. Antievolutionism is one of the key aspects of Seventh-day Adventist doctrine, and it is one of those "fundamentals" concerning which there is no scope for disagreement. However, rejection of evolutionism is a rejection of *a particular* scientific theory, and not a rejection of science *per se*. Once I asked Papan' i Beby, my most important teacher in Adventist doctrine, why, according to the Bible, the animals tabooed in Leviticus 11 were dirty. His answer was revealing:

> "Except with regard to the Holy Sabbath, the Bible does not explain why certain things are right and others wrong. This however, does not mean that we must not ask questions. God wants us to think, but sometimes the answers to our questions are to be found elsewhere, for example in *science* [using the French term]. Concerning biblical food taboos," he concluded, "every single one has been scientifically proven to be unsuitable for human consumption."

Incorporating Science

One of the scientific disciplines that, in the eyes of local Adventists, and Adventists elsewhere, provides much evidence for the correctness of the Bible is modern geology. As I said, evolutionism was often discussed in church, in particular during district meetings that attracted several hundred people among whom were always to be found a few members with a comparatively high degree of formal education. Once the pastor provided the following antievolutionist argument during a Sabbath morning sermon. "There are two books of God," he began, "the Bible and *la nature*. *La nature* always proves the Bible to be right."[7] He then went on to illustrate this point with the following example.

> "Two fossils," he explained—using the blackboard to graphically illustrate what he said—"were once found in two different layers of the same rock. The fossil in the *lower* layer clearly represented a human skull. The fossil in the *upper* layer, in contrast, had been formed by a skull which was similar, yet not identical, to that of humans, and which bore certain animal features. Thus," the pastor concluded, "the theory of evolution is clearly wrong, since according to it, the animal-like skull should have been found in the lower, i.e. older, rather than the upper, i.e. newer, layer of the rock."

I later confronted him with my observation that according to biblical creation, the animal-like skull should not have been there at all, neither in the upper nor the lower layer. To this the pastor replied that the "ugly" face could have been a deformed human skull, possibly the result of some hereditary disease (more on this later).

Church members found further scientific evidence of biblical truth in the field of astronomy. Once the pastor attended a three-week training course in the Adventist center in Antananarivo, the capital city of Madagascar, and brought back a notebook full of the latest astronomical findings. With shining eyes he explained to me the following. Scientists (who had nothing to do with Adventism nota bene) had discovered that the sun had developed into its present form from a fuzzy, nebulous mass. Moreover, the sun would continue to grow to 100 times its present size, and finally, it would become so hot that life on earth would become impossible. At present, the sun is three quarters of the way through its journey. This theory of solar development, the pastor concluded, confirms the development of light out of darkness as explained in the first few verses of the Bible. Furthermore, it also supports the biblical prophecy foretelling the destruction of this earth by a "lake of fire" (Book of Revelation 20: 9–15). On another occasion, while traveling to the town of Toamasina in a *taxi-brousse*, Jimmy, a young Adventist from Maroantsetra, informed me that astronomers had discovered a black hole in the constellation of Orion. This, he went on, was precisely the spot where

Christ will descend when He comes back to earth in the not too distant future. Once again, science confirmed what the Bible had known all along.

Many scientists ridicule the Bible, but in the end, Papan' i Beby assured me, they always had to admit to biblical truth. Such was the case, he related, for the story of the walls of Jericho told in Joshua 6. Scientists had long not taken seriously the biblical claim that the walls of Jericho had collapsed under the sound of ordinary trumpets. However, when the particular structure of these walls was actually examined, it had to be admitted that what the Bible said was perfectly possible; science provided proof of it. Similarly, we read in Isaiah 40: 22 of "the circle of the earth." Hence the Bible told us all along what scientists were later believed to have discovered for the first time, namely, that the earth is round.

Traveling Along

It would be misleading to imagine that most, or even many, ordinary church members in Maroantsetra and Sahameloka have direct access to scientific data such as the number of galaxies in the universe. The pastor has privileged access to such data because of his contact with Adventist centers in Madagascar. These centers pool all sorts of information provided by the global Seventh-day Adventist network, including scientific findings considered relevant to Adventist teachings.

However, highly specific information does travel a long way through the Adventist communication network. The information about the two fossil finds—one a fossil of a human, the other of an animal/human creature—as well as the fact that this was proof against evolutionism, was presented by the pastor in one of his sermons in church. It was thus passed on to all those present, and one has to remember that listening to a sermon is considered by many as study time, and that people take notes of what they hear. District meetings, which often attract several hundred church members, are a particularly good opportunity to spread information to a big audience. Moreover, almost every Sabbath at least a couple of lay church leaders or other members from remote villages attend the service in Maroantsetra town. Those present that morning when the pastor told us about the fossils are likely to have taken this information with them to the countryside. Indeed, the fossil finds discussed earlier were mentioned during more than one church service in Sahameloka while I lived there, although they were not discussed in detail. Church members in Sahameloka were not familiar with the term evolutionism, but they knew that there was a theory that challenged God's creation, and that certain scientific discoveries proved it to be wrong. In fact, the data the pastor, and those after him, were referring to, is known among Creation Scientists as Flood (or Deluge) Geology. This is a theory that uses geological data, particularly fossil finds, to prove the biblical story of the Flood, and which goes back to a voluminous book called The New Geology by the Seventh-day Adventist Price, published in 1923 in the United States (Moore 1993: 46–47).[8] By the 1990s, Flood Geology had traveled from America to the village of Sahameloka in Madagascar.

The Adventist claim, that Sunday worship is against God's will and that it was the *papacy* that introduced it, has traveled a similar route. In 1847, this assertion was first put forward by a man called Bates, a leading member of the Millerite movement, out of which Seventh-day Adventism grew (Hoekema 1963: 96). When I lived in Sahameloka 150 years later, Papan' i Fredel not only knew that Sunday worship was a human invention introduced by "some Catholic priest (*Monseigneur*)," but that this had happened "in the year 321" (see quote on p. 65).

It might be objected that what someone like Papan' i Fredel, who has hardly had any formal education, understands by the term *science*, or what exactly "the year 321" means to him, is completely different to what these concepts express where they originally come from. Thus it is misleading, it could be argued, to speak of the transmission of information, as if the meaning of the information transmitted had remained unchanged on its way from America to Sahameloka. This point raises issues of cultural particularism, which I will address at the end of this book. For the moment, I simply wish to point out that even if "the year 321," for example, has a very specific meaning to somebody who has never had a history class and who thinks of his own life not in terms of calendar years, but in terms of "when so-and-so was beginning to walk" or "when the big storm came," the core of the message—namely that Sunday worship is of human, rather than divine, origin—remains the same. More generally speaking, although it is very likely that information, which has arisen out of a particular cultural context elicits different associations in another context, it cannot be assumed that the message is changed to such an extent as to rule out comparability.

Doing Science

As the above evidence makes clear, for Seventh-day Adventists in general, and also for church members in Maroantsetra and Sahameloka, scientific knowledge does not pose a threat to, but in fact is made use of in support of, biblical truth. That Seventh-day Adventists are emphatically against the theory of evolution does not change this fact; for them evolutionism is simply an incorrect theory. Evolutionism is not seen as the epitome of scientific advance, and its rejection does not automatically imply a rejection of science in general (as many opponents of creationism suggest is the case). Adventists are not concerned with defending religion against science, but rather, from their point of view, with debating one scientific theory against another—namely creationism against evolutionism (hence the term Creation Science).

It is this involvement in scientific debates that I believe is one of the key attractions of Adventism for someone like Papan' i Beby who is so hungry for intellectual activity, but who has been denied access to higher education. Seventh-day Adventism is his way of doing science, allowing him to be an intellectual without a university degree. His thirst for knowledge is not limited to information directly relevant to the Adventist worldview, and he eagerly absorbs almost any information that comes his way. Hence he likes to memorize information he reads in his encyclopedia such as that it was the Roman emperor Vespasian who first introduced public toilets, or what a mausoleum is. There is no doubt that Papan' i Beby's level of self-taught education is highly exceptional. However, it is interesting that Adventist practice should attract and satisfy a person like him.

Although Papan' i Beby is exceptional in many ways, he is not the only member of the local church who is interested in sophisticated discussions concerning Adventist theory. One evening in Maroantsetra, Papan' i Miry, a man of about 50 and a friend of Maman' and Papan' i Beby, came by our house. He did not seem to have come for any particular reason other than to have a social chat. However, after a little while, I overheard the three agitatedly discussing Adventist theory in the light of "the problem of the Malagasy" (*ny probleman' ny Malagasy*), referring to the difficulty the Malagasy have stopping worshipping their ancestors as the church demands. The situation was reminiscent of three anthropologists who meet up socially, but who end up discussing anthropological theory. A similar image forced itself on my mind on a couple of occasions when listening to arguments explaining why Jehovah's Witnesses (of whom there are a small number in Maroantsetra town) were completely and utterly wrong. Since one of the lay leaders of the Adventist church in Maroantsetra used to be with Jehovah's Witnesses, parts of their doctrine have become known among the local Adventist congregation. While, from an outsider's point of view, the differences between Adventist doctrine and that adhered to by Jehovah's Witnesses are relatively minor compared to the similarities,[9] such theological differences were not at all insignificant to the people concerned. Will paradise be in heaven (Jehovah's Witnesses), or on earth (Adventists)? Had Jesus been crucified on a cross (Adventists), or on a stake (Jehovah's Witnesses)? Such were the theological questions that made Papan' i Beby's blood boil. And not only his, but also that of the leader of the small congregation of Jehovah's Witnesses with whom I had some contact, and who tried to convince me that the Adventists had it all wrong. As an outsider to both religions, these debates struck me as the technical discussions of two experts, rather like the disagreements of two academics from the same discipline who squabble over intradisciplinary differences that any outsider would regard as negligible compared to their shared fundamental outlook.

The local church members are keen to absorb scientific information, to discuss Adventist theory in relation to this and to thus be involved in debates over such issues as the origin of humankind. Moreover, they are constantly on the lookout for *new* proof of biblical truth. One day, Papan' i Beby asked me about the Greek Orthodox religion, because he knew that I had lived in Cyprus for some time and that the form of Christianity practiced there was called Greek Orthodox. I told him about the importance of the Virgin Mary for Orthodox Christians and mentioned that she was referred to in Greek by the name *Panayia*, which means "The All Holy." From Papan' i Beby's perspective, the veneration of the Virgin Mary is blasphemy, because nowhere in the Bible does it say that Mary was divine nor that she remained a virgin all of her life. This was clearly further proof that many denominations who called themselves Christians failed to follow the Bible! Papan' i Beby quickly noted the expression *Panayia* on a piece of paper—he even asked me to write it down in Greek letters although he cannot read them—rather like a scientist who has just stumbled over new evidence for his theory. Though I have not heard him use this particular information publicly in church, it is perfectly conceivable that he would do so, in which case one could equally imagine encountering the *Panayia* in Sahameloka and other villages in the Malagasy rainforest.

But evidence of Adventist doctrine does not normally come from such unusual sources. Members of the church in town and in the village discover it all around them in their daily lives. Deteriorating kin relations, for example, were interpreted as a sign of Christ's imminent return, as was the cyclone in the year 2000 that devastated large parts of the district.

Are they Normal Scientists?

The Seventh-day Adventists in Maroantsetra and Sahameloka struck me as what I will call "scientifically minded" for the reasons I have discussed and that I outline again here. First, in their daily approach to Bible study, the emphasis lies on investigation and intellectual comprehension of what is being proposed. Second, being convinced of the truthfulness of Adventist teachings is based on expert knowledge. Third, local church members consider it imperative to match empirical evidence with theory and thus to collect more and more proof of the truthfulness of Adventist teachings.

However, there is clearly a limit to what sincere Seventh-day Adventists can possibly accept as true, and this is why we will have to reconsider the appropriateness of the term "Socratic" in this context. For example, they cannot accept the theory of evolution—whatever proof of it may come their way—because to do so would be to reject the story of creation as told in Genesis, and this in turn would imply to reject Adventism, which is based on a literal reading of the Bible. Therefore, are Malagasy Adventists really "scientifically minded," in the sense defined above?

If one assumes a positivist understanding of science, that is, as the pursuit of knowledge guided by the discovery of facts, the Malagasy Adventists are scientifically minded. However, they are looking at facts within a closed framework of thought determined by Adventist teachings, and they are at pains to squeeze new facts into that framework. Hence the destruction of the Adventist church in Sahameloka during the cyclone was interpreted as a sign of Satan's anger, while the fact that church members' private houses withstood the storm was clear evidence of God's protection. Scholars with a view of science as unrestricted in its openness toward the interpretation of new facts, would therefore *not* agree that the Malagasy Adventists are true scientists. However, if one assumes that scientific inquiry, too, is guided by a particular framework of thought, then one might propose an analogy between the religious practice the local Adventists engage in and what Thomas Kuhn has called "Normal Science" (1996 [1962]).

Kuhn's principal claim is that Normal Scientists—that is most scientists at most times—are not involved in open discovery, indiscriminately accepting any evidence available to them and ready to change their theory accordingly, although they claim they are. Instead they work and think within an accepted paradigm that determines and restricts their vision, rather like a pair of green glasses that make the whole world seem green. Thus Normal Scientific activity is not based on skepticism as is generally assumed, but basically simply confirms what one already knows. Starting from his observations regarding Normal Science, Kuhn develops a theory of "the structure of scientific revolutions." These are caused by "paradigm shifts" and, unlike Normal Science, do lead to genuine scientific progress. However, here I am mainly concerned with Kuhn's analysis of Normal Science. Let us look at his provocative argument in more detail. He defines a paradigm thus:

> [Paradigms are] universally recognized scientific achievements that for a time provide model problems and solutions to a community of practitioners. (1996: x)

Normal Science Kuhn characterizes as

> [R]esearch firmly based upon . . . achievements that some particular scientific community acknowledges for a time as supplying the foundation for its further practice. [. . .] No part of the aim of normal science is to call forth new sorts of phenomena; indeed those that will not fit the box are often not seen at all. Nor do scientists normally aim to invent new theories, and they are often intolerant of those invented by others. Instead, normal-scientific research is directed to the articulation of those phenomena and theories that the paradigm already supplies. (1996: 10, 24)

In other words: Normal Science is "paradigm-based research" (1996: 25) and a paradigm is a framework of thought that is more or less uncritically accepted by a community of practitioners. "Novelty . . . is not a desideratum" (p. 169).

What I want to offer as a suggestion is an analogy between this Normal Scientific activity as interpreted by Kuhn and Seventh-day Adventist religious activity. I have described the local Adventists as scientifically minded because the nature of their religious commitment is based on study and evidence. At the same time though, their search for knowledge is clearly restricted by the fact that they think about, and interpret, evidence within a particular paradigm, namely the literal truth of the Bible. And as with Kuhn's Normal Scientists, what does not fit in the box, is not seen.

Let us go back to the example of the Adventist interpretation of the fossil finds of a human skull in the lower layer of a rock and a human-like skull in the upper, which the pastor interpreted as proof against evolutionism. As the reader will recall, I confronted the pastor with my observation that, according to the theory of creation, the half human/half animal-skull should not have been there at all, neither in the lower nor the upper layer, because God created humans as humans and animals as animals. To this the pastor replied that the "ugly face" might have been the result of some hereditary disease. Being on the lookout for proof of what he already knew—that the Bible is always right—and being somewhat trapped in the paradigm within which he thinks, the pastor did not recognize that his answer to my observation undermined his entire argument. Because if the human-like skull was to be explained away as an abnormality, it could not stand as proof either for or against evolution.

At the same time as limiting practitioners' view, a paradigm does not "explain all the facts with which it can be confronted" (Kuhn 1996: 18) and thus remains "sufficiently open-ended to leave all sorts of problems for the . . . group of practitioners to resolve" (p. 10). For example, it leaves the problem of interpreting these fossil finds with a view to matching evidence with theory. Or it leaves the problem of interpreting an unusually high number of deaths in a particular locality, or of a cyclone devastating one's rice crops.

In the course of his engaged, and engaging discussion, Kuhn likens the activities of Normal Scientists to the process of solving a puzzle, either a jigsaw or a crossword puzzle (p. 35–42); I particularly like the image of the jigsaw. Kuhn makes two main points. First, that the purpose and the thrill of doing a jigsaw lies not in the production of a novel outcome, but in the discovery of *how to get* to the predetermined solution. Second, there are certain rules to the game. For example, one cannot fit the jigsaw pieces in upside down. If one breaks these rules, one can never reach the solution. Like Kuhn's Normal Scientists, the Adventists might be compared to people doing a jigsaw, in that they are first and foremost interested in the *process* of making the picture grow. They also have to stick to the rules, the most important of which is the categorical rejection of "evidence" that contradicts the Bible. The local church members are not concerned with investigating whether or not the Bible is true, they know that it is. They are motivated by a desire to discover the exact content of the Bible, to discover where every piece of the jigsaw belongs and what it contributes toward the overall picture, rather like someone who makes an X-ray of a body in order to see what is inside to be able to understand how it all works and how every organ relates to the body as a whole. This is the fascinating inquiry that Bible study represents.

In chapter 5, I argued that Adventist Bible study in Maroantsetra and Sahameloka is based on the Socratic method of learning, whereby students are encouraged to think about certain questions and to find appropriate answers for themselves by way of thorough study and discussion among each other. The present chapter has shown, however, that this Socratic process of learning takes place within the paradigm of the literal truth of the Bible and that this paradigm sets the framework within which people intellectually operate. How is it possible, one might ask, that the Adventists are engaged in a process of learning, which emphasizes the free play of intellect, and yet all come to think the same? How can it be that the Socratic method of learning leads to such a canonization of knowledge as we find among the local Adventists? Can one really speak of a Socratic process if in the end everyone agrees that God created the world in six days, that the Flood really happened and that exhuming human remains is a bad thing? The answer to this question is twofold.

First, the contradiction between being engaged in intellectual inquiry and being "restricted by a paradigm" is formulated from the outside. It does not exist for the local church members themselves. They accept that the Bible is true and are thus convinced that by studying the Bible they will become able to reach and to fully understand the truth. They do not see the Bible as a paradigm, which limits the possibilities of their inquiry, but as the one book in the world that contains the truth, and that therefore, it is nonsensical to question. For them, approaching truth by studying the Bible is like learning French by studying a French dictionary. The fact that they accept the Bible as their paradigm also means that if, in their studies, they should come across something that they cannot match with Adventist teachings or their personal experience, they would in all probability conclude that they themselves are not knowledgeable enough to fully understand the truth, rather than questioning the paradigm itself. However, it is also important to note that at certain, though admittedly rare, moments, a limit to people's willingness to accept the literal truth of the Bible appears on the horizon; I will recount one such case in chapter 12.

From the perspective of an outsider to Adventism, on the other hand, there *is* a contradiction between the Socratic process of Bible study and the canonization of knowledge, between an open process and a closed result. This contradiction cannot be resolved, but it can be rendered understandable if we again turn to Kuhn's theory of Normal Science. As good Normal Scientists, the Adventists in Maroantsetra and Sahameloka do not seek to *establish* the truth through Bible study, they merely attempt to arrive at it, for the truth is already fixed. Bible study allows them to make the truth their own. Just as a person doing a jigsaw puzzle does not define the picture they are putting together, Bible study does not determine truth. Bible study provides the path, which leads to truth. It is because we are dealing with this type of learning process that the Socratic method of intellectual inquiry is not incompatible with the existence of a highly canonized set of ideas.

The process itself remains Socratic, even if it takes place within a paradigm that predetermines many of the findings. Theoretically, the contradiction between Socratic openness and the canonization of knowledge cannot be resolved. However, in practice, one can exist next to the other.

In a recent publication, Malley (2004) analyzes the nature of "Evangelical Biblicism" among the members of a Baptist church in the United States, most of whom are well-educated professionals. One of his key points is that Evangelical Biblicism is based on a fundamental contradiction between what he refers to as hermeneutic activity on the one hand and biblical authority on the other. By hermeneutic activity Malley means the interpretation of the Bible in order to make it relevant to one's own life. Significantly, there are no specific rules as to how exactly the Bible has to be interpreted and how exactly it has to be meaningful. Indeed, Malley argues, Bible interpretation must be relatively free and flexible in order for the Bible to remain a relevant book for generation after generation across time and space. At the same time, if left unchecked, this free interpretation could go in any direction and possibly even challenge the very authority of the Bible. The exact mechanisms that stop this from happening remain somewhat unclear in the book. Malley seems to suggest that interpretation is kept in check by a combination of avowal of literalism and the general cognitive drive for relevance, the latter making people ignore those interpretations that would make the Bible irrelevant or false.[10] Malley concludes that Evangelical Biblicism "needs both hermeneutic freedom and determinacy" (2004: 123), because "too much hermeneutic freedom and the tradition disintegrates, loosing its epistemological appeal; too little interpretive freedom and the Bible becomes merely an irrelevant historical artefact, rather than the ever-living word of God" (p. 123). Or to put it simply, there has to be a certain scope for individual interpretation, otherwise different people who live in different places and at different times cannot make the Bible relevant to their own lives. However, there has to be a limit to such interpretation, otherwise the Bible becomes a book like any other and thus loses its authority.

I am wary of the tendency in contemporary social science to emphasize, and perhaps exaggerate, the significance of sociocultural context with regard to the acceptance of world religions (see Conclusions). I would therefore not want to *assume* that the same text cannot be meaningful *in the same way* to people in different places at different times—that is an empirical question—which appears to be implied in Malley's argument. However, his analysis and my own are in many ways similar. Especially the emphasis on closely examining the content of a book one has already accepted as authoritative, is striking in both contexts. However, while according to Malley, the attraction of evangelical activity is its *goal*—which is to make the Bible relevant to one's own life—I don't see Bible study, as practiced by the Adventists in Madagascar, as a means to an end. Rather, I want to emphasize the joy of the *process* of Bible study itself. It is precisely because of the excitement of the intellectual inquiry *per se*, though within the limits of a given paradigm, that I have likened Adventist religious activity to Normal Science.

The analogy between Normal Science and Seventh-day Adventist practice that I propose has important limits however. Normal Science, according to Kuhn, has an in-built mechanism that eventually causes an existing paradigm to be abandoned and a new one to be adopted. This is a mechanism that is triggered by exceptional individuals who realize that certain evidence does not match the theory and that, in short, leads, from time to time, to scientific revolutions. Is such a revolution also conceivable within Adventism? First of all, Seventh-day Adventism does not recognize any in-built mechanism, as Kuhn describes for science, which will eventually and inevitably lead to a constant reformulation of what is considered to be true. Because the whole point about biblical truth is that it is eternal. However, it is conceivable—here we move away from Maroantsetra and Sahameloka to places where Adventist doctrine is formulated—that Adventist scholars may come to interpret what is written in the Bible differently. For example, it is theoretically possible for the theory of evolution to be accepted by Seventh-day Adventists if proof of it is found within the Bible. Such a paradigm change (acceptance of evolution) within the ultimate paradigm (the literal truth of the Bible) might be caused, for instance, by the realization that the Book of Genesis had been mistranslated, and that God does indeed tell us in the Bible that He will cause evolution to happen bringing about the existence of ever new creatures on the earth. Such a radical reformulation of Adventist theory would, however, not challenge the ultimate paradigm, that is the literal truth of the Bible as God's word. I must emphasize that all of this talk about possible paradigm-shifts within Adventism is my own speculation; I have no information actually suggesting such a shift to be in the process of occurring. Be that as it may, what is easily conceivable is a paradigm-shift in the biography of individuals, and here we move back to Maroantsetra and Sahameloka. If individual church members should come to the conclusion that Adventist theory is not borne out by the evidence they encounter, they might leave the church. Indeed, this has happened many times in the past in the district, though it is extremely difficult, not to say impossible, to establish why exactly certain members of the church withdraw from it and whether or not this has anything to do with people's view of what is true. However, there is at least one paradigm shift that all the members of the local Adventist church have already undergone during their lives: namely conversion to Seventh-day Adventism.

Toward the end of his analysis, Kuhn suggests that the adoption of a new paradigm—which is what leads to scientific progress—is not primarily based on acquaintance with new scientific proof, but on "faith" in the new paradigm, on faith that it will live up to its promise. Therefore, the adoption of a new paradigm is a question of "conversion." The individual scientist who adopts a new paradigm is not convinced to do so by factual knowledge, but is *persuaded to believe* in the new paradigm (Kuhn 1996: 151–159). In presenting this analysis and using words like "conversion," "faith" and "persuasion," Kuhn clearly suggests, although he does not explicitly say so, that science is in fact much more similar to religion than most scientists would be keen to acknowledge. Seventh-day Adventist practice in Maroantsetra and Sahameloka shows us the other side of the coin: that sometimes at least, "religion" is not all that different from "science," and that the activity of science as it is practiced on a daily basis, if we believe Kuhn, and the type of activity engaged in by the local members of the Adventist church, are related.[11]

An Oddity, or, the Question of Emotional Commitment

The Adventists continually look for proof of Adventist teachings. One central aspect of these is the prophecy of Christ's Second Coming to be followed by a sequence of events that will eventually lead to eternal life in paradise. Christ's return to earth will be preceded by what Seventh-day Adventists call the Sunday law, that is the prohibition on worshipping God on any day other than Sunday. The Sunday law is one of those features of Adventist doctrine that almost all church members, even in remote villages such as Sahameloka, have heard of. They endlessly talk about it, and many daily happenings they interpret as signs, or proof, that the Sunday law and Christ's return will take place "before too long" (*efa tsy ela*)—possibly within the next few years and almost certainly within their lifetime or at least that of their children.[12] Significantly, with the Sunday law will come the persecution of all those who continue to worship God on Saturday as Seventh-day Adventists do. Indeed, local church members imagine their own persecution in concrete terms. I have heard people say how lucky they are—in contrast to other Adventists in other parts of Madagascar and elsewhere—to live near the forest, so that they can hide when the time comes. I have heard people say that once they are hiding in the forest, God will send them water and food. I have heard people speculating on whether or not their non-Adventist kin and neighbors will become their persecutors.

Despite these vivid imaginations, however, when church members talk about the Sunday law and their imminent persecution, they show no emotion and display no fear. They talk about it with a lightness, even, at times, a cheerfulness, which I found astonishing given the fact that what they are envisaging is not someone else's destiny, but their own future suffering. With my host family in town, talk of persecution could acquire a rather theatrical and even comical quality.

On one of the many days when our conversation turned to the Sunday law, Kiki showed me what would happen when it came into force. He picked up our dog's rope and, putting the noose around his neck, started to imitate a person about to be hanged. Changing roles and imitating his murderer, he then said firmly: "Will you still pray on the Sabbath or not?" "I will!" was the equally firm answer. And so the noose was pulled and he was hanged. On another occasion, the family was talking about the misconceived idea that the persecution would begin on New Year's Eve at the dawn of *the year 2000* ridiculing those who believed this. When Kiki (who often played the clown) began to mock the drunk non-Adventists (they would be drunk because it would be New Year's Eve) staggering after the Adventists in order to stab them with knives, the whole family exploded with laughter. Although the point of Kiki's performance was to make fun of the stupidity of those who thought the persecution would occur in the year 2000, and not to mock the persecution as such, I was amazed at the ease and jollity with which the family was dealing with the issue. Kiki had said another time that he thought the persecution was no more than five years away.

I did not observe other members of the church dealing with the issue of persecution as entertainment. But I never felt that people—when they were talking about the Sunday law and how there were signs all around that it would happen before too long—were actually afraid, or even worried, about the prospect of having to run away and hide in the forest or of the possibility of being killed.[13] Also, going back to the Sabbath School discussion I quoted in chapter 5, it is striking that despite the fact that the participants talked repeatedly about "the difficult times," by which they meant the persecution, nobody expressed any fear, and nobody looked afraid as they were talking. The persecution, despite its continual presence in discussions in church and at home, seemed not to move people emotionally.

These observations have forced me to consider the possibility that the local Adventists might simply be reproducing doctrine when they talk about the Sunday law, without what they reproduce actually being very meaningful to them. It is, of course, important to keep in mind that emotions such as fear are not necessarily expressed or visible and that I cannot therefore say with certainty that the local Adventists are not afraid of the persecution. It might also be the case that, despite explicit statements to the contrary, the imminence of the persecution is not felt. These questions must remain unanswered here.

However, let us assume that during the Sabbath School discussion I quoted, talk of the "difficult times" was not charged with emotion, and that the *content* of what people were talking about remained somewhat distant to them. Even if that was the case, the discussion itself was lively and engaged and in that sense moved the participants. Thus even at times, when particular features of Adventist doctrine are reproduced without that content being particularly meaningful to those who reproduce it, people are nevertheless taking pleasure in *developing their argument* and in participating in, and contributing to, a discussion in which they enthusiastically engage.

This observation leads me once again to conclude that at the heart of the attraction of Adventist practice for the local church members, and at the core of their commitment to Adventism, is the very *process* of study and of intellectual engagement. Like people doing a jigsaw puzzle, the local Adventists are primarily excited by making the picture grow, perhaps even more so than by its beauty. Perhaps the discussion that Sabbath morning was a truly *academic* discussion, rather like we imagine what might have taken place at Plato's academy; a discussion, in other words, not for the purpose of coming to particular conclusions, but for the purpose of a participatory search for knowledge.

Chapter 7

Text and Learning

In chapters 5 and 6, I have discussed the Adventists' emphasis on Bible study, knowledge of the Bible and comprehension of biblical text. In this chapter I will analyze how this focus on studying text relates to a much more general Malagasy approach toward writing and learning.

The Bible and Other Books

Written text and literacy have enjoyed a long and prestigious history in Madagascar. The oldest written documents we know of are the so-called *Sorabe*, or Great Writings.[1] These are a series of books that are in the Malagasy *language*, but that are written in Arabic *script*. They are in possession of the Antaimoro of southeast Madagascar, a people with historical connections to the Arab world.[2] Some *Sorabe* contain information on the mythical origins of the Antaimoro, while some are works of medicine, geomancy, divination and astrology. Before the arrival of the first Christian missionaries in 1820 and the subsequent scholarization of a substantial part of the population, Malagasy society was generally nonliterate, and the Antaimoro were unique in their scribal tradition. It was not only the esoteric knowledge contained in the *Sorabe*, but also the Antaimoro's writing ability that gave them influence and power in pre-Christian times before literacy became widespread. Antaimoro scribes, diviners and medicine men were employed by many of the other peoples all around the island during that period (Deschamps 1959: 27; Dez 1983: 111). But their writing skills became particularly important when the Merina kingdom of the central highlands began to expand toward the end of the eighteenth century, turning into an elaborate, centralized state with a complex administrative organization. Merina kings brought Antaimoro scribes to settle at their court in order to take their advice on a number of matters, including auspicious times for military action. The Antaimoro's counsel was based on the information contained in the *Sorabe*, and their status on their exclusive access to these writings. Antaimoro also acted as secretaries for the rapidly growing administration of the Merina kingdom (Bloch 1986: 14), and they even taught some Merina officials to read and write. Moreover, there is evidence that they opened a school in the capital Antananarivo around the year 1800 (Bloch 1968: 286–287). Thus long before Christianity came to Madagascar, there was a great interest in written text and literacy in the country.

In the 1820s, LMS missionaries made their first attempts to set foot in Madagascar in order to embark on their program of spreading the gospel, which they intended to do largely by way of teaching the Malagasy how to read the Bible. King Radama was very skeptical toward the *religious* program of the missionaries, but he was keen on some of the particular skills the missionaries would bring with them, especially literacy in the Roman script (Ellis, W. 1838: chapter 10; Raison 1974; Raison-Jourde 1991: 287). Because of his political alliance with the British at the time (Bloch 1986: 16–17), Radama considered the introduction of the Roman script as far more promising for his kingdom than access to the Antaimoro's *Sorabe*, because knowledge of the Roman script would enable "communication with foreign powers" (Raison-Jourde 1995: 292). Under the condition that the missionaries would indeed bring technical expertise, and especially literacy, into the country, the king allowed them in (Ellis, W. 1848: 275).

Once the missionaries were in Madagascar, their primary goal was to translate the Bible, to print it and to teach as many Malagasy as possible to read and write so as to make the Bible available to them. It was first published in 1835. However, Christianity was soon seen as a threat to royal authority and the power of the monarchy. Radama's successor, Queen Ranavalona I, understood the Bible to be the book of the royal ancestors of the foreigners, and thought of Christianity as their cult: by worshipping Jesus, she reasoned, the Malagasy were made to forget about their own royal ancestors. Thus between 1836—that is one year after the publication of the Bible—and 1861, all foreign missionaries were expelled from Madagascar and Malagasy Christians suffered several waves of persecution (see Ellis, W. 1848: chapters 12 and 13; Raison-Jourde 1991: chapters 3 and 4). Obviously, the Bible was in these years an object that one could only possess at a risk.

But this did not signal the end of the importance of written text. In reaction against the foreigners' book of royal ancestries and genealogies, a number of Merina began to produce manuscripts that mirrored what they understood the Bible to contain. What they began to write down were *their own* ancestral genealogies and accounts of *their own* history. In order to fight Christianity, then, they used the missionaries' own tool, namely written text (Bloch 1989b: 22–24).

However, the policy of rejecting Christianity ended in the 1860s when the Merina royalty accepted Protestantism as their state religion. Ever since, Christianity and the Bible with it have played an immensely important role in Madagascar.

In highland Madagascar, the written word has been highly prestigious at least since the time when the Antaimoro scribes worked at the Merina royal court. However, one must not assume that what literacy has come to mean in the highlands is necessarily also what literacy has come to mean elsewhere in Madagascar. In fact, the main point of Bloch's discussion of literacy in Madagascar, referred to above, is to show—in critical response to Goody's theory of the "great divide"—that literacy *in itself* does not have any particular quality and does not carry with it any particular implications. What writing and literacy exactly mean in a given society always has to be looked at contextually (Bloch 1989b, 1993b).

Bloch describes how, among the Zafimaniry, who live a long way from Maroantsetra, almost all kinds of texts, including government communications and adverts for bras, are "presumed to come from an immensely powerful beyond and because of this they are taken to be true without question" (1993b: 103). I am not sure that this holds true to the extent described by Bloch in the area of Maroantsetra. Although people do proudly display all kinds of magazine advertisement on their walls, this strikes me more as an effort at decoration than anything else. It does not reveal any particular view people might have about the nature of these pictures or the text that goes with them. However, what Bloch describes for written text in general, is certainly true in the area of Maroantsetra with regard to books, and in particular the Bible. Let me mention in passing, that this means that the acceptance of the Bible as literally true is not at all exceptional in Madagascar and in no way restricted to those Malagasy who belong to what we term "fundamentalist" churches.

It would be a mistake to assume that the status of the written word as revealing authoritative knowledge is juxtaposed to a lack of such status of the spoken word. In Madagascar, there is not only a long tradition of attributing wisdom and truthfulness to written language, but also equally to certain forms of spoken language (Bloch 1968, 1989b). This is so especially with regard to traditional oratory (*kabary*), which Malagasy elders perform masterfully and through which the wise words of the ancestors are transmitted to new generations. *Kabary*, as opposed to ordinary language, is characterized by allusive, decorative speech and is extremely rich in proverbs, metaphors and other stylistic devices (see Bloch 1971, 1975, 1989b, 1993b; Keenan 1975). Bloch argues that since its first publication in 1835, the Bible has been perceived by the Malagasy as essentially of the same nature as *kabary*, because its style of language is recognizably that of oratory, not ordinary daily talk, and because the Bible's content comes from an immensely powerful source from "beyond," like that of *kabary*, which comes directly from the ancestors (Bloch 1989b). It was, among other reasons, because the Bible was perceived to be a very special *kabary*, Bloch argues, that it became regarded an authoritative and wise source of knowledge.

Is the Bible a Book?

Christianity relies on truth revealed through words. Robbins describes how for the Urapmin, a recently Christianized people in Papua New Guinea, this causes a problem, because the Christian idea of truthful speech clashes with an indigenous notion among the Urapmin that words, whether written or spoken, cannot be trusted (2001a). As we have seen, the Malagasy Seventh-day Adventists do not have this problem. Neither are they in the situation described by Engelke in his analysis of a group of apostolics in Zimbabwe (2004). These people basically perceive the Bible to be a tool of colonial power; hence they reject it and take pride in referring to themselves, in complete contrast to the Malagasy Adventists, as "the Christians who don't read the Bible." At the same time as rejecting the *written* Bible though, the Zimbabwean apostolics construct a discourse that reduces text to an infinitely inferior channel of communicating with God than "direct" communication through performed speech. In the case of Madagascar, the arrival of Christianity and the importance of the Bible preceded colonial rule by several decades, and by the time Madagascar became a French colony in 1896, Christianity had become an indigenous institution. In contrast to the situations described by Robbins and by Engelke, the Malagasy Adventists' emphasis on the Bible and its acceptance as a source of truth is unproblematic in the local society. Indeed, the Adventists share the generally held view of books that attributes an authoritative quality to them. And some members of the church are actively engaged in the business of selling books.

*   *   *

At the time of my fieldwork, a dozen members of the Adventist church in Maroantsetra town were employed by the church as professional door-to-door booksellers.[3] This Adventist activity was in fact the only source of books, or any other written material, in town, except for what pupils receive at school and a few pamphlets the Protestant and Catholic churches provide. As there is almost no likelihood of books being affordable for rural people, none of the local booksellers ever tried their luck in the countryside; thus, what follows only concerns Maroantsetra town.

One of the Adventist booksellers was Maman' i Ominò whom I sometimes accompanied on her rounds. Dressed in her very best outfit, Maman' i Ominò spent much time walking around town, knocking at the doors of well-to-do members of society (such as rich Chinese merchants or the director of the local electricity board) who might possibly be able to afford one of the books she carried in her bag. For the books she had on offer were very expensive,[4] and their prices by far exceeded the financial means of Maman' i Ominò herself, the other Adventist booksellers and the great majority of the members of the Adventist church. Moreover, practically all of these books were written in French, which most of those who sold them, and I guess many of those who bought them, could not read at all, or only a little.[5] Most of the books sold were from a French publishing house (Vie et Santé, in Dammarie-lès-Lys) which, although not explicitly declared to be Adventist, clearly has close affinities to the church. These books are primarily produced for European readers and concern such things as healthy nutrition, including tables about the vitamin and protein content of different foods. But to people in Maroantsetra, the recipes presented would not make much sense even if they could read them, nor would they have the required ingredients—muesli, strawberries, fresh vegetables, soya milk—to prepare them. One of the most popular books Maman' i Ominò sold was a publication that gave advice on how to deal with daily stress symbolized by an overpowering clock on the cover. As with strawberries and muesli, however, having to rush from one place to another was not exactly among the daily problems of the local population.

The prize book for both sellers and potential buyers was a massive French *Catholic* Bible with golden page edges and rich in colorful illustrations of Popes and cathedrals. I was extremely surprised that the Adventist church would distribute a Catholic Bible that glorifies the papacy so despised by Adventists. The answers given by Maman' i Ominò and by Papan' i Beby regarding this question were evasive, suggesting something along the lines of "it is still a Bible and it is beautiful" (Maman' i Ominò) and "one has to know what the enemy produces" (Papan' i Beby). This Bible cost the equivalent of a civil servant's monthly salary, and so most people who decided to purchase one had to pay for it in installments. Selling one was extremely good business for a bookseller.[6] It was everyone's dream, including the members of the Adventist church, to own such a Bible. Even Papan' i Beby hoped to be able to buy one one day, despite his contempt for the Catholic church in general and the Pope in particular, a contempt he seized every opportunity to express.

For local people, books often have an almost mysterious aura about them, simply by virtue of being books. Indeed it seems, that it is this aura of authenticity that makes the books Maman' i Ominò and others sell so desirable for the town's population. This aura is much more important than the books' content, which many buyers are unable to read, and which, even if they could, would be unlikely, except in the case of the Bible, to make much sense to them. The purpose of buying any of these books is quite clearly possession and display. In fact, people sometimes bought books that were still wrapped up in plastic solely on the basis of descriptions of what was to be found inside.

What is particularly interesting with regard to the book selling business is the fact that the members of the Adventist church share the perception that books are primarily valuable because they contain written text and so inspire awe and the desire to have them in one's house. No act of learning is associated with these books. Maman' i Ominò, a very enthusiastic and involved member of the Adventist church, thought it a great shame that she could not afford to buy any of the books she sold, although she was perfectly aware that their content was well beyond her level of literacy, particularly her literacy in French, which was limited to a few words. She did not feel sorry that she could not *read* them, but sorry that she could not afford to *buy* them. Like other people in town, the local Adventists approach books in general with awe, and do not consider it a priority to study them or understand them.

*   *   *

We can conclude then that the Adventists' relationship to books is similar to that of other people in the area and elsewhere in Madagascar. This being so, their relationship to books is curiously disconnected from the Adventist emphasis on studying and comprehending the Bible's *content*. The disconnection occurs between Bibles used for Adventist Bible study, on the one hand, and all others books, including the Catholic Bible, on the other. Ironically, the much-desired Catholic Bible is treated by members of the Adventist church with considerably more awe, if they ever get close to one, than the Bibles they use for daily study.

To be sure, the Bible is the epitome of all books, for Adventists and other Malagasy Christians alike, because, more so than any other book, it is thought to come from "an immensely powerful beyond" (Bloch 1993b: 103). And the truthfulness of its content is clearly not at stake. But while other books—and oratory (*kabary*) that, as I explained, is perceived to be of essentially the same nature as written text—are approached with an attitude of respectful acceptance, the Adventists approach God's "great *kabary*" in the Bibles they study in a spirit of intellectual analysis. Hence during Adventist Bible study sessions, the Bible's consistency and inner logic, and how it relates to everyday life, is constantly analyzed and discussed.

Bibles used for Bible study, then, almost form a category of books in their own right, a category that is approached significantly differently to any other, including Bibles *not* used in Adventist practice. Thus one might ask: although the Bible is the book of all books for the local Adventists, do they actually perceive of it as a *book*?

Adventism and School Knowledge

In comparing how the Adventists' focus on Bible study relates to general ideas among the local population concerning texts, we have found a strong continuity with regard to the perception of books as prestigious and as containing authoritative truth simply by virtue of being books. At the same time, although the Bible is the most authoritative of all books, it does not fit into the general category of books, because unlike any other book (including Bibles for possession and display), it is approached as a book to be studied rather than admired. Thus with regard to the relationship to text we find both continuity and novelty in the Adventists' approach.

I now turn to the issue of how the Adventists' emphasis on Bible study relates to local perceptions of learning. One question that is likely to have risen in the reader's mind is whether Adventism is not a substitute for poor schooling opportunities in the area. To answer this question, let us look at the issue of the relationship between Adventism and schools more closely.

Two different suggestions could be put forward. First, one might argue that Adventism is a way to get the education local people are otherwise denied, a possibility to learn what they failed to learn at school. Second, one could point out the different styles of learning practiced in local schools and during Adventist church services respectively and suggest that the Adventists are dissatisfied with the *method* of learning found in schools. Before I can discuss these issues, I must briefly describe the local situation with regard to formal education.

School Performance

Compared to many other countries in the Third World, Madagascar has a very high level of elementary schooling.[7] However, there are vast differences in the levels of scholarization in different parts of the island. This is largely due to the impact of the Christian missions, which, from the beginning of Christianization in the nineteenth century, concentrated their efforts on the populations living in the central highlands. Generally speaking, these are to this day the most literate areas.

In the district of Maroantsetra, most people attend several years of primary school, with a much smaller proportion also attending secondary school, which is only available in town. Beyond the level of the French *baccalauréat*, Maroantsetra has nothing to offer and those few students who pursue further studies have to go to other towns. Few people in the area are entirely illiterate, but many nevertheless struggle with writing and sometimes reading as well.[8]

While the quality of schools in Maroantsetra town leaves a great deal to be desired—with teachers available only for some exam subjects—in the countryside it is much worse. In Sahameloka, as in most other villages of that size, there is a primary school where the children theoretically receive five years of education. In reality, however, lessons are very often cancelled because of the teacher having gone to town or being busy with the rice harvest, or other equally urgent business. I was told that a couple of years ago, Sahameloka's schoolteacher failed to come to work for a period of several months, due to the fact that he was staying in another village with relatives. Given the inadequacy of schooling in rural areas, it is extremely rare for someone from the countryside to proceed to secondary education in Maroantsetra and, I believe, practically unheard of to continue beyond this.

Older residents in the district recall that access to schools and the quality of teaching in the countryside too, used to be better a few decades ago than it is now, and indeed, older people are often more literate than the young. The effects of the postcolonial governments' neglect of many rural areas are becoming increasingly noticeable.

Indeed, these days, many pupils seem to learn astonishingly little at school. Mezaquei, the 9-year old boy of my family in Sahameloka, was not able to read or write a single word except his own name, and this after he had already repeated *five* times the first class of the village primary school. It has to be acknowledged, that he had missed much of those five years of schooling, partly because he continually found some excuse or other that allowed him to skip school, and partly because of the long absences of the village's teachers. Beby, the 15-year old girl from my family in town was, after several years of learning English, unable to hold even the simplest conversation. The only thing she could actually say was that her name was Beby, and that she was fine, along with the corresponding questions. Nevertheless, her notebook was full of complicated English grammar, which she had copied from the blackboard during lessons, and which she was struggling to learn by heart for the exams. Teaching to a large extent consisted of the teacher writing vocabulary and grammar on the blackboard that the pupils copied studiously and memorized. They seemed, however, to comprehend only little of what they learnt.[9] Thus, from a contemporary Western point of view of learning, teaching did not appear to produce the desired effect.

Maths was another case in point. Florentin, a middle-aged member of the Adventist church in Maroantsetra, had been trained as a teacher. When I knew him, he worked as a civil servant at the *Perception Principale*, which belongs to the Ministry of Finance. Yet he was unable to work out how many years he had been with the Adventist church, despite knowing that he was baptized in 1987 and that we were now in the year 1999. Papan' i Silivie in Sahameloka knew that he was born in 1964, but he was at a loss to calculate his age.[10] The fact that these examples all concern members of the Adventist church does not generate a distorted picture, because with regard to their performance in school subjects, the Adventists appear to be no different to the average person in the district.

One area about which many local people seemed to have particularly little knowledge is the world beyond Madagascar. Neither newspapers nor internet connection are available in the district, not even in town. Many people have a radio, also in the countryside, but they tend to only listen (when they have batteries, that is) to the local radio station, which mostly just plays popular songs. Thus one of the few potential sources of information about the world outside Madagascar are schools.

Knowledge of "Andafy"

During my stay in the region of Maroantsetra, as well as when traveling in other parts of Madagascar, I always found the Malagasy people to be very much interested in information about the world *andafy*, the world "beyond the sea" (Abinal et Malzac 1993: 37). *Andafy* is used to refer to any place outside Madagascar, whether it be Mauritius, Africa, China or Europe. The people who live *andafy* are generically called *vazaha*, although, usually, this term is used for White people, especially the French.[11] Everywhere I went in Madagascar, I found myself bombarded with questions concerning what people *andafy* ate, how long it would take and how much it would cost to go there by airplane, what people wore, and whether it was true that there were places entirely populated by *vazaha*. Whilst being interested to find out more about *andafy*, many Malagasy I have met, in particular rural people, have but the haziest of ideas of the world beyond Madagascar. Many, for example, believe that the world consists entirely of islands.

The members of the Adventist church in Maroantsetra and Sahameloka were no exception in terms of their lack of knowledge about the world beyond the sea. Take a look at the conversation I had with Papan' i Fredel and Papan' i Tahina shortly after my arrival in Sahameloka. The point of quoting this discussion will become clear shortly. Papan' i Fredel attended local primary school for a few years; he is in his late 40s. Papan' i Tahina is in his early 20s. He is of Betsileo origin on his father's side and so was sent to Ambositra, a Betsileo town in the Malagasy highlands, for a couple of years of secondary school. Papan' i Tahina was one of two Adventists from Sahameloka who had attended more than five years of primary school. Our conversation went like this:

Papan' i Fredel: Where exactly are you from?
Me: I am from Switzerland.
Papan' i Fredel: Right, but from which country?
Me: Switzerland is a country; it lies next to France [if people know anything about *andafy*, it is normally related to France].
Papan' i Tahina: Does Switzerland also belong to France, like Madagascar?
Papan' i Fredel: We don't belong to France any longer, don't you know that!
Papan' i Tahina: Oh really [embarrassed], I didn't know that, I thought we still belonged to France [Papan' i Tahina was born ten years after independence].
Papan' i Fredel: Which direction does one have to go to reach *andafy* [cardinal points are very significant all over Madagascar]?
Me: Well, that depends, there are many different places *andafy*. If you want to go to France or Switzerland for example, you have to go north.
Papan' i Fredel: Really! I thought *andafy* was to the south of Madagascar [Maroantsetra lies in the north of Madagascar, and so local people often think that almost everything else lies further south].
Papan' i Tahina: Where is Africa?
Me: That's to the west of Madagascar.
Papan' i Tahina: Do the Karany [Malagasy-Indians] also live with you in the north?
Me: No, the place where the Karany and the Chinese live lies to the east of Madagascar.

Papan' i Tahina: Where is Asia?
Me: That's precisely where the Karany and the Chinese live.

At this point, I got up and drew a rough map of the world into the sand, which probably did not make much sense to either of the two men I was talking to. I proceeded to point out the different continents, including America.

Papan' i Tahina: This is where America is? But in which *kontinanta* [continent] is it?
Me: America is a continent. A big mass of land like that, comprising many countries, is called a continent.
Papan' i Fredel: Egypt is an island, isn't it?
Me: No, Egypt is part of the African continent, it is a country in the north of Africa, and there are other countries next to it.
Papan' i Fredel: Isn't there a president called Bill Clinton somewhere?
Me: Yes, that's right, he is the president of America.
Papan' i Fredel: Is Mauritius as far away from Madagascar as where you come from?
Me: No, Mauritius is very close to the east of Madagascar, it only takes something like an hour to get there by airplane [this was a meaningless answer since neither of the two men had ever seen, let alone travelled in, an airplane].

The conversation continued for about half an hour in the same style. For Papan' i Tahina, who spent a couple of years in the highlands doing secondary education where geography was certainly taught as a subject, the complete lack of knowledge about the world beyond Madagascar was somewhat surprising. However, it was not only knowledge of basic world geography that entirely passed many local people by. I was often asked questions such as whether there were mountains, trees and rivers *andafy*, just like in Madagascar, whether thunder and lightning also existed where I came from, or whether the moon would also shine at night. And many people, in town as well as in the countryside, were very surprised when I told them that indeed it would. When people heard that the *vazaha* do not necessarily eat rice every day, as they themselves do, and that bananas, breadfruit, pineapples and coconuts do not grow everywhere in the world, they sometimes expressed pity for the *vazaha*, for it seemed to them that they must have practically nothing to eat.

Is Adventism a Substitute for School Knowledge?

Papan' i Tahina was the only member of the Adventist church in Sahameloka who had ever lived outside the district. His literacy was very good and mainly because of this he was a lay church leader. In that capacity, he had no problem whatsoever giving a sermon in church, a sermon that he had written himself, that required a high degree of Bible expertise and that combined numerous references from the whole Bible. Papan' i Tahina does not know what a continent is, but he can sketch the history of humankind, from creation to the Flood, to Jesus, to today, with ease. Papan' i Fredel, who thinks that other countries all lie to the south of Madagascar, knows that the Pope is presently preparing the implementation of the Sunday law, and that Sunday worship was ratified by some "*Monseigneur* in the year 321.*" The point here is not to make the Malagasy look ignorant. Rather, it is to show that, although there are, of course, exceptions, such as Papan' i Beby, there exists an immense gap between church members' expertise in biblical and Adventist matters, on the one hand, and their lack of the kind of knowledge one learns at school, on the other. It would be tempting then to conclude that Adventism is a substitute to make up for the poor schooling opportunities in the area.

Much of the literature on Seventh-day Adventism would seem to propose precisely such an instrumental link between Adventism and access to education.[12] In countries where the Adventist church actually does provide schooling for people who would otherwise receive none, access to education may well be a strong incentive for church membership. But this is clearly not the case in the district of Maroantsetra.

However, it is true that the reading skills of many Adventists in Maroantsetra and Sahameloka have improved considerably as a result of regular Bible study. The most striking example is that of Emanuel, a man in his late 50s. Emanuel never went to school, and he was completely illiterate when he joined the Adventist church in Maroantsetra as a young man in 1972. However, with the help of other members of the church, he began to learn to read and write and kept practicing over the years. When I met him 26 years after his initial conversion, he was an elected leader of the church in Maroantsetra. He read absolutely fluently and in general gave the impression of being a very sophisticated man, dressed in a stiffly ironed white shirt and a suit on the Sabbath, giving lengthy sermons while putting his glasses on, and taking them off, and putting them on again. His manner, as he spoke to the audience, was very scholarly indeed. His case was sometimes referred to by others, with pride, as an example of the potential achievement made possible by Bible study. Emanuel was clearly an exception, but several other church members, too, told me that before joining the church, they had never had anything to do with "paper," and that their reading abilities had much improved since. However, unlike in Emanuel's case, for many their literacy remains too limited to have any practical impact on their lives. After nine years of involvement with the Adventist church, Papan' i Claude, for example, still needed the support of his son when he had to deal with a contract (to do with buying land or cattle). As I mentioned earlier, he still struggled to sign his name.

But there are other arguments that undermine an instrumentalist explanation of Adventism as an alternative to formal schooling. In a sense, it is surprising that the local Adventists know so little about the world beyond their own experience. For one thing, they are members in a church with a marked international organization and international contacts. They also hear about places beyond Madagascar during many church services, when "testimonies" from Russia or Thailand are read to them. Moreover, everything that is related in the Bible, which the Adventists spend hours studying, happened *andafy* (beyond the bounds of Madagascar). And in the Bible, there is plenty of talk about Jesus walking through cornfields, Moses being abandoned by a river, or the Sermon on the Mount. So why should church members have been surprised, as they were, when I told them that *andafy*, there were people farming land and that indeed there were mountains and rivers? I interpret the fact that church members do not infer this kind of information about the outside world from the Bible as suggesting that what they seek to learn through Bible study is *knowledge of a different nature* to the sort of thing one learns at school.

The disconnection between Bible study and formal schooling is also illustrated by the fact that church membership does not seem to change people's view of the value of schools. As with many other people in Sahameloka, adult members of the Adventist church are often very lax about whether or not their children attend school. Mezaquei continually found, or invented, some excuse or other for not attending school—he was already late, he couldn't find his tiny, worn-out blackboard and so on. Sometimes, he set off for school, only to be discovered later on in the morning sneaking up behind us as we went into the forest. Perhaps this is not surprising behavior for a 9-year old. What was, however, surprising to me was that his parents hardly ever scolded him. Sometimes they did a bit, but his nonattendance at school had no real consequences at all. Several others among the teenage Adventists in the village had quit school after just two or three years and nobody made a fuss about it.[13] The attitude of the Adventists toward their children's school attendance reflected the attitude of the village as a whole. Their approach to schools was no different to that of non-Adventist villagers. Of course, if it were the case that the Adventists perceived of the church as "our own school" substituting for public ones, then they would obviously not insist on their children going to the village's primary school. However, like everyone else in Sahameloka, the Adventists always claimed and emphasized that schooling was terribly important. They also did not stop sending their children to school altogether. Their involvement in the Adventist church simply did not affect the way they related to schools. Public schools and Adventism were not brought into connection with each other.

Moreover, the church members themselves never made an explicit link between the inadequacy of formal schooling and what they might hope to achieve through Adventism. Poor school performance did not enter into conversations concerning the attraction of Adventist practice. Remarks such as "Before joining the church, I had never had anything to do with 'paper' " were always only made in response to a question of mine about the relationship between their experience at school and Adventist Bible study.

What the ethnographic evidence shows is that for church members in Maroantsetra and Sahameloka, there is a marked disconnection between the knowledge they gain through their involvement in the Adventist church and the kind of knowledge acquired at school. They do not expect to learn the things they never learnt at school through involvement with the church. If school knowledge and Adventist knowledge are treated as two different types of things altogether, the latter cannot be interpreted as a substitute for the former.[14]

Turning now to the second possible suggestion, that the Adventists may be dissatisfied with the *method* of teaching at their schools, the difference between school methods and the Seventh-day Adventist approach to studying the Bible is indeed very striking. While formal schooling largely consists of teachers speaking and writing things on blackboards and students being silent, copying in their notebooks and learning by heart what is on the blackboard, Adventist Bible study, as I have shown, is based on a fundamentally different approach, namely that of equal participation by all in a process of Socratic learning. And the ethnography clearly demonstrates that the local members of the church are very keen on that approach. Does their enthusiasm for Bible study then perhaps reflect a dissatisfaction with the method of learning they are familiar with from their school days? It might be tempting to arrive at such a conclusion, especially coming from a contemporary Western approach toward learning, which the Adventist method of Bible study closely resembles. However, there is no evidence that this is actually the case. As I explained earlier, reflections on the methods and the quality of teaching at local schools never entered local Adventists' discourse about why they were attracted to Adventism or what they considered particularly valuable about it. The emphasis put on the excitement and value of Bible study was never juxtaposed to, or accompanied by complaints about, the inadequacy of local forms of tuition. Thus although from a contemporary Western point of view, pupils' performance in subjects taught at school is poor, one cannot assume that the local people share that notion. The only thing local people are clearly dissatisfied with is the frequent absence of teachers, but they do not perceive Adventism to be related to that problem or to provide its solution. Thus to argue that the members of the church are attracted to Adventist Bible study because they consider that it employs a superior teaching method to that used in formal schooling, would be to impose on them the contemporary Western view of learning. The people concerned keep the Adventist church quite separate from schools, and we as analysts should not muddle up these two spaces of learning by suggesting that one is a substitute for the other. Indeed, some of those church members most enthusiastic about Adventist Bible study are also among those most emphatically *pro* formal schooling and hence most determined to give their children the best possible education from public schools.

In sum: From the local Adventists' perspective, the church and the school are two separate, unconnected places of learning. However, there is also a conceptual link between them to which I now turn.

Studying and Potency

Literacy is highly significant among the members of the Adventist church for obvious reasons: the better a person can read, the easier it is for him or her to study the Bible. Furthermore, it is the most literate members of the church who are thought best equipped to be lay leaders as well as to take on other duties such as chairing Sabbath School discussions. But a good command of the written word is not directly linked to authority. The decision to entrust the most literate members of the church with certain roles and duties is primarily a pragmatic one.

However, literacy is not just seen in an instrumental light, and in this respect Seventh-day Adventists do not differ from other people in the area. In order to explain this, I need to say a little bit more about local people's view of *vazaha* (all foreigners, but particularly White people). Since I was one such *vazaha*, one who suddenly entered their lives, people were more or less forced to relate to me in some way or another. And the ways in which they did so were highly revealing.

What follows does not specifically refer to members of the Adventist church, but to the local population more generally.

As elsewhere in Madagascar, local people are generally very impressed with what they refer to as the *fahaizana* of White foreigners. *Fahaizana*, and the related verb *mahay*, are difficult to translate, because they have many shades of meaning.[15] However, the core of *fahaizana/mahay* is the idea of being competent and knowledgeable and, as such, powerful.[16]

Whenever the Malagasy speak of the *vazaha* (White foreigners), the expression *mahay* (to know, to be capable, to be on top of things) is not far away, and often there is a sense of awe, as well as of *vazaha* superiority and, accordingly, Malagasy inferiority on the part of the speaker. The *vazaha* are knowledgeable and capable (*"Mahay ny vazaha e!"*); the Malagasy are not. Even down to daily objects, *vazaha* used as an adjective denotes superiority over things defined as *malagasy*. Thus a spoon made of cheap, thin aluminium is called a "Malagasy spoon" (*sotro gasy*), whereas a "*vazaha* spoon" (*sotro vazaha*) is a much more solid, shiny, and also more expensive object. Many similar expressions referring to something valuable as *vazaha* and something badly made as *malagasy* are used in daily life.[17] Knowledge

There are innumerable manifestations of the *fahaizana* of the *vazaha*, the knowledge of White foreigners, but they are basically of three kinds: technical, medical, environmental.

In Sahameloka especially, my Olympus 140-zoom camera would elicit statements of great admiration for the *fahaizana* of the *vazaha* ("Look, what incredible *fahaizana* they have!"), especially because it could take pictures all by itself when set up accordingly. My tape recorder and especially my tiny, but powerful, microphone that I used for recording conversations, produced similar reactions. After I had turned the tape recorder off, those who had been recorded always loved to listen to their own voices through my headphones. This was a big thrill for young and old alike and probably the most attractive feature of the whole procedure. As soon as the "listen through the headphones" part had begun, lots of children would normally gather and beg to be allowed to listen too through those funny little things one puts in one's ears. I do not think anybody in the village had ever listened to anything coming through headphones before, and so not surprisingly, people were enormously excited at this new display of the *fahaizana* of those living beyond Madagascar. But even much simpler things were considered evidence of such knowledge/capability. Not long after I had arrived in Sahameloka, I received a musical New Year's card from a friend in Europe. When you opened it, it played a song! From the moment my "singing letter" (*taratasy mihira*) arrived in Sahameloka, to the moment I left the village six months later, it was shown to almost every visitor who came into our house. The popularity of my singing letter became so great that I had to hide it and deny its existence in order not to have the whole village at our doorstep. Whoever had the privilege to be shown the miraculous thing though, first stared at it in disbelief and, after the mystery of how it worked had been revealed, then listened to the Christmas melody, making repeated statements to the effect of how impressive the *fahaizana* of the *vazaha* was.

By virtue of being a *vazaha*, I was assumed to be an expert in all sorts of areas. Once somebody from Sahameloka presented me with a broken camera. When I told the man that I had not the faintest idea how to mend it, he was visibly disappointed. Equally, I was expected to have knowledge of medical matters and so, while living in Sahameloka, I was often consulted as a "doctor." Once I was shown an obviously very ill child who was completely covered in blisters. To my untrained eye, the child looked like it had a serious skin disease, but neither did I have any clue as to what exactly the baby was suffering from nor did I have any appropriate medicine with me. And so I could not do anything except apologize to the baby's father, saying that unfortunately I had no medical training whatsoever and that I was therefore at a loss to help his child. He did not seem to believe me, because *vazaha* have *fahaizana*.

Fahaizana is technical know-how and medical expertise, but it is also potency of a very general nature. This became particularly clear when local people speculated about *vazaha*'s control over nature. One day, again in Sahameloka, I had joined a group of people who were discussing the forthcoming solar eclipse in Madagascar. There was a lot of publicity about this event and people were warned through the radio not to look at the sun, unless they had a pair of special glasses provided for such purposes. As a result of this awareness raising campaign, people in Sahameloka were terrified that they would all go blind. At one stage of the conversation, the wife of the village president asked me: "Is this [the eclipse] something human beings [meaning *vazaha*] do? God does this sort of thing, doesn't He?"[18] She was not quite sure. After cyclone Hudah had hit the area in April 2000, destroying much of local people's harvest and forestland, not to speak of the village itself, I heard similar speculations as to whether the cyclone had been sent by *vazaha* or by God. The vazaha were also assumed to be in complete control of their own living space. Many people suggested that the environment *andafy* (beyond the sea), where the *vazaha* live, must consist entirely of concrete buildings and cars and, unlike eastern Madagascar, must be completely "clear" (*mazava*), that is void of dark spaces such as forest. It was this view of the world *andafy* that caused people to be surprised when they were informed that *andafy* as well, there were people who farm land.

It is important to note that, although *vazaha* in general are perceived to have *fahaizana* much superior to the average Malagasy, *vazaha* potency is not thought of in essentialist terms. In other words: *vazaha* are not born with *fahaizana*. So, how do they end up so knowledgeable, capable of constructing such miraculous things as a camera that can take pictures all by itself? What causes *fahaizana*? The answer to this question will bring us to the heart of the matter concerning the relationship between local concepts of learning and Adventist Bible study.

During my stay in Sahameloka, I learnt to do various different tasks in which the villagers engaged. One of these was to plait women's hair in the local fashion. The first couple of times I did this, loads of people gathered around and watched me plaiting. When I managed to do it fairly well, if not perfectly, everyone immediately concluded that I was quick at learning how to plait hair because I was educated, because I had gone to school and studied for years. Many of them had seen me reading thick books or writing with what they considered an incredible speed, and thus it was the common view that I must be a very educated person. Whatever task I embarked upon to learn, whether it was plaiting hair, planting rice or weaving a fish trap, the reaction was invariably the same. People always commented that I was good and quick at learning, even if I felt I wasn't at all, because I had studied, because I was educated (*ólo avy nianatra malaky mahay raha; ólo mahay taratasy malaky mahay raha*). Although it is of course obvious to people in Sahameloka that writing and reading are not at all the same thing as planting rice and require quite a different kind of expertise, it was the former that accounted for the latter. My ability to write quickly and to read thick books completely merged in their eyes with my ability to learn to plait hair or to weed a rice field.

Having gone through higher education and being good at reading and writing has, for contemporary Westerners, nothing to do with the ability to learn how to plant rice. On the contrary, pen pushers are assumed to be no good at manual work. Not so for people in Maroantsetra and Sahameloka. For them, the fact of having studied is the basis of *all* learning ability and the basis of a capability, or potency, of a very general nature. Literacy is the visible epitome of such potency. Thus the answer to the question "What is the cause of *fahaizana*?" is simple: it is education, and it is because the *vazaha* are educated that they have *fahaizana*.

I have chosen to speak of potency, rather than power, because *fahaizana* is not political or economic power, although such power may well result from *fahaizana*, as indeed people in Madagascar observe to be the case with the *vazaha*. In Foucault's terms, power/knowledge are of course inseparable. However, I prefer to speak of "potency" to highlight the fact that *fahaizana* is not conceived of as power in the narrow sense of socioeconomic power; rather, it denotes unspecific capability. Of what exactly the *vazaha* are knowledgeable, or what exactly their *fahaizana* is, people in a place such as Sahameloka are not quite sure. The *vazaha* are assumed to know all the things that are out there to be known, whatever these things may be. Although their *fahaizana* becomes visible through such things as a singing letter or a camera, *fahaizana* is a general quality rather than any set of particular skills.

Mianatra

The word that is used to refer to the activity of studying and learning, and of hence becoming educated, is *mianatra*. *Mianatra* is the road toward *fahaizana*, toward the kind of potency that those living outside Madagascar are thought to have. This is also the word used to describe what one does at school, and it is the word the Malagasy Adventists use to describe Adventist Bible study.

The dictionary entry for the verb *mianatra* reads: "Apprendre, étudier, imiter, contrefaire" (Abinal & Malzac 1993: 37). Thus *mianatra* has two basic meanings: on the one hand to study and to learn, on the other to imitate and to copy. It will be obvious to the reader at this stage of the discussion that what pupils do in school often tends to be *mianatra* in the sense of copying, while what the Adventists do during Bible study is mostly *mianatra* in the sense of studying. Of course, to construct this distinction between "*mianatra*-copy" and "*mianatra*-study" is already, to a certain extent, to misrepresent the concept of *mianatra*, because the crux of the matter is precisely that *mianatra* is both the type of activity one engages in at school and the type of activity the Adventists engage in during Bible study. And it is because both these types of activities are seen as a form of *mianatra*—and as such they are associated with the kind of very general potency I discussed above—that they are valued. It is the activity of *mianatra* that is crucial, and not necessarily the level of achievement. Even if Beby knows precious little English after several years of instruction, it is a jolly good thing that she does *mianatra*. Thus contrary to a modernist type of conclusion that local schools are basically a failure, they are in fact valued by local people as places where children are engaged in the process of *mianatra*. And it is also the process of *mianatra*, of Bible study, which the members of the church consider to be the essence of Seventh-day Adventism.

Conclusion

It might be useful to recapitulate the argument of this chapter step by step. The topic has been the relationship between the Adventist focus on Bible study, knowledge and comprehension of biblical text, on the one hand, and locally salient notions of books and learning, on the other.

With regard to books, I first noted a view of written text as coming from an immensely powerful "beyond" and of thus containing authoritative knowledge. This view can be traced back to at least the eighteenth century and is salient in many parts of Madagascar including the area of Maroantsetra. Adventist practice, with its emphasis on studying the Bible, resonates extremely well with this high regard for the written word and, especially, books. Indeed, the local Adventists share the strongly held idea that books are awe-inspiring. This is demonstrated particularly well by the way they relate to books sold around town by a number of Adventist booksellers employed by the church. However, parallel to this continuity in terms of attitudes toward books, we encounter an element of novelty in that Bibles used for daily Bible study are not treated like any other book, including Bibles *not* used for Bible study. While the most important aspect of other books is the fact that they are books, the whole point about the Adventist Bible is the fact that it is a book whose content and truthfulness should be carefully studied.

Then we moved on to the question of the relationship between Adventism, on the one hand, and school knowledge and learning more generally, on the other. Two main points emerged. First, from the perspective of local Adventists, the church and the school are two separate spaces for learning, so that learning in one of these spaces does not substitute for, or make redundant, learning in the other space. Second, what one does both in school and in church is to *mianatra*. To *mianatra* is to do something that is highly valued by all local people, because it is thought to lead to potency. It is equally valued by the local Adventists for whom the activity of *mianatra*, of Bible study, is the key attraction of the Adventist church. Thus we encounter continuity between the local and the Adventist emphases on the importance of *mianatra*. Both *mianatra* in school and *mianatra* in church lead to knowledge and understanding and, in that sense, to potency (the very general capability to be in control).

There is, however, a specifically Adventist twist to the story, because the potency church members aspire to develop through Bible study is knowledge/power of a specifically Adventist nature. But before I can explain what exactly this specifically Adventist potency is, I must discuss the role of Satan in the Adventist universe.

Chapter 8

The Great Controversy

↳ struggle between God and Satan

Satan plays an incredibly important role for Seventh-day Adventists in Madagascar. Everything that happened in the past, that is happening at the moment and that will happen in the future is a manifestation of the struggle for power between God[1] and Satan. In the Adventist literature, this fight is known as "The Great Controversy." Although only few church members in Maroantsetra and Sahameloka are familiar with this expression, they are all clearly aware of its message and interpret human history, the present state of the world and the misfortunes, big and small, which strike them in daily life, in light of it. Nothing happens by chance; everything is either a manifestation of God's love and protection or else the work of Satan, interchangeably referred to as *Satana* or *Devoly*.

The cyclone that struck Sahameloka in April 2000 exemplified the Great Controversy. The Adventist church was razed to the ground, while the Catholic one was hardly damaged at all and the Protestant one only needed its roof repaired. Satan had chosen his targets carefully. At the same time, church members remarked that none of their own houses, in contrast to many others in the village, had been completely destroyed. As the cyclone had howled above our heads making the corrugated-iron roof shake and lift, the whole family had fallen on their knees praying to God for protection. The house withstood the storm undamaged like only a few others in the village, a clear sign that God had heard them. Two days after the cyclone, the water had receded enough to make it possible for people to go and inspect the damage done to their fields and their land in the forest. The family had been badly hit. Much of their rice harvest had been destroyed, and hardly a clove tree still stood upright. Satan had targeted them, because they were Seventh-day Adventists.

Within the grand historical scheme of events, which are also determined by the Great Controversy, every single person is conceptualized as a vehicle by use of which God and Satan carry out their struggle for ultimate power over the world and the universe. Indeed, people's minds and bodies are the primary sites where world history is constantly being made.

Knowledge of Satan's role is universal among the members of the local Adventist church, and the views and interpretations described in this chapter are commonly shared. With regard to Satan's role, there is a significant overlap between Seventh-day Adventist official doctrine, as expressed in numerous publications, and local conceptualizations. While what I am interested in here is the latter, the degree of correspondence between the two is indeed striking. Why this is so, is, however, not the topic of this study.

How Satan Operates

God's and Satan's Angels

Although invisible to the human eye, there are at all times two angels (*anjely*) sitting on the shoulders of every person. On the right shoulder sits one of God's angels, on the left, one working for Satan. As people go through life and are faced with decisions to be made, God's and Satan's angels whisper inaudibly into the ears of their hosts trying to win them over to their respective side. Each time one of the angels that sits on people's left shoulders wins this continual tug-of-war, "Satan is happy, but Jesus cries" (*faly i Satana, mitomany i Jesôsy*), and vice versa. Kiki once told me, with great admiration, of a Seventh-day Adventist pastor he had met, who was always careful not to lean his *right* shoulder against a wall lest God's angel should be made uncomfortable—although of course he knew that angels can sit on air. This act of consideration toward his good angel was the pastor's daily way, so Kiki explained, of signaling to Satan that he had no chance to win him over. The two angels sitting on a person's shoulders keep a written record of battles lost and won, so that when the Last Judgment comes, their books can be presented to God.

While good and bad angels literally sit close to people's *minds*, in some situations the struggle between God and Satan is of a distinctly *bodily* nature. A particularly vivid and dramatic example that I witnessed one Sabbath morning in Maroantsetra illustrates the embodiment of the Great Controversy.

Denise's Baptism

That morning, almost two hundred people were about to be baptized as Seventh-Day-Adventists.[2] Among them was Denise, a young woman who had been a spirit medium since childhood. Spirit possession (*tromba*)—together with several other traditional practices, in particular exhumation and cattle sacrifice—is interpreted by the Adventists as the work of the devil. Hence Denise was perceived as having served the devil for many years, and consequently now to be firmly under his grip. In fact, the spirit who possessed her had "bought her life" (*voavidiny ny fiainako*). As a small child, she had physically died: her body was cold and she had stopped breathing, Denise told me. Her parents were already preparing for the burial when the spirit brought her back to life. In return, she was to serve him (it was a male spirit) for the rest of her life. Denise had fulfilled her side of the bargain so far, but now she wanted to get rid of her spirit. This was because the spirit had not allowed her to marry the man whom she loved, and Denise increasingly felt that the spirit was making it impossible for her to lead a normal, happy life. After years of toying with the idea of joining the Adventist church, she had therefore finally decided to get baptized.

As everyone gathered in the church and the pastor took those to be baptized through the first part of the baptizmal ritual, which culminates in their acceptance of the Adventist creed,[3] Denise suddenly stormed out of the church, screaming, ran through the courtyard and finally collapsed under a shelter. Several people followed her as she fled and were now kneeling beside her holding her trembling body down, and loudly begging God to help her defeat her spirit (i.e., Satan), who was obviously trying to stop her from getting baptized. Eventually, she calmed down and went back into the church. Satan had lost this battle. However, the fight over her person was not over yet. Later, as she was about to get baptized through full immersion in the sea, the pastor spoke intense prayers with and for Denise. He and three other church members held her firmly as the big moment approached, supporting her in the physical struggle that she was about to experience. Everyone present held their breath for they all knew that the spirit was powerful and might actually kill Denise for having provoked him in such a way. The only thing that could help her now was her firm commitment to God. Was she going to be strong enough? The pastor later told me that those supporting her had felt her body trembling with the spirit's last effort to keep control over her life. But God was stronger and Denise had proven her will to follow Him. And so when she reappeared from under the water, she threw up her arms toward heaven shouting "Hallelujah!" Relief, excitement and a sense of victory and jubilation took hold of the crowd. That morning, Denise literally embodied the power struggle between God and Satan.[4]

Satan's Omnipresence

From the grand schemes of world history to the minutest, mundane detail of daily life, everything on this earth and beyond is touched by the Great Controversy. There is no person or thing that could not potentially become a site of war. Members of the Adventist church interpret illness, violence, corruption, consumption of alcohol and drugs as evidence of Satan's machinations, as they do any behavior considered to be immoral, such as not respecting one's parents. Satan is held responsible for the very existence of death—it was he who tempted Adam and Eve—as well as for the death and suffering caused by accidents or natural disasters. People recognize multiple levels of causation in the same way as the Azande, so well described by Evans-Pritchard (1937). However, from the point of view of the Seventh-day Adventists in Maroantsetra and Sahameloka, ultimately all evil stems from the devil. Like for the Azande, there is no such thing as a stroke of fate.

When one day in Maroantsetra the house of a couple, who had recently shown interest in becoming members of the Adventist church, burnt down, church members interpreted this event as Satan's warning to the people concerned, although they did not dispute that the fire had spread from the hearth. During my stay in Maroantsetra, I rented a small house in which there was a wardrobe where I kept my clothes, books and notes. Among my books were dictionaries and novels, but also a number of Adventist publications, in particular a book by the Adventist prophetess Ellen White, which had been given to me as a present by an American Adventist couple who had visited Maroantsetra while I lived there. Rather strangely, only the book by Ellen White got covered with mildew, while my novels and dictionaries remained in perfect condition. To Maman' and Papan' i Beby, this was not an accident at all, or due to the particular quality of the paper, but very clearly Satan's doing. From their perspective, it was obvious that inoffensive material such as dictionaries would not attract the anger of the devil, while a book written by Ellen White, one of his main adversaries, would.

God's Apprentice

God and Satan are thought of as being of almost equal strength—*almost*, because in the end, God will win, as the Bible foretells. Furthermore, they fight with the same kinds of "weapons." Why is this so? The reason brings us to the Seventh-day Adventist theory of how evil came to exist. This was explained to me on several occasions by different members of the church, both in town and in the village, and I was astonished how "correctly" they all reproduced this particular part of global Adventist doctrine. This is how it goes: before the creation of life on earth, God had created a great number of angels, one of whom was Lucifer. At first, Lucifer was a good angel serving God like all the others, but as time went on, a greed for power grew within him, which made him want to challenge God and control the universe himself. So Lucifer, from then on called Satan, started a conspiracy among God's angels and finally managed to win over one third of them to his evil intentions. It is these angels that sit on people's left shoulders helping Satan to tempt humankind.

What is particularly relevant in this theory explaining the origin of evil is the fact that Satan was God's apprentice, as it were, prior to his fall. Hence, Satan knows God's ways (*ny fomban' Andriamanitra*) which, as Maman' i Ominò eloquently explained to me, he copies and imitates in order to operate powerfully and effectively in this world. In the quote below, Maman' i Ominò refers to the fact that spirits who possess local people often impose a taboo to eat crab or shrimps on their mediums.

> Satan knows all of God's secrets. Adventists don't eat shrimps, they don't eat crab. Satan has stolen these secrets! The reason why he has stolen these things is simple: he knows God's rules, and so he stole them and imposed them on people as his own. Many people suffer from liver disease. What does the doctor tell them not to eat? Crab and shrimps, because these make the disease even worse. Satan knows this! What is not good for us? Crab and shrimps! They are not good for our health. And so one must not eat them. That is why people really believe in Satan, they really believe in him strongly! Because Satan used to live in heaven, he knows that one must not eat crab and shrimps.[5]

Maman' i Ominò continued her discussion of how Satan steals God's secrets a little later comparing spirit possession—the preparation for which involves the marking of various things with white chalk—with the tenth plague of Egypt and the Passover as told in Exodus 12.

> [The spirits tell their mediums] to mark their houses with white chalk, and then the mediums do this. When the children of Israel left Egypt, what happened? [God said to them]: Mark your houses! Because the Israelites slaughtered a lamb and God told them to mark their houses [with the lamb's blood]. Mark every door, he said, so that I won't enter your houses. Because I will kill many people, I will kill the first-born of everything in this town. It's exactly the same with the spirits. Satan [in the guise of a spirit] tells people to mark their houses [with white

chalk], so that when his angels pass by, they see who is theirs. When God's angels passed by [the houses of the Israelites], what happened? They saw the marks on the houses.[6]

Similarly, Maman' i Ominò went on, spirit mediums have to go through a ritual called *barisa* that involves having "holy water" (*rano masina*) poured over them. From the Adventists' perspective, *barisa* is clearly an imitation of the ritual of baptism, called *batisa* in Malagasy, and as such another striking example of how Satan has stolen God's secrets. It is precisely because Satan has learnt his job from God Himself that he is in command of such powerful tools as healing and "baptism."

The Written Word

In a similar vein, Satan has copied the written word as a powerful method of communication. One Wednesday evening, the pastor brought a very unusual document to church in Maroantsetra that he then proceeded to agitatedly discuss at length. The document in question was a sheet of paper with text on both sides, *signed by "Lucifer"*! This document came directly from the devil himself, the pastor explained to the amazed and completely gripped congregation. It revealed Satan's plans to make Christians, and especially Seventh-day-Adventists, stray from God's path. The document especially encouraged people not to fast and not to pray. But not only that; it also mentioned a conference of all Satanists to be held in the near future. The agitated nature of the pastor's explanations made it obvious that he had no doubt as to the authenticity of this message.

When I asked him the following day where exactly this document had come from, and how the Adventists of all people had got hold of it, the pastor explained that it came from a church in Zaire, where a group of Satanists had formed the so-called *Eglise du Satan*. This group of Satanists in Zaire had also published a revised version of the Bible, the pastor went on, which had been stripped of important books and passages, notably the Books of Daniel and Revelation, which are among the most important for Seventh-day Adventists. The document he had presented in church was addressed "à tous les Satanistes" and had only by accident (or was it God's interference?) fallen into the hands of members of the Adventist church in Zaire who subsequently distributed it among members of their church in different countries.

At first, this might sound like a rather bizarre, and to some readers perhaps even ridiculous, story. However, if we adopt the Adventists' perspective in which Satan is as real as God and, moreover, is a specialist in copying God's ways, it becomes immediately obvious that to accept the document the pastor brought to church as authentic is perfectly logical. If God chose the written word as a powerful medium to make His will known (remember the authority that accompanies written things in Madagascar in general) why should the devil not make use of this efficacious "evangelical" tool, too? And indeed, this was precisely how the pastor and other people responded to my doubts concerning the authenticity of Lucifer's signature.

God and Satan as Moral Persons

God and Satan not only use similar "weapons" to fight for their respective causes, they are similar in other ways, too. Both are highly personified and, to a certain extent, humanized in the Adventists' way of thinking about the power struggle that goes on between them. God is believed to have the body of a man, because He created Adam "in his image." Satan's physical appearance was less clear to my informants. They were unsure whether "he" was male or gender-neutral like an angel (gender is not grammatically marked in the Malagasy language). However, he (or perhaps it) is certainly thought of as having a human-like body with a head, shoulders and arms.

Moreover, God's and Satan's minds are strikingly similar and are reminiscent of the minds of human beings. The tug-of-war between God and Satan is not primarily understood to be between two *sources* of power, but to be between two competing *personalities* guided by motivations, intentions and feelings characteristic of humans, such as love and hate, the craving for power, envy and revenge, sympathy and protection. The way in which both Satan and God make their presence felt on earth is also often strikingly mundane, as though thought up by a human brain. One might wonder, for example, why a being as powerful as the devil should bother to make mildew grow on my book; doesn't he have more important things to do? Or one might be surprised that the Creator of all things should depend on His angels' records at the time of the Last Judgment. The reason why the two most powerful beings in the universe resort to such pragmatic means is that they are perceived to be, and act, very much like (im)moral persons.[7]

Satan's character is indeed reminiscent of that of a cunning politician who uses intrigue and trickery to fool people and to make them believe his lies. This was brought home to me on one occasion when the pastor and Papan' i Beby discussed the machinations of the devil. In particular they discussed how the recent economic boom in the area—on the surface due to a sudden increase in the price of cloves on the global market—had made many people act selfishly and immorally, spending lots of money on alcohol, prostitution and the like. Satan uses many tricks to help his wicked cause, from making mildew grow on an Adventist book to influencing the world economy.[8]

A Matter of Choice

We have seen how absolutely everything that happens in this world, from the great sweep of world history to the minutest detail of every-day life, is, from the Adventist point of view, a manifestation of the power struggle between God and Satan. It is because God's arms and Satan's tentacles reach every corner of human existence that there is no neutral space that one can possibly occupy. Hence, according to the local Adventists, everyone must choose either God or Satan as their "master" (*tompo*). The option of not making such a choice does not exist. God and the devil are each other's antithesis and accepting the authority of one implies rejecting the other. If they are like day and night, then dusk and dawn—being in a state of uncertainty or transition—are dangerous times during which one is exposed and vulnerable, as Denise's story illustrates. There is no safe in-between area.

To make a choice is not only a necessity; the ability to choose is also considered a precious gift. If God had wanted, He could have made robots, but He did not. Instead He created humans who can choose between Good and Evil. Indeed the very existence of evil is based on Lucifer's ability to make such a choice. Moreover, as we saw in chapter 6, to make a conscious and informed choice for God, is an important criterion that distinguishes Seventh-day Adventists, in their view, from other Christians such as local Catholics and Protestants who "just believe" without properly understanding *why* they choose what they choose.

Interestingly, the pastor once explained during a church service that both young children and slaves would not be held responsible for their actions at the time of the Last Judgment, because they had no choice. This is how his argument went: children up to a certain age are too young to make a conscious choice for or against God, which is why Seventh-day Adventists only practice adult baptism. Children whose parents go to paradise will go with them. But the children of parents who fail to be among the saved, will not themselves have to suffer punishment like their parents. Instead, they will be painlessly annihilated and will vanish as though they had never existed. Their memory will be erased, too. Similarly, slaves, the pastor continued (using the word *andevo*), are denied free choice to act as they wish. Thus, at the time of the Last Judgment, they will neither go to paradise nor will they suffer punishment. As with young children whose parents fail to be among the saved, their existence will be wiped out, since they cannot be held responsible for their actions as full persons, who act out of free choice, can. It is important to keep in mind that the pastor was not referring to descendants of slaves (some of whom were sitting in the audience) and, as we saw in an earlier chapter, that descendents of slaves have become full persons in this part of Madagascar. But because at the Last Judgment, all human beings who have ever lived will be judged, the pastor referred to slaves who lived in former times whose final fate will also be decided at the time of the Last Judgment.

In other words: full human personhood, in Adventist discourse, is dependent on the ability to choose. Hence the necessity to choose between the authority of either God or Satan is not perceived as a burden, but as an expression of the privilege of being human.

Clarity of Mind

Satan does not only promote wickedness and immoral behavior. His machinations also *deceive* people so that they cannot see clearly, so that their minds become obscured. To make a choice for God, is, for the Adventists in Maroantsetra and Sahameloka, not only a choice for the good, but equally importantly, it is a choice for clarity of mind.

In chapter 6, I used Kuhn's metaphor of solving a jigsaw puzzle to illustrate the significance of the process of studying, this process being more important than any novel outcome. However, the Adventists do not only derive joy from the process of doing the jigsaw, they also get excited watching the picture develop and grow. They are also motivated in their religious commitment by the anticipated satisfaction of seeing the entire picture with all its colors and shapes. The picture the Adventists want to see is, quite simply, the truth: the truth about the world and life "beyond," the truth about human nature and the forces at play in the universe.

What makes the process of seeing the truth so difficult is the fact that it has been intentionally hidden by Satan, whose master plan is promoted by his agents on earth—Darwinian scientists and the mainstream churches for example. When Catholics and Protestants go to church on Sunday, they fall prey to Satan's deception, because the truth is that God wants us to worship on Saturday. When mediums think that they are possessed by the spirit of a dead person, they are, in reality, possessed by the devil masquerading as the spirit. This, however, one can only find out through careful Bible study. It is only when one actually reads and studies Exodus 20 that one realizes that

Saturday, and not Sunday, is the day God wants us to respect as holy. A bag full of muddled jigsaw pieces, to borrow Kuhn's metaphor once again, contains the whole picture, yet we cannot see it without making the effort of turning over every piece, examining it and putting it in its correct place. The truth is there in the Bible, but we cannot see it unless and until we study what the Bible says.

To study the Bible is to literally uncover the truth buried beneath Satan's veil of lies. To study the Bible is to penetrate through a mist of deception, to remove the Satanic veil that blurs our perception of reality; it is to make the truth appear clearly. Seventh-day Adventist practice is like an "archeological process" (Caplan 1987a: 17). The archeologist knows that the vase is in the ground, yet she has to dig it out through hard work, effort and patience. Bible study, conducted in a Socratic style, is to unearth the vase, and to bring it into the open for everyone to see.

When trying to convince other people of the value of Adventism, during proselytizing weekends in the countryside for example, local members of the church promise that those who join the church will acquire knowledge. What this promise means is that they will acquire knowledge that will enable them to see and to understand how they have been misled into accepting as true many things that are actually not true at all. It is a promise to see behind Satan's veil of deception (although, of course, those listening know nothing of the Great Controversy at this stage and might not immediately understand what those speaking mean by "deception").

Conversion to Adventism is sometimes conceptualized by members of the church as moving from a state of mental sleep to a state of being mentally alert. One person said:

> I was like somebody who is unconscious, I was like someone who sleeps, but then suddenly wakes up. I was still asleep when I moved to the other place [converted]; it was only when I arrived there [when I had become firm in my commitment], that I woke up.[9]

During one Sabbath School I witnessed, two different kinds of inspiration (*tsindrimandry*) were discussed: inspiration by God and inspiration by Satan. The discussion can be summarized as follows. "Satan inspires people in their sleep. For example, he makes them dream of a dead relative who demands that a cow be slaughtered for them. Thinking that it was indeed their dead relative who spoke to them when in fact it was the devil in disguise, they are terrified and do what the 'spirit' demands, lest they should be struck by some misfortune. Satan takes advantage of the fact that people are easily deceived when they sleep, when their mind is not quite alert. In contrast, the prophets chosen by God are startled as though from deep sleep when seized by His inspiration and suddenly feel wide awake." In other words: church members feel that their choice for God is a choice for an unclouded vision of reality, a choice for clarity of mind.

Parry has discussed how in the Brahmanical tradition knowledge is "recovered" from sacred texts rather than "discovered" (Parry 1985: 205). The Brahman's engagement with sacred texts is not a matter of creating new knowledge, but a matter of accessing knowledge that has long been revealed by the gods. This is also true for the Adventists, since the truth is readily available in the Bible if one only cares to study it. In contrast to the Brahmans, however, the Adventists have a distinct sense of having to rescue the truth from beneath a cover that has been intentionally laid upon it—the cover of Satan's deception. In this sense, they have to uncover the truth; this is the ultimate aim. The road that leads to the truth being fully uncovered and brought into the light, however, involves a process of discovery that, I suggest, is comparable to the Normal Scientific process (Kuhn 1996).

As long as people are deceived and misled, they fall prey to Satan's control over their minds and, as a result, their actions. Thus penetrating through the mist of Satan's deception is to rid themselves of that control or, to put it differently, to gain knowledge/power or potency, as discussed in chapter 7. It is this kind of potency—the potency of seeing beneath the veil of falseness and of seeing reality as it is, laid bare—that the members of the church aspire to gain through the process of Bible study.

The potency acquired through the process of *mianatra* (studying) in church is not an issue of power in its narrow sense. The members of the church are perfectly aware that studying the Bible will not make them richer, it will not provide them with cheap medical care and it will not give them possession of agricultural machines. The Faith Gospel, which states that God blesses His people with material riches, and which seems important in many New Churches in Africa (Gifford 1998), is not relevant here.

It is not a question of trying to access the potency-cum-power (*fahaizana*) of the *vazaha* (White foreigners) either. Both *vazaha-fahaizana* and Adventist potency are based on superior knowledge, but the potency necessary to break through Satan's veil of deception is of a different quality to the *vazaha* potency necessary to master technology and medical science or to control the environment. However the *method* that is thought to lead to both types of potency is the same, and that method is to study (*mianatra*) and thus to become knowledgeable in a very general sense. *Mianatra* provides the road toward understanding and mastering things through superior knowledge. The Adventists travel along this road, yet at a certain point they go in a specifically Adventist direction. And the potency they gradually achieve by traveling along this road of study has a specifically Adventist quality and is interpreted in a specifically Adventist way. It is interpreted as the intellectual potency to penetrate Satan's web of lies and to thus stop being deceived.

Chapter 9

The Construction and Rejection of Ancestral Religion

We have seen how Satan is omnipresent in the world of the local Adventists and how his influence is felt in numerous kinds of ways. However, in Madagascar, Satan's favorite trick is to act in the guise of the ancestors. In order to realize what a drastic statement this is in the Malagasy context, one needs to fully understand the significance of the ancestors for Malagasy people.

The Significance of Malagasy Ancestors

The relationship between the living and the dead and the presence of the ancestors in people's lives is of the utmost importance all over Madagascar. This is reflected in the fact that there is hardly any study of a Malagasy society that does not, in some way or another, deal with the ancestors.[1] The ancestors figure in people's past, present and future lives as they do in past, present, and no doubt future writings on Madagascar. However, the relationship between the living and the dead is not always easy, because Malagasy ancestors are of an essentially ambiguous nature. They are a source of blessing upon which the well-being, prosperity and indeed the lives of the living depend. But they are also difficult (*sarotra*), because they demand many things from their descendants, cruelly punishing those who fail to fulfill their demands.

Maurice Bloch, whose work to a large extent initiated the social anthropology of Madagascar, has focused on ancestral blessing (*tsodrano*) as a source of life, in particular in his work on the Merina of highland Madagascar (Bloch 1994a [1971], 1986, 1989a). He has discussed in great detail the notion of a timeless ancestral order and its ritual creation in the face of the human condition of mortality.

Bloch has shown how the image of the ancestral order legitimizes the authority of elders by naturalizing power relations. He has also discussed how Malagasy people willingly participate in the ritual creation of this image, because the ancestors are perceived to be the source of blessing and thus of health, prosperity and fertility not only for those in positions of power, but for *all* of their descendants, too.

The importance of ancestral blessing as a source of life, which is sought through ritual communication with the dead, cannot be stressed enough and has been widely confirmed and illustrated by numerous case studies from all around the island.[2] However, recent ethnographies (in particular Astuti 1995, Cole 2001 and Graeber 1995 [but see Graeber 2001: 232–239]) have focused on the other side of the ambiguous nature of Malagasy ancestors discussing how they are not only a source of blessing, but also a problem. As these ethnographies show, it is often difficult for living people to fulfill the demands of the ancestors, because these demands constrain people's actions, movements, possibilities and pleasures in life. Hence, in an attempt to square their own desires and needs with those of the ancestors, the living and the dead enter into a dynamic process by which they negotiate their respective views and wishes.

The anthropological study that perhaps discusses this process of negotiation most emphatically and centrally is Jennifer Cole's analysis of Betsimisaraka sacrifice (2001). Cole illustrates the process of negotiation by showing, for example, how during the ritual the Betsimisaraka modify or remove certain taboos that were imposed on them by their ancestors, but that have become too difficult to keep. What is also sought and received through the very same ritual process, however, is the consent of the ancestors to the changes proposed by the living.

The ambiguity of the nature of the ancestors as both a source of blessing and a problem, epitomized in the works of Bloch and Cole respectively, is present throughout the anthropology of Madagascar, and indeed in the writings of both of these authors. What is central for the present study is the fact that the ancestors are perceived to be the fount of life and that their blessing is vital for all human endeavors, even if obtaining that blessing is not always easy.

In the area of Maroantsetra, the most important ritual practices through which ancestral blessing is sought are exhumation and cattle sacrifice. Exhumation[3] takes place five to seven years after a person's death and involves the coming together of large numbers of kin and other people, the sacrifice of a cow or bull, a ritual meal and sometimes extensive festivities, depending on the social status of the deceased. In the central act, the dead person's physical remains are exhumed (by now, only the bones and the skull are left), carefully and tenderly cleaned, wrapped in several layers of cloth, and finally put to rest in, mostly individual, sarcophagi (*hazovato*).[4] Two or three years later, a cattle sacrifice is performed for the same ancestor. Cattle sacrifice (*rasa hariaña*, literally: the sharing of wealth) is conceptualized as giving the ancestors their share of what their descendants have only been able to obtain thanks to their blessing, and involves the ritual consumption of the sacrificial meat by the community of the living and that of the ancestors. Only when both exhumation and sacrifice have been performed for a particular ancestor is "the work done" (*vita ny asa*) and the peril of ancestral wrath, at least temporarily, removed.

The Diabolization of the Ancestors

One of the most important studies of new forms of Christianity in contemporary Africa is Birgit Meyer's analysis of Pentecostalism among the Ewe of Ghana (1999). One of Meyer's concerns is to find out why Pentecostal churches are so successful among the people she studies. To answer this question, she conducts a careful comparison between a mission church founded by German Pietists in the nineteenth century and two more recently founded churches in the Pentecostal tradition that split away from the mission church. Meyer concludes that the main reason for the success of the Pentecostal churches is the fact that the mission church fails to take seriously people's fears of witchcraft and evil spirits. In contrast, the Pentecostal churches provide space for addressing, and dealing with, such fears. The way they do this is primarily through the image of the devil, who acts as a broker between indigenous ideas and new Christian concepts. The existence of such phenomena as witchcraft is not disputed by Pentecostalism, but these are reinterpreted as a manifestation of the devil. In this way, indigenous concepts of the "supernatural" are integrated within Christianity, and people's fears are taken seriously.

We encounter the exact same process of the integration of indigenous concepts through their diabolization among the Adventists in Madagascar. Adventists do not participate in either exhumation or cattle sacrifice, even for their closest kin. They refuse to take part because, in their view, the act of communicating with the ancestors, as one does during these rituals, is equivalent to collaborating with Satan. The diabolization of the ancestors in the Adventist discourse involves two propositions.

The first proposition is that the dead are nothing but a pile of rotting bones (*maty dia maty* [Dead is dead!]*! tôlaña fò* [It's just bones]*!) and that the ancestors, as such, do not exist. Once again, note how radical a statement this is in the Malagasy context.

There are several Bible passages, which state clearly that when people are dead, they are *dead* (*maty dia maty*), as local church members endlessly emphasize. In Ecclesiastes 9: 5–6 in particular we read:

> "For the living know that they shall die; but the dead know not any thing, neither have they any more a reward; for the memory of them is forgotten. Also their love, and their hatred, and their envy, is now perished; neither have they any more a portion for ever in any *thing* that is done under the sun" (emphasis in the original).[5]

This and other, similar passages are among the best-known and most often recited by the Adventists in Maroantsetra and Sahameloka, and many of them can pick up their Bible and find such passages with ease.

Once I attended a sacrifice that took place in Sahameloka on a Saturday morning. Although Maman' and Papan' i Claude understood that I needed to attend such rituals for my studies, this time they were worried because it took place on the Sabbath. To make my attendance at the sacrifice acceptable to them, I had to promise that I would join them in church in the afternoon, as I did. After the church service, Papan' i Silivie and Papan' i Tahina, two young, very committed church members, took me to one side and inquired: "Did you ask the people responsible for the sacrifice (where, as always on such occasions, a bull had been killed and then consumed by both the community of the living, and the ancestors, to whom certain parts of the sacrificed animal had been offered) whether the ancestors *had actually eaten* their part?" When I replied that I had not, unfortunately, asked this question, which the two men obviously considered to be very significant, they offered me their own answer:

> The Malagasy really believe that the ancestors eat the meat offered to them at sacrifices. But is it not patently obvious that that isn't actually the case? Because after all, everyone can see with their own eyes that nothing at all happens with the ancestors' share of the sacrificed animal, and that all of it is still there at the end of the ritual. How could the dead possibly eat anything, since they don't have a mouth to eat with any more?! But [shaking their heads about the absurdity of such a notion] the Malagasy think that the ancestors actually eat their share!

On another occasion Dadin' i Miry, who had just turned to Adventism after some forty years of being a spirit medium, pointed out that the ancestors could not possibly eat any of the meat offered to them in sacrifice, because their stomachs were already rotten, and that clothes brought to their graves to keep them warm would likewise rot.

Now, if the ancestors are just "dead stuff" (*raha maty?!*), if they are "just bones" (*tôlaña fò*), as local Adventists often say, how can they possibly affect the lives of the living either by blessing them or by striking them down with misfortune? There is no denying, as local Adventists admit, that people who fail to do "the work for the ancestors" (*ny asan-drazana*), that is exhumation and sacrifice, and those who break ancestral taboos, *do* fall ill or even die; everyone can think of examples. And it is also undoubtedly true that people prosper when their ancestors bless them. Listen to a story Papan' i Fredel told me one afternoon in Sahameloka. He was telling me how, long before he became an Adventist, he had gone to offer rum to the ancestors.

> I shook hands with one of my ancestors. His hand was very, very cold! One didn't see him, because this happened at night; one mustn't call the ancestors before it's dark; when night comes, when it starts to get dark, that's when one calls them. [*Me: Did you really feel his hand?*] Yes! I felt it, yes! And we also offered rum [he mimes putting down a bottle]. We heard how the ancestor took the bottle. We heard how he drank: "cho! cho! cho! cho!." We heard him drinking the rum, we heard him drinking the rum! Later on, when the ancestor was gone, we saw that although we had heard him drinking lots, the bottle was only a tiny bit less full. But what was left was not strong rum any longer; the strength of the rum had gone.[6]

Papan' i Fredel has clearly no doubt about the existence of "ancestral" power, even now that he is a committed Adventist. Thus there is a paradox of, on the one hand, the ancestors being nothing but a pile of rotting bones, and, on the other hand, their presence and influence being clearly felt. The Adventists' second proposition solves this paradox: the power to affect people's lives, supposedly exercised by the ancestors, is in reality the devil's power at work and not that of dead forebears. Thus it was not Papan' i Fredel's ancestor, who drank the rum they offered, and whose hand he shook, but the devil in disguise.

It is primarily because Satan has copied God's ways and has thus come into possession of powerful tools such as healing, that he is able to fool the Malagasy. His profound influence on people's lives—making them ill or well, giving or depriving them of children, making their land fertile or barren, making them rich or poor—means that people are easily deceived. Now that Papan' i Fredel has become an Adventist, he understands this perfectly; his explanation of the devil's trickery is highly typical:

> God tells us that it is not the ancestors who speak to you, but that the devil pretends to be God. When the devil was thrown down to this

earth, he wanted to get all the glory for himself and to replace God.
And if one does not believe this, one will say: "It is the ancestors who
speak!" But, if one believes in the word of God, one says that it is the
devil who speaks with the voice of the dead. That is how I understand
it. And when I started to study the Holy Scripture, I had to say that this
is true. Surely, the dead are not able to speak, but the devil—God's
enemy who wants to get all the glory for himself—he speaks with the
voices of many people, and he knows how to make people ill. When
people fall ill, they are easily deceived and so they say: "The ancestors
have power." But if one then gives him [the devil] a bull or a cow [in a
sacrifice to the "ancestors"]—he who has made you ill in the first
place—then the person will recover, and so one says: "The ancestors are
real!" Because as soon as the sacrifice is done, people recover! That's
what people think. One really recovers, because it was the devil in
the first place who made you ill. But when he receives his cattle, he
will leave the person in peace and they will recover. Because they
followed him.[7]

Note the emphasis on deception, and on Bible study as the way to
discover the fact that this is an issue of deception. Numerous other
church members offered almost identical explanations of why people
are deceived by the devil, always using phrases that evoke pretence and
disguise on the devil's part (such as *malaka sary* [to copy], *misandoko*
[to pretend]).

The demonization of indigenous concepts and powers is a process
that has been documented in numerous contexts of Christianization
in Africa, Latin America, Asia and elsewhere.[8] In contrast to many
modern Catholic and Protestant denominations that tend to interpret
phenomena like "ancestor worship" as old-fashioned superstition—
quite in contrast to the early missionaries for whom the devil was real
(Bloch 2002: 134)—Seventh-day Adventist doctrine, globally and as
it is understood locally, emphasizes the reality of "ancestral" power by
associating it with the devil. Thus, ironically, such doctrines reinforce
precisely those indigenous concepts that are their main targets. In
Meyer's words:

> [D]emonisation by no means implies that the former gods and spirits
> will disappear out of people's lives. As servants of Satan they are still
> regarded as real powers that have to be dealt with in a concrete way—
> rather than as outmoded "superstitions," as modern Protestant theology
> would have it. (1999: xvii)

The two propositions involved in the demonization of Malagasy
ancestors through the local Adventist discourse are two sides of the
same coin, one doesn't make sense without the other. However,

sometimes, there is also an element of ambiguity involved. Think back to Papan' i Silivies's and Papan' i Tahina's statement referring to how ridiculous it was to think that the ancestors actually had eaten their share of the sacrificial meat, proof of which was the fact that everybody could see with their own eyes that the ancestors' share was still there at the end of the ritual, and that obviously nobody had eaten it. Significantly, they did not suggest—unlike Papan' i Fredel in his story about the rum offering—that although the meat was still there at the end of the ritual, it had lost its taste and strength. Rather, they suggested that nothing at all had been going on. In such statements, there is an element of denouncing ancestral power as an illusion full stop, as superstition, rather than deception. In contrast, Papan' i Fredel does not question the reality of the power he felt—the cold hand, the "cho, cho, cho" he heard—but he interprets this experience from the perspective of someone whose blindfold as to the true identity of the "ancestor" has been removed.

Most narratives I obtained echoed Papan' i Fredel's interpretation, but the type of "disenchanted" view as expressed by Papan' i Silivie and Papan' i Tahina was also voiced by numerous members of the church. Moreover, many Adventists hold both these views at the same time, moving between one and the other. In many of the narratives I recorded, one and the same person talks at some stage of the alleged ancestral power as nonsense, while at another stage emphatically insisting on "the real existence of Satan" (*teña misy i Satana*), proof of which is the power of the "ancestors."

Being familiar with the literature on Malagasy cultures and societies before I left to do fieldwork, I was convinced that I would be studying the ways in which the Malagasy Adventists *combine* traditional practices related to the ancestors with their Adventist faith. I was wrong: neither do traditional and Adventist concepts and practices merge into a new, syncretic form, nor do they coexist as socially related, yet incommensurable traditions of knowledge as Lambek suggests is the case with Islam, spirit possession and sorcery in Mayotte (Lambek 1993). From the point of view of the members of the Adventist church, one cannot work for the ancestors *and* be a sincere Adventist, because to do so would be to serve God and Satan at the same time. Indeed, the fact that Seventh-day Adventists do not participate in exhumation and cattle sacrifice is one of the crucial factors that distinguishes them, and sets them apart, from the rest of society. Moreover, nonparticipation in these rituals is one of the most important criteria by which the Adventists assess each other's commitment to the church. A person attending every Sabbath church service, but also attending exhumations is not considered a proper

Adventist. As I mentioned in chapter 2, the pastor in Maroantsetra made the commitment not to participate in such practices part of the creed, to be accepted before baptism. After having read point 3 of the creed, he always briefly stopped to explain that to "renounce the sinful ways of the world" meant staying clear from both exhumation and cattle sacrifice.

The Construction of Ancestral Religion

The insistence on not taking part in exhumation and cattle sacrifice is part and parcel of a much more general rejection of what the local Adventists refer to as *fomban-drazana*. What exactly is rejected?

What the local Adventists mean by *fomban-drazana*, when they talk about what they reject, is a great number of practices among which figure prominently: exhumation, cattle sacrifice, vows to one's ancestors, spirit possession, divination and witchcraft. For other local people, who have nothing to do with the Adventist church, these practices are not at all one and the same thing, and they are not referred to by one generic term. In Adventist parlance, however, all of them are lumped together as manifestations of Satan's influence in this world. In fact, the terms for practices such as spirit possession, divination, witchcraft and exhumation are often employed interchangeably, Adventists not differentiating between them.

The term *fomban-drazana* literally means "the ways (or the customs) of the ancestors." And this is precisely what is normally, in non-Adventist contexts, understood by *fomban-drazana*: namely everything that the living generations have learnt from their ancestors. In the ordinary usage of the term—in the area of Maroantsetra and elsewhere in Madagascar—*fomban-drazana* represent a way of life. Respecting and bowing down to elders, performing oratory or planting rice are as much examples of *fomban-drazana* as invoking one's ancestors in ritual. All of these are considered "the ways of the ancestors": *fomban-drazana*. This does not, of course, mean that things designated as "of the ancestors" are necessarily particularly old (cf. Bloch 1994a [1971]; Feeley-Harnik 1991; Cole 2001), but it does mean that they have moral legitimacy by virtue of being associated with the ancestors.

Thus the term *fomban-drazana* as employed by local Seventh-day Adventists, with its specific meaning referring to an amalgam of things they consider to be the devil's work, is a novel construction on their part. The Adventists have not invented the term *fomban-drazana*, but they have given it a completely new meaning. In Adventist parlance, *fomban-drazana* does not refer to "that which the ancestors have passed on to us," as it does in ordinary talk. Instead *fomban-drazana* refers to practices that involve what we might call "supernatural" phenomena such as communication with one's ancestors or the presence of invisible power; "supernatural" in the sense that these phenomena are not straightforwardly of this earth. Such a usage of the term *fomban-drazana*, in contrast to its ordinary usage among Malagasy people, creates the idea of "religion" as being something apart, separated from such activities as farming rice or showing respect to elderly people, as "disembedded."

I call the Adventist construction of *fomban-drazana* a disembedded notion of "religion," because by treating "supernatural entities," in particular the ancestors, as separate from other spheres of life like kinship, this construction is clearly modeled on Christianity. In the ordinary Malagasy worldview, such a concept of disembedded religion is, however, inappropriate, in particular with relation to the ancestors. With regard to the relationship between elders and ancestors in Africa more generally, Kopytoff pointed out long ago that ancestors are basically perceived of, and treated, in much the same way as elders, except that they are dead and thus cannot be seen (1997 [1968]). The ethnography of Madagascar confirms this point; Malagasy people do not relate to their ancestors as supernatural beings completely different to elders, rather they communicate with dead forebears in particular circumstances in ways that are reminiscent of the way they relate to elders (Bloch 2002; see also Astuti 2000).

By introducing a clear-cut distinction between phenomena that are visible to the eye and others that are not, by representing such practices as exhumation and cattle sacrifice as a separate, "religious" matter concerned with the "supernatural," the Adventists Christianize *fomban-drazana*. And by so doing, they create an opposition between two alternative "religions": one, Seventh-day Adventism, which is true, and the other, *fomban-drazana*, which represents the worshipping of Satan and thus, needless to say, is to be rejected as "false religion." As two alternative systems that are, however, similar in nature, Adventism and *fomban-drazana* are constructed as comparable.

It is not by accident that members of the Adventist church sometimes pointed to explicit parallels between *fomban-drazana* (as false religion) and Adventism. The comparability of the two systems and the fact that Satan copies God's ways makes this inevitable. For example, Papan' i Beby once explained the following analogy to the participants of a Sabbath School discussion.

"When someone falls ill," he began, "the Malagasy sometimes sacrifice a bull to their ancestors so that the sick person may not die. Thus in cattle sacrifice, the life of the animal is exchanged for the life of a person. The death of the bull brings human life. The same exchange of death for life happened when Jesus Christ died in order to save humankind. His death will bring us eternal life.

Other people drew a similar parallel between "praying" (*mivavaka*) and "invoking the ancestors" (*mijoro*), because, as Maman' i Beby said, both are to ask for help and protection (*mangataka*). The difference is simply that the ancestors' religion is nothing but a deception, while God truly exists.

I also call the Adventist construction of *fomban-drazana* (modeled on Christianity) the construction of disembedded religion because of the prominence of the word *mino* in this discourse. For the moment, we might translate *mino* as "to believe" in the sense of "accepting as true."[9] *Mino* is not a word that Malagasy people would normally use in relation to their ancestors, because one doesn't "believe" in one's ancestors as one does not "believe" in elders. The word *mino*, then, is normally associated with the Christian religion. However, when the local Adventists talk about people's relationship to the ancestors, including their own former relationships, they very often use the word *mino*. Thus when talking about their own past experiences with ancestors and their own former "false beliefs," they would refer to the times "when we still believed in the ancestors" (*tamin' ny zahay mbóla nino [past tense of mino] ny razana*), by which they meant "when we still accepted the ancestors as real." These former times they contrast with "now, that we don't believe in the ancestors anymore" (*efa tsy mino ny razana amin' ny izao*), by which they mean "now, that we have come to understand that the ancestors are but a deception." Likewise, when describing how their non-Adventist compatriots follow the "false religion" of *fomban-drazana*, they would claim that "the Malagasy believe in ancestors" (*mino ny razana ny malagasy*) or, which to them is roughly the same, that they believe in spirit possession (*mino ny tromba*) or in traditional medicine (*mino ny fanafody gasy ny malagasy*). According to the local Adventists, the non-Adventist Malagasy accept all of these things as real while they themselves know that such things are not really "real," but are rather manifestations of the devil's power. Maman' i Ominò summarized all the "false beliefs" she used to share with other Malagasy saying: "the Malagasy really believe in Satan" (*teña mino azy, mino azy tanteraka*). In short: to accept the ancestors, and other "supernatural" entities, as real, to believe in *fomban-drazana*, is to be ignorant of the fact that all of these things are but a cover for Satan's power. To "believe" in *fomban-drazana* is to lack the potency to see beneath Satan's veil of deception.

Chapter 10

Clarity

In the lives of the members of the Adventist church in Sahameloka and Maroantsetra, Bible study is the most important religious activity. Adventist Bible study is not a matter of the truth being taught by a higher authority, but of everyone discovering the truth for themselves by way of investigation and dialogue. Because of its use of a Socratic type of Bible study, which involves a continual process of Normal Scientific discovery, local Adventist practice is distinctly intellectual. The central question this book addresses concerns the nature of the attraction of Seventh-day Adventism for church members in Maroantsetra and Sahameloka. The answer to this question, in a nutshell, is that it is the intellectual excitement linked to the process of studying the Bible that is the key to local people's commitment to the Adventist church. Bible study does, however, not only provide intellectual excitement *per se*. It is also seen as the road toward understanding the truth revealed through God's wise words. Knowledge of the truth is available there in the Bible, and yet the Bible remains silent unless and until we make the effort to make it speak by reading and studying it. And the achievement of this process is indeed great. To study the Bible and to truly understand what it says is to see behind Satan's veil of deception. Not only does Satan promote wickedness and evil, he also intentionally hides the truth from humankind thus denying us a clear view of reality. The principal result of Satan's power is the fact that people are deceived into accepting as true that which is not. In Madagascar, this is so in particular with regard to the alleged power of the dead. It is only through the activity of *mianatra* (studying) that one can develop the intellectual potency to "dis-cover" the truth from beneath Satan's deception. Therefore, Bible study is perceived by the local Adventists to be the road to clarity. I began this book with the image of Papan' i Loricà studying the Bible by candlelight for hours on end. We can now understand what keeps him awake and motivated: it is the excitement of the process of discovery and learning in which he is engaged at that moment, it is the thrill of traveling *the road* to clarity. On top of that, Papan' i Loricà's vision of the world becomes ever more clear, the more he learns, and so it is also *the clarity* of where the road leads him that motivates him to go on.

To stop being deceived by Satan is one aspect of the clarity of the Adventist view. The road of Bible study, however, leads to clarity in more than one sense.

The Adventist Notion of Clarity

The local members of the Adventist church pride themselves on knowing and understanding why they follow God, rather than "just believing," as Catholics and Protestants do in their view. This emphasis on knowledge, rather than "belief" (to which I will come back shortly), is not only an expression of the subjective interpretation of Adventism as primarily a matter of expertise, but also implies that one *can know* God's truth. This aspect reveals quite a different facet of the Adventist notion of the clarity, of—in Malagasy—the *mazava*, that the Adventist road leads to. Let us first look at the Malagasy concept *mazava*.

Mazava

Mazava connotes a very powerful concept in many places in Madagascar and captures a variety of meanings, all of which are associated with clarity and light.[1] *Mazava* is normally used as an adjective that can (in one of its senses) refer to something being clear in the sense of having been properly understood. For example, when people explained a Malagasy word to me, one that I did not understand yet, they would inquire, at the end of their explanation, whether that word was now *mazava* (clear) to me or not, in other words, whether I had understood what it meant. Similarly, when my Adventist friends pondered possible reasons for my failure to get baptized, they would ask: "Is there something which is not *mazava* to you yet?" (*Misy mbóla tsy mazava aminao?*). Among the Zafimaniry, whose homeland lies in the thick forest in another area of Madagascar, *mazava* denotes open space, which the Zafimaniry have cleared as a basis for their livelihood. For the Zafimaniry, good, clear views over cultivated land, which is praised for how *mazava* it is, are a symbol of human achievement and progress (Bloch 1995a).

In Seventh-day Adventist discourse, the word *mazava* is also associated with light and clarity. First, *mazava* denotes the kind of clarity I have already discussed, that is the intellectual potency to see behind Satan's deception and to gain an undisturbed, clear view of reality. *Mazava* is also used as a noun in Adventist talk referring to "all that which is clear and true," and in some contexts, it is even employed to refer to God Himself. In this sense, the Adventists contrast "The *mazava*" to "The *maizina*," which can refer to darkness, ignorance, evil forces and, in some contexts, the devil. To study the Bible—to travel along the road to clarity in this first sense of the word in Adventist discourse—is thus to move from a self-perceived state of ignorance and darkness toward life in an "enlightened" world, toward *mazava*.

Light as a metaphor of the Christian faith, and darkness as its opposite obviously echoes standard Christian rhetoric. But, the Adventists also see themselves as moving toward an "enlightened" world in a sense that goes much further than the standard Christian interpretation. When we explore this second aspect of the Adventist notion of clarity, of the *mazava* that the road of Bible study leads to, we leave the bounds of mainstream Christianity. In order to understand this second, much more unusual, aspect of the clarity represented by the Adventist view, we must first examine two future moments in time foretold by Seventh-day Adventist doctrine. The first one concerns the millennium.

What Happens During the Millennium?

One of the central aspects of Seventh-day Adventist doctrine is the distinction between the first and second death, and the first and the second resurrection. All humans must die as a result of the original sin; this is the first death. All the righteous dead, however, will be resurrected at Christ's return *prior* to the millennium, and together with the righteous living, will ascend to heaven and never die again. All those who have failed to follow Christ will be resurrected *after* the millennium, but only to receive the Last Judgment and then be annihilated forever and cease to exist; this is the second resurrection and the second death, which only the unrighteous have to suffer. Not many members of the Adventist church in either Maroantsetra or Sahameloka would be able to give even an approximate account of these future events, although they have certainly all heard the details of this Adventist prophecy at some stage or other. One central aspect of the prophecy, however, is well known, and that is the purpose of the events *during* the millennium when all righteous people will live together with Jesus in heaven. Maman' and Papan' i Beby once illustrated the millennial scenario to me by way of a thought experiment that went like this:

> Imagine Maman' i Beby arriving in heaven. She tries to find Papan'
> i Beby since, on the basis of his pious life on earth, she is certain that he
> must be among the saved. But she fails to find him, and nobody else
> who knew Papan' i Beby has seen him either. Doubts arise in her mind:
> "Might God have made a mistake in this particular case? How could
> He not have saved Papan' i Beby who dedicated his life to Him?" The
> only way her doubts can be removed is for God to show her, to *prove* to
> her that His judgment is indeed just.

Nobody really knows how exactly God will do this, Papan' and Maman'
i Beby continued; but they imagine a kind of massive cinema screen
on which—in the unlikely case that Papan' i Beby should indeed fail
to be among the saved—God will show a sort of film, which will
demonstrate that Papan' i Beby secretly committed adultery or that
behind his devout Christian appearance, he was, in reality, a witch. The
purpose of the millennium is thus to make God's judgment absolutely
clear—*mazava*—to everyone and to remove any potential doubt in
the minds of the saved as to the justice of God's judgment.[2] Although
I do not think that many members of the church have such a well-
designed image of the events that will occur during the millennium,
they do always emphasize that God, in some way or another, will
prove and explain His justice and that there will be no more doubt of
whatever kind. In other words, everything will be made absolutely
clear—*mazava*—and people will understand why things are the way
they are.

Life in Paradise

The second future moment in time I want to consider is life in paradise
after the millennium and after the final annihilation of evil and death.
People's mental images of paradise are likely to be very splendid in
general—they talk of its golden streets for example—but there is one
aspect of the anticipated splendor, which is of particular importance
for the present discussion. And that is the fact that God Himself will
come out into the light for everyone to see. He will sit on His golden
throne in paradise and He will be of flesh and blood. People will be
able to touch Him and speak to Him. Church members often talked
about this aspect of life in paradise, and when they did, their eyes
would shine with the anticipation of actually *seeing* God with their
own eyes. Reconsider the following extract from the Sabbath School
discussion I cited at length in chapter 5.

It is like with a competition. If one doesn't know what the first and second prizes are, people will hesitate to take part. But if they know what they can win, they will rush to take part. If people know that the first prize is a bicycle, then everyone will want to take part. You see, it is just like that with us knowing what is waiting for us in paradise, knowing for example that the blind will see, the deaf will hear and that we will see God sitting there. But it is not really the fact that the blind will see and the weak will become strong which is so fantastic about this place [paradise], but that we will *see* God living together with us. [Someone else: Yes, that's exactly right!] What we have long been wondering about is: what is Jesus really like? What are his hands which had the nails in them like? What is God's life like? And what is His name? [. . .] All of that we will *see* there!

I conclude from these reflections on the millennium and life in paradise that what interests and moves church members most about the future is the anticipation of finally *seeing* things entirely *clearly*, rather than the promise of bliss as tends to be emphasized in definitions of millenarianism.[3] In other words, they anticipate complete clarity and "enlightenment," complete knowledge of that which is true. This is the *mazava*, the clarity, that Bible study leads to. However, there is still more to be said about the local Adventists' idea that, at the heart of the religion they have embraced, is the potential to know and to see clearly.

Beyond Modern Belief

Asad has convincingly demonstrated that the idea of there being such a thing as Religion, of which one can find different manifestations in cultures around the world—the idea of Religion having "an autonomous essence" (1993: 28)—is a product of the history of European Christianity (Asad 1993). Therefore, the attempt to define "Religion" independently of particular social and historical contexts is an ethnocentric nonstarter. Asad has identified a number of developments relating to the nature of Christianity, which took place in the course of the seventeenth and eighteenth centuries in Europe, and which eventually led to the development of the modern notion of religion. One of these developments is of particular interest for the present discussion, namely the shift from the concept of Christianity as something founded on *knowledge* of religious doctrine, the life of saints and so on, to a concept of Christianity that is founded on *belief* in God and that "emphasizes the priority of belief as a state of mind" (1993: 47). Belief in this modern sense is a matter of private conscience, an inner state (Needham 1972) concerning things whose truthfulness is thought not to be empirically accessible, not to be knowable. Christian religion has thus become a mysterious matter of the heart and as such, cannot be understood, or argued for or against, rationally.

Many scholars, among them Pouillon (1982), have noted that the concept of belief as just discussed only makes sense within a framework, such as that provided by modern Christianity, which is based on a duality between an empirically accessible world and another transcendental world that is not empirically accessible and that one therefore has to believe in, in the above sense. Many cultures, however, do not make such a distinction and hence do not have a concept of disembedded religion, or a concept of supernatural entities that one has to believe in. As we saw in chapter 9, this is also the case in Madagascar where ancestors are thought to be pretty much the same kind of thing as people except for the fact that they are dead and not visible. Asad, however, has convincingly argued that the preoccupation with belief as a private matter of the heart is not only a specifically Christian phenomenon, but also a relatively *modern* Christian concept.

When one compares this modern concept of Christianity (based on belief as a matter of the heart) with the Malagasy Adventists' idea of what their religion is all about, one realizes that there is a huge gulf between these two concepts. For church members in Sahameloka and Maroantsetra, true religion is not at all based on this modern notion of belief concerning matter whose substance is not empirically knowable. Rather, from their point of view, the core of their religion is the acquisition of knowledge and intellectual comprehension of truth through the process of Bible study. In that sense, their notion of the nature of Adventism departs from what is usually thought of as being characteristic of modern Christianity.

The distinction between this world and another world, and the promise of a better life in the other world, has been described as a key attraction of world religions (Hefner 1993a: 34), and also of salvationist movements such as Seventh-day Adventism. Yet for the Malagasy Adventists, life in paradise does not imply a vision of a mysterious or supernatural world—of another world—but rather of a world that is as empirically accessible and clear (*mazava*) as planting rice is in this world. Life in heaven during the millennium will be as real as life is on this earth; God sitting on His golden throne will be as real as a person sitting on a chair is now. Thus the very distinction becomes invalid; the typically modern Christian dualist worldview between this world and another world beyond the knowable reality, is not applicable.

Christianity is not new in Madagascar and not new to most local Adventists. What is new to them is their acquaintance with a version of Christianity that lacks the idea of an *intrinsically unknowable* hereafter. What is new to them is the realization that the Christian "transcendental" world is actually of exactly the same nature as the activity of farming or the material reality of the house across the street. Only, it lies in the future. In other words: the Adventists' vision is not only clear, *mazava*, but what they see is perfectly knowable and *will* be empirically accessible.

Ironically, in the sense that Adventism does not essentialize the difference between the visible and the invisible, it is in fact closer to the traditional, ancestor-based worldview than to mainstream Christianity.

It is also interesting to note that one of the recurring features in definitions of "fundamentalism" is anti-secularism. This means precisely that people we think of as "fundamentalists" are against the separation between a religious and a secular sphere. The incorporation of "science" into "religion," which has been noted as typical of "fundamentalists" in general, makes this clear.[4] Although it is not usually presented in these terms, such anti-secularism implies that "fundamentalists" critique the modern Christian dualist view of the cosmos. The "fundamentalist" objection to secularism is a refusal to accept disembedded religion, a refusal of the idea of there being such a thing as "religion" in the sense of a separate aspect of society relating to supernatural/invisible phenomena.

That church members in Maroantsetra and Sahameloka consider the acquisition of a clear view as a key element of Seventh-day Adventism is also confirmed by the retrospective discourse (of those who used to be Catholics or Protestants) about why they were dissatisfied with mainstream Christianity. The following statements are representative. "When I was a Protestant, things were not very *mazava* (clear) to me (*tsy mazava tsara be*)." "The Catholics don't explain [literally: reveal] well about God (*tsy mañambara tsara be mikasika an' Andriamanitra*)." "The Catholics simply say 'The Catholic religion is true' (. . . *amin' ny Katolika akao, milaza fò 'Marina ny fivavahana Katolika'*)." "They just believe (*mino fò zare*)." Such statements not only express a critique of mainstream Christianity from the perspective of those who have left it. They also imply a dissatisfaction with the modern emphasis in Christianity of religion as a nonintellectual sphere of human experience. In the modern concept, the most important thing for a believer is to feel close to God; what goes on in someone's heart is what really matters, even to God Himself! To exactly understand God's ways, however, is not only not of primary importance, but is indeed considered impossible beyond a certain point. For the Malagasy Adventists, there is no such point beyond which the realm of the unknowable begins. For them, "religion" is about knowing and understanding God's truth as we see it in front of our eyes in the here and now, and as we will see it in the hereafter. When the local Adventists say in a derogatory tone that their Catholic and Protestant coresidents or kin "just believe in God," they may not necessarily mean that mainstream Christian belief is "just a matter of the heart." However, such statements certainly do imply that mainstream Christians accept something as true without understanding why they do so, that mainstream Christianity is, in other words, a matter of blind faith. And this is precisely what the local Adventists, at least retrospectively, are dissatisfied with. In statements such as "With the Protestants, things are not at all *mazava*," or, phrased positively, "The Adventists explain things really clearly," we can see a desire for an intellectual comprehension of "religion" which, in the view of the local Adventists, is neglected by mainstream Christianity, but which Seventh-day Adventism provides.

The End of the Need to Trust

The Adventists in Maroantsetra and Sahameloka have a concept of Christianity based on knowledge rather than faith. Does this mean that they do not have any kind of religious "belief" at all? In order to answer this question, we must first look at the Adventists' usage of the word *mino*, which, when used in religious terms, is normally translated as "to believe."[5]

In Adventist usage, the verb *mino*, and its related noun *finoana*, have at least four different meanings. Meaning one: *mino* is used to refer to other Christians accepting God and the teachings of whatever church they belong to without properly understanding why they do so. To "just believe" in this sense, as opposed to the Adventists' informed choice of God, has a negative quality. Meaning two: *mino* is employed in the Adventists' discourse about *fomban-drazana* as false religion. In this sense, to "believe" in the ancestors (*mino ny razana*) is to be deceived by Satan and hence to lack clarity of mind. This second meaning of *mino* is linked to the first in that both refer to a state of mind that is characterized by a lack of comprehension of the truth. Meaning three: the Adventists' own differentiation of themselves from those who *mino* captures the idea that the here-and-now and the hereafter are of essentially the same nature and that both are empirically accessible.

At this point, it might seem as if the local Adventists have, from their own point of view, nothing to do with the notion of *mino*. Significantly, however, they also use the word *mino* in a fourth sense, to express their own relationship to God. But when they say that *they* "believe" (*mino*) in God or Jesus (*mino Andriamanitra, mino i Jesôsy izahay*), what they mean is not simply that they accept the true, rather than a false religion, but something rather more specific. It is this fourth sense in which the local Adventists employ the word *mino* to which I now turn.

What will happen at Christ's Second Coming and the sequence of events that will follow thereafter are perfectly knowable and will be empirically accessible. However, they are not so at the moment. After all, as local Adventists admit, nobody has actually ever seen God. Therefore, the Adventists, too, have no option but, for the time being, to *mino*. *Mino* used in this sense, expressing the Adventists' own relationship to God, does not denote belief in the modern Christian sense as a matter of the heart, but denotes trust in the fact that the straightforward reality of that which one has not yet seen with one's own eyes (*tsy hita maso*) will be revealed to human senses in due time.

Papan' i Beby once illustrated this meaning of *mino* and its related noun *finoana* to me in the following way. He was chopping firewood, while I sat nearby and we were discussing what exactly it meant to say that the Adventists have *finoana*. In order to illustrate the meaning of *finoana* to me, he picked up a particularly thorny branch from his pile of wood and told me to stretch out my open hands, palms up. When I had done so, he held the branch just above my hands, and told me to close my eyes and then to clench my fists, which I did after a moment's consideration that I might prick my fingers. But of course he had pulled the branch away before I hurt myself. "You see, this is *finoana*," Papan' i Beby triumphantly exclaimed, delighted that his experiment had been successful. Because although I could not see with my eyes closed whether or not he had pulled the branch away, I had trusted him.

When church members in Sahameloka and Maroantsetra speak of their own *finoana* in God, they do not refer to "belief" as it is understood in mainstream Christianity (despite the fact that they use a word that is normally translated as "belief"). While mainstream Christian belief is beyond any empirically knowable reality, for the Malagasy Adventists, *finoana* denotes trust in the promise that the truth about the world—which, unfortunately, one has not seen with one's own eyes yet—will be revealed and made accessible to human senses. After Christ's return, the need to trust—the need to *mino*—will cease to exist, because everything will be clear (*mazava*). But for the time being, one has no option but to trust in the wisdom and authority of the Bible as God's word with this trust being continuously nourished by new evidence of the Bible's truthfulness. Although the subject of *finoana* is not empirically accessible at the moment, it is intrinsically knowable, and it is essentially of the same nature as those things one has already seen with one's own eyes. When Malagasy Adventists say, that they *mino* in God or Jesus, they refer to their trust in the fact that what is foretold in the Bible, particularly in the Book of Revelation, will materialize, in due time, in exactly the way it has been foretold. Only in this sense, do they "believe" in God. To "believe in God" means to trust that they will see the *mazava*.

Not Everything Is All That Clear

At this stage of the analysis, what emerges is an image of clarity. One of the main goals of this book is to understand what, from the point of view of local members of the church, the world looks like through Adventist spectacles; and through these spectacles, the world looks amazingly clear. The Adventist world looks strikingly clear not only because the future will offer complete clarity, as discussed. Already in the present, one's mind is also no longer obscured, but one can see clearly which forces are at play in this world and beyond, and one can see clearly Satan's many ways of deception, the epitome of which in Madagascar is *fomban-drazana* in the sense of "false religion." The clarity of the Adventist vision is thus located both in the present and in the future.

However, the Adventists in Maroantsetra and Sahameloka are not only members of the Adventist church, and their identity is not solely defined by that membership. They are real people. They do not live in an Adventist ivory tower from the safe heights of which they can gaze down upon the world. They do not live in isolation from the rest of society, so—at the same time as being committed members of the Adventist church—they are also members of ancestries, kin groups, localities and also of a nation. In daily life, they have to deal with ordinary problems and manage their lives, like everyone else around them who is not in the Adventist church. As "ordinary" Malagasy people, as villagers, kin, friends and neighbors, Adventists do not always necessarily look at the world through their Adventist spectacles. This fact introduces a considerable amount of uncertainty as to who the Adventists feel they are, how they should interpret the world and how they should act in daily life. Because they are both Seventh-day Adventists and "ordinary" people, they are constantly switching between two registers. The vision is clearest when only the Adventist register is on, such as during church services. But as soon as the "ordinary" register is switched on as well, the clarity of the vision is disturbed. A person cannot cut him or herself in two, so the situation of both registers being simultaneously on is the situation the local Adventists find themselves in during much of their everyday lives. It is almost as if they were wearing a pair of spectacles one lens of which was an Adventist one, the other an "ordinary" one. The picture that such a pair of glasses would produce would be rather muddled, unclear and contradictory. Thus, ironically, although the Adventist vision on its own is extremely clear, in combination with the "ordinary" vision, it is very complicated. The end result for local members of the Adventist church is having to face new types of uncertainties, uncertainties to which they were not exposed before their commitment to the church. It is to these new uncertainties produced by the simultaneous presence of two different "ways of being" that I turn in the final part of this book.

Part III

Uncertainties

In chapter 9 we saw how the concept of *fomban-drazana* is reformulated through Adventist discourse, coming to represent "false religion" to Adventists. We also saw how the local Adventists reject practices designated part of this type of *fomban-drazana*, in particular exhumation and cattle sacrifice.

In her study of Ewe Pentecostalism, Meyer (1999) discusses how the diabolization of indigenous concepts is the result of translating biblical concepts such as God, sin and Satan into Ewe language that, because the Ewe did not have these concepts, lacked equivalent terms. In the course of this process of "translating the devil," the Christian concept of Satan was aligned with what the foreign missionaries considered to be heathen religion. From the missionaries' point of view, their translation of Christian concepts into Ewe was successful. But this did not necessarily mean that the Ewe understood the translated concepts in the way the missionaries intended, since their meaning was transformed in the process and adjusted to Ewe understandings (see also Rafael 1993).

The exact same process of aligning indigenous concepts with Satan has taken place in Madagascar through the presentation of the Seventh-day Adventist concept of the Great Controversy to the Malagasy Adventists in the Malagasy language. The result of this translation process is the construction of *fomban-drazana* as false religion. However, the local Adventists continue to be Malagasy people and they continue to understand *fomban-drazana* according to the ordinary usage of the term referring to everything the living generations have learnt from their forebears. And when understood in this sense, they are wholly in favor of following "the ways of the ancestors" and indeed, consider it imperative to do so. For example, they consider showing respect toward one's seniors, and in particular toward elderly people, a key element of moral behavior. For the Malagasy Adventists, then, the process of translating the devil as *fomban-drazana* is highly ambiguous and entails considerable uncertainties as to the moral nature of this concept. We will encounter such uncertainty in several places in chapters 11 and 12, but the issue of the double meaning of *fomban-drazana* for Malagasy Seventh-day Adventists will only be fully explored in the final conclusion.

Chapter 11

Making Choices

The simultaneous presence of the Adventist and the local vision of the world often make it difficult for the members of the church to decide how they should act in daily life. This is the subject matter of the final two chapters before we come to the conclusions of this book. Chapter 12 will focus on the social relationships among Adventists as well as the social relationships between them and their non-Adventist neighbors, friends and in particular kin. The present chapter examines how the life of an individual is marked by the simultaneous presence of the Adventist and the ordinary Malagasy view of things. Of course, a person's individual life is not separable from his or her social relationships. It is only for the purpose of analysis that I have disentangled the two.

Commitment to Seventh-day Adventism is not just a matter of going to a certain church on a certain day, it is a lifestyle. Church membership has an influence on one's life that extends far beyond strictly religious matters. Every day, every week, every year, every stage of one's life is to some extent influenced by the fact of being an Adventist.

There is, of course, considerable variation regarding the influence church membership has on different people's individual lives, depending partly on specific duties within the church (which vary greatly), and partly on personal commitment. I cannot do full justice to these differences. What follows should be understood as a representation of the daily life of a "typical" member of the local Adventist church, that is someone who is seriously committed, but who does not hold any special office such as being a lay leader.

Although Adventism exerts considerable influence over people's daily lives, it should be remembered that Adventism does not override everything else. Adventism is not the *only* commitment people have and it is not necessarily their dominant mode of life in all situations. Much of what the local Adventists do is not affected by their membership of the church. Growing up, going to school, getting married and starting one's own household, working, having children, grandchildren . . . the Adventists go through life much like everybody else.

In short: the local Adventists' lives are shaped both by Adventist values and activities, and by those of the society they grew up and live in. Neither is clearly dominant, neither pushes the other completely to the side. Because of the simultaneous presence of two different ways of being and two different ways of looking at the world, the local Adventists feel uncertain in many situations as to what exactly they should do, especially when faced with having to make important decisions in the course of their lives.

It would, however, be misleading to suggest that everything to do with Adventism immediately causes problems for local church members or their kin and neighbors. A substantial part of the Adventist way of living can easily be integrated into people's lives as rice farmers or town dwellers without causing anybody to take offence. It is to the unproblematic integration of Adventism to which I turn first.

Unproblematic Aspects of the Adventist Way of Life

There are four aspects of the Adventist way of life that are unproblematic in the sense that they do not cause any clash with locally important concepts or practices. The first of these are most Adventist practices in church and at home.

Unproblematic Practices

One of the most obvious impacts of commitment to the Adventist church on people's daily lives is the practice of repeated prayer. The day begins and ends with a silent prayer said while kneeling down beside one's bed with one's head bent down. A prayer is spoken prior to every meal in the day and sometimes also afterward. Some people even say a short prayer before eating a snack, such as a banana, while working in the forest. Prayers are also spoken before someone sets out on a special venture such as a trip to town or a longer journey, a visit to the hospital or missionizing work. These prayers ask for spiritual strength, for the success of the venture that one is about to undertake, or for the safe return of those about to leave. The activity of praying punctuates the day, periodically marking and bringing out people's religious commitment.

As unproblematic as repeated prayer is the activity of Bible study, both in church and at home. Regular attendance at church services throughout the week—twice in the evening, and once during the day on the Sabbath—also presents no problems in and of itself. The payment of tithes, too, is unproblematic from the point of view of its compatibility with local culture. Church members are, in theory, expected to pay tithes, for their cash income and for the value of their produce. I do not know whether or not people actually do this, since only the pastor sees the content of the little envelopes provided for this purpose, and he is not allowed to give out any information regarding the contributions made. But my impression is that paying tithes was looked at rather pragmatically in Maroantsetra and Sahameloka. "It's not an obligation, but one ought to do it" (*tsy tsy maintsy, fa tokony*), Papan' i Beby once explained to me, although his family in fact always paid their tithes. In Maroantsetra, quite a few people, but by no means all, did hand in their envelopes and thus presumably gave some money while in Sahameloka, where agricultural products were not considered relevant to tithing, this was a rare sight. What is important here is that those Adventists who wish to pay tithes can do so without causing any problem to themselves or to others.

Let me briefly add a few words about the financial aspect of church membership at this point. Despite the expectation that tithes be paid, giving money or material to the church is always a voluntary act, and there is little pressure exerted on church members to do so. On the other hand, membership of the Adventist church, at least in the district of Maroantsetra, does not result in any material or financial advantages such as free medical care or schooling. Thus, potential economic benefit would never stand up as an explanation of the attraction of the church as has sometimes been suggested for Seventh-day Adventism in other contexts.[1] The only financial advantage church membership entails are savings in ritual expenses, which admittedly can be substantial—the value of a bull for example or lots of rice and rum for the guests at an exhumation or a sacrifice. The high ritual expenses are in fact lamented by many non-Adventist local people. However, despite such lamentations, local people do not dare not to perform an exhumation or sacrifice simply for financial reasons, because the danger of ancestral wrath is too great. For the local Adventists, not performing ancestral rituals is, in the end, one of the main *problems* they face in their lives, and not an *attraction* of the Adventist church. This is so because the fact that they refuse to take part in ritual work done for even their closest kin causes significant social tensions which, as we will see in chapter 12, by far outweigh the material gain involved in not performing ritual work.

Dietary Rules

The second aspect of the Adventist way of life that is unproblematic in terms of possible social implications are dietary rules. Seventh-day Adventists follow the food prohibitions given in Leviticus chapter 11. The notion of dietary taboos is easily compatible with local practice. Taboos (*fady*) of all kinds, including those relating to the consumption of food, are prevalent throughout Madagascar. Almost every Malagasy family has specific dietary taboos, which are often said to have been instigated by one of their ancestors for a specific reason. So Adventism in this respect is not introducing a new concept, but merely changing the menu plan. Former ancestral food taboos are dropped, new Adventist ones adopted. In fact, in Sahameloka these food taboos have hardly any impact since people almost exclusively live off rice, leaf broth, bananas and sometimes a chicken, none of which are *fady* for Adventists. The impact on our diet in Maroantsetra was slightly greater, since we were not allowed to eat shrimps and other crustaceans, which are generally popular and widely available at the market. Pork is hardly eaten in this part of Madagascar, and so the prohibition on eating it did not pose a problem either.

Staying Away

Another aspect of the Adventist way of life that does not result in any particular problems or tensions is the nonpractice of spirit possession, divination and "Malagasy medicine" (*odygasy*) involving the consultation of a traditional healer. The Adventists' lack of involvement in these practices is unproblematic, both for the Adventists themselves and for other people, because—unlike with regard to exhumation and sacrifice—it is not considered imperative for everybody to engage in spirit possession, divination or traditional medicine. In fact, it was only a small minority of local people who were involved in spirit possession, for example, with many Protestants disapproving of it as well.

Seventh-day Adventists also do not celebrate any of the traditional Christian festivities (Christmas, Easter, Pentecost), not because they disagree with their significance, but because they consider their timing to be of Catholic doing and to lack any evidence in the Bible. Adventists also go their separate way on New Year's Eve, partly because, according to Adventist theology, the year ends at sunset rather than at midnight, but more importantly because the Adventists disapprove of the heavy drinking generally involved in local turn-of-the-year parties. Instead, the Adventists have their own, quiet celebration of the New Year after sunset in church. They don't seem to object to the date of the beginning of the year itself. It should be noted, however, that neither Christmas nor Easter nor New Year's celebrations are socially very significant events in the local society. Thus the fact that the Adventists go their separate way on these occasions is not seen to be problematic.

Moving Toward the Problematic

Among the Adventist consumption taboos, there is one that, although not problematic in itself, can become so because it amounts to a public statement of belonging to the Adventist community and, implicitly, of not belonging to the non-Adventist community. This is the prohibition to drink alcohol.

Lambek has suggested that one has to understand taboos "less as facts than as acts" (1992a: 246). He interprets the keeping of a particular taboo as a "performative act in the sense that it brings into being and maintains—embodies—a particular [. . .] moral state" (1992a: 253). Following Lambek, I want to suggest that by abstaining from alcohol, the Adventists make a statement to themselves and to others about who they are and, equally importantly, about who they are not (anymore).[2]

The difference between being a teetotaler, on the one hand, and not consuming shrimps or other types of food, on the other, is that alcohol consumption forms part of socially significant activities, while eating crustaceans does not. Local families regularly call on their close and more distant kin to join them harvesting rice or to help with other big jobs that need doing such as collecting palm leaves in the forest for roof building. On such occasions, the generous provision of alcohol is the helpers' pay at the end of a hard day's work, and it is likely that numerous people will get drunk. For the local Adventists, this is a problem, because even if they don't drink themselves, they do not consider it proper to be part of an occasion involving the excessive consumption of alcohol. For the same reason, it is difficult for them to call on their non-Adventist kin to help them with a day's work, because these kin clearly expect to be offered large amounts of rum in return for their efforts. My family in Sahameloka once offered to provide a meal of chicken instead of alcohol, which, too, would have been quite a treat for many people. Yet, the offer was rejected. There is no rule that a person must drink alcohol; but there is a rule that at certain social gatherings, alcohol must be provided for those who wish to consume it. Thus the Adventists' teetotaling attitude is problematic not because they themselves do not drink alcohol—which nobody would mind—but because it excludes them from certain social activities that necessarily involve alcohol consumption. Moreover, such joint working endeavors of kin often take place on a Saturday, in which case the Adventists cannot take part anyway. Their absence at such collective events does, however, not go unnoticed by their non-Adventist kin.

Every three months, the Seventh-day Adventists perform communion, which, in Adventist practice worldwide, is followed by a ritual during which the baptized members of the church wash each other's feet in imitation of the Last Supper (this is the only gender-segregated practice in the church). In Maroantsetra, this ritual normally takes place during an Adventist district meeting, which tends to attract several hundred, and sometimes up to a thousand, church members mainly from the countryside. This means that the actual service has to be held in the open for lack of space inside the church. The ritual of communion-cum-footwashing is, like being teetotal, not problematic in itself, but can become so because of it being a public statement. Only baptized members of the church are allowed to take part in this ritual, creating a distinctive sense of inclusion in the Adventist community. During the ritual, the baptized church members are indeed a "club of the religiously qualified" (Weber's definition of a Protestant sect ["Verein der religiös Qualifizierten"; my translation; 1920: 221]). It was only during communion that it was ever politely suggested to me that, as a non-Adventist, I should sit at the back. After having washed each other's feet, all the church members gather in a big circle. From this I was likewise excluded (I was allowed to stand nearby and observe). After several songs and prayers, the circle is dissolved by way of a snake-like movement (with the circle moving back on itself), during which everyone shakes everyone else's hand. Especially when standing in the circle, the sense of being part of the Adventist, as opposed to any other, community is palpable. And since the footwashing as well as the singing and praying that follow always take place in the open—and since the Adventist church is in the center of town—the sense of exclusive community thus created is visible to bypassers as well.

Baptism represents a similar situation. The Malagasy Adventists distinguish between *intéressés*—people interested in Adventism—and *membres*. Although an "interested person" may in fact be more committed than a member, the dividing line between them, marked by baptism by full immersion, is clear. Since baptism ought to be the result of a conscious and properly thought-through decision by the person concerned, Seventh-day Adventists only practice adult baptism, which in Madagascar is interpreted to mean people at least 14 years old.[3] Children are believed to be without sin anyway and thus there is no need for them to be ritually cleansed.

Intéressés can participate in Bible study and other activities in church, but only baptized members are allowed to take on duties and offices and to play a leading role during church services. Although baptism is not considered an automatic ticket to heaven, it does mark one's inclusion in the local, and the global, community of Adventists. As such it represents an important turning point at the end of a sometimes lengthy process of deciding whether and when to join the church. But baptism is not only a statement to oneself; it is also a public marker of one's identity. It was not by chance that mass baptisms in Maroantsetra took place in the sea rather than inside the church, and that they were preceded by a march through the center of town. To get baptized is to publicly announce: "I have made up my mind." And indeed, baptism is considered by the local church members as a signal of the definite end of any involvement with *fomban-drazana* (exhumation, cattle sacrifice . . .).

Being Torn

Repeated prayer, Bible study, the nonconsumption of shrimps and pork and nonparticipation in Christmas celebrations do not involve confrontation between Adventist and "ordinary" local conceptions and are thus unproblematic not only for the wider community, but also for the Adventists themselves. This is, however, not so in situations when Adventist and "ordinary" rules and values are conflictive, or at least different, in which case individual Adventists are forced to navigate their way through these conflicting demands. Such navigation at times involves a considerable amount of uncertainty.

The Choice of a Spouse

One decision every Adventist has to make and that involves consideration of both Adventist and traditional rules, and the weighing of these against each other, is the choice of a spouse.

The only Seventh-day Adventist decrees regarding marriage require monogamy and legal recognition of the union. However, the global church also strongly discourages members from marrying a non-Adventist spouse. The only traditional marriage rule is that of exogamy. The exogamy rule is not clearly defined, but it is simple in principle: as long as anybody alive knows, or suspects, that a potential couple is related, either through their mothers' or their fathers' side, the couple are considered kin and as such cannot marry each other. Consequently, young men in search of brides often consult elders for the purpose of making sure they do not marry one of their kin out of ignorance.

With regard to monogamy, the local Adventists accept the Adventist decree. In the rare cases when a man has more than one wife, he must give up all of them except for one before he can be baptized (I know of one such case in Sahameloka; polygamy, though not unknown, is rare in this part of Madagascar). For young people looking for a spouse, then, there are two rules: "do not marry kin" and "marry within the church." Thus, ideally, the future spouse of a young Adventist starting to make plans to get married will be another church member, or at least someone not disinclined toward becoming one, who, at the same time, is not kin. In theory, these two rules are perfectly compatible, but in real life it is not always easy for young people to find a spouse who fulfills both criteria, and whom they like enough to marry, especially as people tend to find their partners in nearby villages. In case of conflict between the criterion of exogamy and that of church affiliation, the former, as an imperative local rule, clearly has more weight than the latter. Local Adventists consider marriage between church members to be the ideal, not only because they aspire to spiritual harmony between the two spouses, but also because of potential pragmatic problems, such as the religious education of their children, which may arise if only one of the spouses belongs to the Adventist church. But because this ideal can not always be realized, and because the rule of exogamy must not be compromised, it is acceptable in the region of Maroantsetra for an Adventist to be married to someone not belonging to the church, as long as their relationship is legalized. Failure to respect the exogamy rule is not looked upon so kindly. There was one young couple among Sahameloka's Adventists who were considered by everyone to be kin, albeit distant ones. This definitely caused eyebrows to be raised. In fact they had met at an Adventist meeting, and when later weighing up the local as opposed to the Adventist rule, they had, untypically, decided in favor of the latter.

There were a few church members I knew whose spouses had a different church affiliation or no religious affiliation at all. This tended to turn out to be a problem, and, in one case I am familiar with, resulted in a young man leaving the Adventist church altogether. Another case concerned one of the most committed members of the church in Maroantsetra who was married to a woman who was herself an equally committed member of the Jehovah's Witnesses (he, too, used to be a Jehovah's Witness, but then converted to Adventism; she didn't follow). They had four young children and I understand there was a certain amount of quarrelling between the two about who was going to take the children to church. However, as far as one can know, they seemed to live quite happily with their different church affiliations, which obviously did not do any harm to their respective religious commitment.

It is also important to note that the Adventist requirement of civil marriage[4] does not substitute, but instead supplements, the traditional marriage ceremony (*orimbato*). The local Adventists are entirely in favor of the latter as it does not involve communication with the ancestors, but simply represents the public announcement of a marriage and of the contract between the two families involved. They are also in favor of traditional marriage, because it is "good" ancestral custom. Traditional marriage is *fomban-drazana* not in the Adventist sense of "false religion," but *fomban-drazana* in the ordinary sense referring to everything the living generations have learnt from those who lived before them.

Working the Land

Concerning the choice of a spouse, Adventism basically adds a rule, which young church members ought to consider on top of other existing rules, but this addition is essentially nonconflictive. In contrast, the activity of working one's land confronts the members of the church with a fundamental incompatibility between Adventist and local concepts.

It is almost impossible to overemphasize the significance of the concept of land being passed on from one generation to another in Madagascar. One of the most important aspects of honoring one's ancestors is to farm the land one has, ultimately, inherited from them.[5] The Adventists share this concept.

However, working one's ancestral land is not only a matter of sowing and harvesting rice; what is equally important is to farm the land on the proper days, following ancestral rules. And this is where the problem for local Adventists lies, because Adventist and "traditional" work days do not correspond at all.

The Adventist rule is simple: work six days of the week and rest on the seventh, the Sabbath (Saturday). The prohibition to work, and to handle money, on the Sabbath is the most important of all Adventist *fady* (taboos) and may only be compromised if someone needs urgent help.

Traditional rules are more complex. The concept of there being particular days of the week when it is *fady* to work one's land, is as prominent throughout Madagascar as are consumption taboos. There are two kinds of work day taboos. The first one is ancestry-specific (*andro fady*), that is, a particular ancestry is not allowed to do any work on a particular day of the week, especially on their rice fields, but sometimes in the forest as well. The second is specific to particular pieces of land (*fadin' ny tany*) that must not be worked on, by anybody, on certain days of the week. There is always a particular reason for both types of taboo, such as one of the ancestors having been bitten by a crocodile while working on a Tuesday causing this particular ancestor to pronounce it *fady* for his descendants to work on a Tuesday. Often, the precise reason for the *fady* is not known by those who follow such work day taboos, yet it is undisputed that they were given to people by their ancestors and that therefore they must be respected. Transgression of a work day *fady* entails a serious risk of provoking the anger of the ancestors and hence of misfortune. People can easily come up with examples of such ancestral punishment. Every ancestry has its own work day taboos; but in Sahameloka, these invariably concerned Tuesday or Friday, less often Thursday or Sunday, but never Saturday. On the contrary, Saturday is considered by the local population a very good day for working, which is why joint working endeavors were often undertaken on Saturdays.

In principle, membership of the Adventist church invalidates both types of traditional work day *fady*. This is so not because there is anything wrong *per se* with not working on a Tuesday, but because following such ancestral *fady* implies that one attributes to the dead the power to punish those who do not follow their rules. However, while living in Sahameloka, I observed that most local Adventists continued to keep the *fady* of their respective ancestries. When asked explicitly about this, they would always claim not to keep ancestral taboo days, but I often found them at home on such days in spite of such claims. Why they stay at home is not entirely clear. The reason they give themselves, when confronted directly, is that they haven't gone to work on the fields for the sake of good kin relations. Transgression of a *fady* may trigger indiscriminate reprisal, affecting not only the transgressor, but anybody subject to the particular *fady* being ignored. In addition, most of Sahameloka's Adventists are young people and keeping ancestral *fady* is a matter of respect toward their senior kin. Moreover, being young, they often work land that is not their own yet, and so, by disregarding ancestral taboos they would risk losing the basis of their subsistence.

My host family in Sahameloka seemed to oscillate between keeping and not keeping their ancestral taboo days. Mostly, the rice fields were not visited on a Tuesday as it is *fady* for both Papan' i Claude's and Maman' i Claude's family to do so. For Papan' i Claude, Friday was also *fady* to work, and for Maman' i Claude also Sunday, but the family considered neither of these two days as strong (*mahery*) a taboo day as Tuesday and thus basically ignored them. From time to time though, they also went off to their rice fields on a Tuesday, clearly hoping, however, that nobody would notice. One such Tuesday, unfortunately, Maman' i Claude's father, who is neither in the Adventist nor any other church, turned up for a visit—of course, Tuesday is his work day *fady* as well and so he has time on his hands. He was not pleased, to say the least, to find out that his daughter was working the land he had given her on a Tuesday, because, as I said, disregard for taboos may not only entail punishment of the actual transgressor, but may result in indiscriminate reprisal for anybody who is subject to a taboo. On their return from the fields, Maman' i Claude was visibly embarrassed about what had happened and anxious about the possible consequences of her behavior.

Pragmatic considerations certainly play a role in making the Adventists decide whether or not to work on a particular day. However, we must also consider the possibility that the local Adventists are actually unclear as to what is the right thing to do. As I said earlier, the activity of working the land is inseparable from doing so on the proper days. The work and its timing are two sides of the same coin. But while working the land is *fomban-drazana* in the sense of "following ancestral custom," and is thus morally right (as are traditional marriage ceremonies or respecting elders), the keeping of ancestral taboo days is also associated with *fomban-drazana* in the sense of "false religion" and is thus highly problematic. It is the simultaneous presence of both these interpretations of what it is to work one's ancestral land, which causes uncertainty among local Adventists as to whether or not they ought to respect traditional taboos.

Finally, we must consider the possibility that the clarity of Adventist teachings does not always result in equal clarity of the local Adventists' interpretation of matters. This is illustrated by the issue of where Adventists want to be buried.

The Graveyard Issue

In chapter 9, I discussed two Adventist propositions related to the process of the diabolization of alleged ancestral power. The first proposition is, the reader will recall, that "the dead are nothing but a pile of rotting bones" and that therefore, it is ridiculous to attribute them with any power to affect living people's lives, as Malagasy people generally do. However, there are at least some moments when local Adventists, contrary to their explicit assertions, seem to be not all that sure as to the state of the dead.

Such uncertainty was particularly noticeable with regard to one issue that the members of the church in Sahameloka repeatedly discussed among themselves, namely the question as to where they themselves should one day be buried. Many of them expressed the wish that the village's Adventists have their own burial ground, rather than being buried among their kin. The desire for an Adventist burial ground, where people would be buried irrespective of ancestry, stems from the fact that the members of the church know perfectly well that their non-Adventist kin will eventually exhume them, even against the Adventists' explicit will. They will do so as a means of self-protection against potential ancestral wrath, for they are sure that the Adventists, too, like everybody else, will become powerful ancestors able to strike the living with misfortune if displeased. I know of two cases in the area where a child of Adventist parents was exhumed by its non-Adventist kin against the explicit will of its parents.[6] However, in spite of this being a serious concern for Sahameloka's Adventists, they do not raise the issue of a separate burial ground with their non-Adventist kin, since they know perfectly well that the elders would never give permission for such a project. But if the Adventists think, as they endlessly emphasize, that the dead are nothing but rotting bones, why should it make any difference to them whether or not their own bones, or those of their children, are exhumed? If for them exhumation is simply a pointless exercise of digging up a bundle of bones, why should they be so concerned about it? When I put this question to Papan' i Silivie, who was particularly concerned about, and eloquent on, this issue, he hesitated a few moments, seeming to look to Maman' i Claude, who was also present at that discussion, for help with answering the question. Finally he replied that it was taboo (*fady*) for Seventh-day Adventists to be exhumed, because this would suggest that there is more to bones than just bones, which in turn would be equivalent to invoking the devil. However, I am sure that what I was witnessing at that moment was an instance of uncertainty as to the state of the dead, an uncertainty that was the result of Papan' i Silivie and Maman' i Claude looking at the world through their Adventist spectacles, while at the same time also continuing to look at human remains in the way their non-Adventist kin do, namely as something infinitely more than just a pile of rotting bones.

Powerful Land

I have referred in this chapter to numerous decisions the Adventists have to make in the course of their everyday lives, and to how these are influenced by Adventist values and rules as well as "traditional" ones. The kinds of decision I have discussed so far concern situations and problems on which the church takes an explicit view, although this does not necessarily mean, as we saw, that it is always entirely clear to local church members how they should act. Decision-making processes are, however, even more ambiguous and marked by even more uncertainty when local Adventists are confronted with problems that Adventist doctrine does not directly address. In order to illustrate this point, I have chosen the example of "powerful land."

Papan' and Maman' i Claude owned a piece of semi-cleared forest a long way from Sahameloka, which they thought of as a kind of fall back for when their land close to the village might have become impractically small due to its division among kin. The piece of land next to theirs was owned by a man who had entirely cleared the forest on his patch, built a proper house on the cleared land and who had now lived there for several years by himself. One morning, this man turned up at our house and offered to sell his piece of already nicely cleared forest land to Maman' and Papan' i Claude. The reason why he wanted to move away was because the land had turned out to be "powerful" (*mahery*). Land said to be powerful is thought to be controlled by a supernatural force called *tsiny*, which is responsible for the misfortune and bad luck afflicting the people living on it. The present owner of the land in question complained about constant illness. Since there is nothing one can do about "powerful" land other than to abandon it, he wanted to move away. However, he quite understandably preferred to sell the land rather than let it lie fallow. He approached Papan' and Maman' i Claude for two reasons. First, he assumed that they might be interested to buy the land since his land joined up with, and had many advantages over, theirs. Second, he knew that nobody would buy allegedly "powerful" land except for, possibly, Adventists, who, he was aware, thought themselves to be protected from such forces by God. The offer was indeed very attractive for Papan' and Maman' i Claude. But at the same time, they felt extremely uncertain as to whether they dared to buy *tany mahery* (powerful land). They knew of another piece of "powerful" land that had had a negative effect on the three different families who had lived there in succession, but on which a fourth, *Adventist*, family, had since lived without encountering any problems. Yet they were also clearly afraid to buy the land and expose themselves to its power. For an entire week, the issue was discussed back and forth: "Shall we? Shan't we? Shall we? Shan't we?" Maman' and Papan' i Claude were losing sleep over this problem, and the decision they finally reached did not put an end to their uncertainty. They decided to buy the land and give it a try. But this decision was clearly a risk. If no misfortune hit them, they would keep it; if it turned out still to be "powerful," they would attempt to sell it, possibly to migrants who are thought to be less vulnerable to attacks by local *tsiny*. Maman' and Papan' i Claude by no means dismissed the possibility of the land being *mahery*. But they hoped that God would protect them from the force of the land if they accepted this test of their courage. However, so they repeatedly told themselves, they would have to be especially diligent in their Bible study and always attend all church services, in order to secure God's protection. As it finally turned out, they never bought the land, because it was too expensive, while they had hoped it would be cheap because of it being "powerful."

The problem of having to decide whether or not to buy "powerful" land is not one that local Adventists face very often. However, in the course of time, they do encounter numerous situations that necessitate the same kind of process of navigating one's way through a sea of conflicting signals.

Chapter 12

Kinship

In September of 1999, a fire swept through a town in northern Madagascar where sapphires had recently been found, which had therefore attracted large numbers of migrants from different parts of Madagascar intent on trying their luck prospecting. Many of these migrants had become members of a New Church called "Jesus Saves" (Jesosy Mamonjy). As the fire ravaged the town destroying people's houses, Jesus Saves converts ran to their new meeting hall and prayed that it be spared from the flames. They made no effort to help their neighbors to extinguish the fire. Moreover, to the anger and distress of the local population, they had built their new hall on the *eastern* side of the town's lake totally disregarding the fact that it was strictly taboo (*fady*) to construct buildings there. Such inconsiderate behavior, as Walsh tells us in his account of events (Walsh 2002), was shocking to the town's inhabitants and created a deep gulf between Jesus Saves Christians and the rest of the local population. Had the Seventh-day Adventists in the district of Maroantsetra heard of the migrants' conduct, they would have been equally shocked, because their attitude to community living is completely opposed to this. On one occasion in Sahameloka, a young boy failed to return home by the time it got dark. As he had still not been found by about nine o'clock, by which time most villagers were in bed, the *anjoma*—a large sea shell used by the village president for the purpose of attracting people's attention—was blown. Everyone immediately came out of doors to see what was wrong. As people learnt what had happened, a troop of young men was put together in order to find the lost child. The search party was successful and came back into the village an hour or so later, carrying the little boy like a hero on their shoulders, singing songs of joy and togetherness to which everyone still up joined in with. It went without saying that the village's Adventists participated in the search just like everyone else, and that they formed part of the celebrated unity.

This chapter explores from different perspectives the social relations the local members of the Adventist church are involved in. In a prelude to the key questions to be addressed, I will briefly look at how Seventh-day Adventists live within the wider local society of which they are part. We will see how, in complete contrast to the aggressive behavior of Jesus Saves members described by Walsh, the Adventists in Maroantsetra and Sahameloka make every effort to blend in with their social environment and to not offend anybody, if at all possible, while remaining truthful to their religious commitment.[1] Then we move on to issues of kinship to which the bulk of the chapter is dedicated, exploring, on the one hand, the relationship between members of the Adventist church and their non-Adventist kin and, on the other hand, the nature of the relations among the members of the church.

Prelude: Living within the Wider Society

The first indication that the local Adventists do not live in isolation from the rest of society is the fact that, neither in town nor in any of the district's villages, are they spatially segregated, but instead continue to live within established settlement patterns after their conversion to Adventism. I have never heard of any Adventist family even making an attempt to do otherwise.[2] They interact with their neighbors on a daily basis, be these Adventists or not, much like everybody else. When Maman' i Beby needed some washing powder or soap, she called on our neighbors' little girl, sending her off to buy what she needed and sometimes rewarding her with a slice of pineapple or some other goody. When our lemur, whom we illegally kept as a pet, got caught high up in the lychee tree (he was attached to a string), we called the boy from next door to climb up the tree and get the terrified animal down. Similarly, our neighbors in Sahameloka borrowed tools from us and used our washing line. Papan' i Beby's relationship with his work colleagues was not clouded by the fact that he was the only one who was ever seen working on a Sunday, but never on a Saturday. During our daily trip to the market, Maman' i Beby would always keep stopping and chatting to people who had nothing to do with the Adventist church, and she spent many an afternoon visiting a neighbor in hospital or other people she knew. The children of both families in which I lived had Adventist and non-Adventist friends alike, and there was no attempt on the part of their parents, or those of their friends, to stop such interaction. It was a non-Adventist girl who regularly came to pick up Beby on her way to school and who often plaited her hair.

Kiki often played cards with his mates from school on our veranda, and the young boys of my family in Sahameloka were always playing with their neighbors' kids.

Not only are church members friendly to other people, they also make an extra effort to fulfill their social roles and duties as neighbors and coresidents. In contrast to exhumations and sacrifices, during which people ritually invoke their ancestors, wakes and funerals in this part of Madagascar do not involve the invocation of, or communication with, ancestors, at least not in an explicit and visible sense. Therefore, these are the only mortuary-related practices Seventh-day Adventists can, and do, attend. Arguably, the members of the Adventist church *construe* such events as wakes and funerals to be free of "ancestor worship," in order to be able to attend. Indeed, they are very careful to do *at least* their expected share when participating in the wakes and funerals of close and distant neighbors, friends and acquaintances, work colleagues and others. In fact, it has always been my impression that they were extra alert not to neglect their social obligations in this respect thereby sending out a message that their nonparticipation in exhumation and cattle sacrifice was not intended to disrupt social relations.

Unfortunately—from the Adventist point of view—Protestant and Catholic weddings in Sahameloka almost always took place on a Saturday. Because of the prohibition to do any kind of work during the Sabbath, Adventist kin cannot help with cooking or other preparations. However, they—as well as many Adventists not closely related to the groom or bride—would always make a point of contributing money to the event and of attending the wedding meal at lunchtime between the first and second part of the Sabbath church service. On one occasion, the morning part of the Sabbath service ended early and the afternoon part started late, explicitly so as to enable church members to attend the wedding that was taking place that day.

What, and, Who, are Kin?

Membership of the Adventist church in Maroantsetra and Sahameloka has little impact on the daily relationships church members have with neighbors, friends and other people with whom they interact. But what are the implications of church membership on the relations between kin? We have already, at numerous points, encountered the Adventist prohibition to participate in exhumation, cattle sacrifice and other ritual practices that involve communication with the ancestors. And I have already noted that in the Malagasy context, where the relationship between the living and the dead is extremely important, such nonparticipation is the source of considerable tensions between Adventists and their non-Adventist kin. It must be added though, that the tensions thus caused are not equally prominent throughout the year. Ancestral rituals usually take place during the course of a four-month period (December–March), and so the tensions aroused by the Adventists' nonparticipation come to the fore during that time. During the rest of the year these tensions, though not absent, are muted.

In this chapter I am concerned with the impact of these tensions on the day-to-day relations between Adventist and non-Adventist kin, or, in other words, the impact the Adventists' refusal to ritually relate to their dead kin has on the relationship between the living.

Kin Are Kin

There is a generic term in Malagasy used to refer to all one's kin on both one's mother's and one's father's side: *havana*. In defense of Fortes's view that kinship is intrinsically moral, Bloch (1973) has discussed how, among the Merina of highland Madagascar, being *havana* implies unconditional, long-term reciprocity, security and support. This is also true in the area of Maroantsetra, as it is elsewhere in Madagascar. Like other Betsimisaraka (cf. Cole 2001: 71), people in Maroantsetra reckon kinship through both their father's and their mother's descent lines, "as far back as anybody can remember," people say, and they refer to all of these people as their *havana*. *Havana* are people one has the right to rely on by virtue of being *havana*. If someone falls ill in Maroantsetra or Sahameloka, it is their *havana* who care for the patient, who pay for the necessary expenses, who bring food to the hospital and who clean the patient's body. If somebody needs financial support or a place to stay, it is kin one approaches for help. Acting as kin is not a matter of choice, but a matter of course. It is not a voluntary, but a compulsory, commitment that one cannot shed except in the most unusual circumstances. In other words, *havana* are connected, but also stuck with each other, by the very fact that they are *havana*. Although in reality kin quarrel quite a lot and there is a fair amount of conflict among them, the ideal, at least, is mutual, unconditional support.

The Adventists' refusal to participate in "ancestral work" (*asan-drazana*) done for even their closest kin often entails severe social consequences. These can range from covert tension among kin, to open conflict and, in rare cases, to the disinheritance of members of the Adventist church. The degree of conflict depends on a number of aspects, but there is no doubt that joining the Adventist church carries the potential to provoke serious trouble. This is recognized by everyone in, and outside, the church. For some who are considering the idea of joining the church, potential trouble with kin is a deterrent important enough to stop them from actually doing so. Others—like the young man from Sahameloka called Christa whom I introduced in chapter 4—leave the church soon after having joined it because tensions with their kin turn out to be unbearable. Many people, however, are willing to accept the social costs involved in being a Seventh-day Adventist.

The situation for those who join the church and remain in it varies considerably. In some cases, their relationship with their non-Adventist kin is seriously damaged, sometimes to the extent that everyday contact becomes virtually nonexistent even among kin who live in the same village. Under normal circumstances, such a situation is quite unthinkable. Papan' i Claude is a case in point and I will come back to him later in the chapter. However, in the great majority of cases, both sides make an effort to iron out the tensions caused by the problems surrounding the ancestors as much as possible, because, after all, one is *havana*. Although around the time when an exhumation actually takes places, the relations between Adventist and non-Adventist kin may be rather frosty, during the rest of the year, they visit each other regularly, share meals, chat, look after each other's children and so on. The Adventists' willingness to keep ancestral work day taboos (*fady*) certainly helps promote good will, although, as we saw, the Saturday problem remains unresolved.

One morning in Sahameloka, before setting off to work in the fields, we were reading the daily Morning Watch, a short passage from the Bible that serves as a kind of thought for the day. That morning it read: "If any man come to me, and hate not his father, and mother, and wife, and children, and brethren [brothers], and sisters, yea, and his own life also, he cannot be my disciple" (St. Luke 14: 26).[3] Consternation all around. After a few moments' silence filled with a deep sense of incomprehension and even embarrassment at what was being suggested in this verse, Maman' i Claude finally said: "That is not clear to me" (*tsy mazava amin'nahy*), an expression that is often used to state disagreement or disapproval, perhaps comparable to the English "I don't get it!"

> "You know," she continued after a moment's reflection, "the Bible is like a forest: there are all kinds of trees and plants in a forest. There are many, many good trees in a forest, but there are also many which are not all that good. And so it is with the Bible. Most of what is written in the Bible is good and true, but there are some verses

which are not all that good. It is just like with a forest. One has to choose the good ones."

Maman' i Claude's interpretation of the passage in question is clearly unorthodox as it challenges the literal truth of the Bible—this was one of the extremely rare moments I witnessed when the paradigm of the literal truth of the Bible was rejected by a member of the church—and someone like Papan' i Beby, not to speak of the pastor, would have been quite shocked at Maman' i Claude's statement. However, this particular Bible verse is certainly a bad tree in her eyes. And this is so, because it attacks one of the most crucial principles of the social organization of Malagasy societies, namely kinship.

Indeed, kinship ties continue to play a very important role within the lives of the local Seventh-day Adventists. The following example provides a strong case in point.

Kiki's Journey

At the time of my fieldwork, Maman' and Papan' i Beby and their children had lived in Maroantsetra for 18 years. Kiki and Beby were born there and had never lived anywhere else. The family originates from another town further south along the east coast and has no kin in Maroantsetra or anywhere nearby. Because of this, and also because of the family's intense participation in church affairs, most of their social contacts are with other Adventists. However, in the course of the past years, the family has experienced many disappointments regarding these contacts, or at least this is how things look from their point of view.

While I lived with them, Kiki was in his penultimate year at school approaching his *baccalauréat*, and he intended to continue his studies at a university thereafter. However, there was a shortage of teachers at his school in Maroantsetra, and certain subjects, English for example, were simply not taught even though they were on the curriculum for the *baccalauréat* exams. Therefore, Kiki's parents, who place great value on the formal education of their children, decided to send him to the town of Toamasina, which is the capital of the eastern province of the same name. Toamasina is very close to where Maman' and Papan' i Beby originally come from and where many of their kin live, *none* of whom, however, are Seventh-day Adventists. Having decided to send Kiki "back home" for the final year of his secondary education, the question arose as to where exactly they should send him to stay. Following Betsimisaraka kinship rules, the proper place for Kiki to stay would have been with Papan' i Beby's younger brother Gervain. Gervain, because he is Papan' i Beby's younger brother, is

Kiki's "little/younger father" (*papa hely*), and in that capacity, Gervain is responsible for Kiki just as if Kiki was his biological son. However, Gervain is away from home for most of the year due to the fact that he is employed on a French ship, which takes him to far-away countries. Theoretically, Kiki could have stayed with Gervain's wife who lives in Toamasina throughout the year. Unfortunately though, from the point of view of Kiki's parents, her lifestyle is rather dubious: she drinks, she smokes and in general does not lead a lifestyle deemed respectable by Kiki's parents. In short, Gervain's wife was not exactly going to provide the perfect environment for a young Adventist, so Maman' and Papan' i Beby reckoned. Therefore, in order to avoid possible bad influences on the boy, Kiki was sent to stay with Maman' i Beby's brother who, despite not being an Adventist, leads a lifestyle that is acceptable to Kiki's parents. By taking that decision, they passed over not only Papan' i Beby's younger brother Gervain. They also passed over another of Papan' i Beby's close relatives in town, namely his nephew (the son of his elder sister) who, in their family, is second in line after Gervain in his responsibility to care for Kiki. Papan' i Beby's nephew promptly complained about Kiki not staying with him. Kiki's parents had chosen not to send their son to stay with him because he, too, consumed a considerable amount of alcohol, while Maman' i Beby's brother with whom Kiki was sent to stay, only drank at parties. Although drinking at parties is not ideal either in Adventist eyes, it is within the limits of acceptable behavior. A few weeks after Kiki's arrival in Toamasina, after having heard the complaints voiced by Papan' i Beby's relatives, it was finally decided that Kiki would stay principally with Maman' i Beby's brother as planned, but that he would spend the weekends with Papan' i Beby's nephew. And this is what happened in the end.

I have summarized a decision-making process that took several months to mature, during which time Maman' and Papan' i Beby discussed the problem as to whom Kiki was to stay with in Toamasina over and over again. Among all his relatives, there was no really suitable place for him from their point of view, and the solution they found was clearly a compromise. At no point, however, was the possibility of sending Kiki to some *unrelated Adventist* family even considered, despite the difficulty in finding an appropriate home for Kiki among their kin. Given the situation and taking into account the family's strong involvement in, and commitment to, the church for 18 years, one would have expected the possibility of sending Kiki to stay with other Adventists to be, at least, considered. However, it never was.

Kiki's journey shows clearly how relations between the Adventists and their non-Adventist kin remain of central importance despite the strain put on them by the Adventists distancing themselves from ritual practices. What the example of finding a home for Kiki illustrates is exactly the unconditional, long-term reciprocity typical of the relationship between *havana* (kin). And because support among kin is unconditional, because it lies in the very nature of kinship, it continues to exist between Adventist and non-Adventist kin even when the latter are at a loss to understand, or find it difficult to accept, that the former refuse to take part in kin-based ritual practices such as exhumation and cattle sacrifice.

In my account of Kiki moving to Toamasina, I have left one detail unmentioned, namely the fact that Kiki's parents never even bothered to inform their relatives of his impending arrival, let alone to ask them whether he could come and stay. I repeatedly asked Maman' and Papan' i Beby whether they had written to their relatives in Toamasina. "No, that is not necessary, we are family" (*fianakaviana*), they replied. And so, one day in September, Kiki and his father packed their bags and set off on their strenuous journey southward. Upon their unexpected arrival at their relatives' house, they were, so Papan' i Beby assured me afterward, greeted enthusiastically and Kiki was welcomed as a new member of the household as if it meant nothing to have someone sleeping and studying in one's living room—which is where Kiki had to stay for lack of other space—for an entire year. Not only did Kiki arrive without any previous warning, but it went without saying that his relatives would pay for his food, clothe him and cover other expenses that might arise during the time he would stay with them. It is this kind of support one has a right to expect of one's *havana*, and in particular of one's close family (*fianakaviana*). Despite the difficulties of finding a suitable home for Kiki, it was unthinkable for Maman' and Papan' i Beby not to send him to stay with kin. Equally, the latter expected them to do so, as the "fight" over who exactly Kiki was going to stay with illustrates. If Kiki's parents had sent him to an unrelated Adventist family, this would have been very offensive to their relatives in town; it would almost have amounted to a declaration of wanting to break kin relations.[4]

Head of Ancestry

Within his father's ancestry, Kiki is not just anybody, he is its future head. Papan' i Beby is currently head of their ancestry, but for the time being his older sister has been entrusted with carrying out his duties in that capacity. This is because Papan' i Beby has lived away from home for many years and because he is not expected to return until retirement in another ten years or so. It is also because his only brother Gervain is away most of the year. However, Papan' i Beby must always be consulted about the concerns of his ancestry, and before any decisions can be taken, his kin must still obtain his approval. This is also the case concerning ritual practices, which the Adventists consider to be the work of the devil.[5] With regard to these, however, Papan' i Beby avoids his duty by telling his kin that he does not wish to be involved in any decisions to do with tombs or ancestors.

In his generation within the ancestry, Papan' i Beby is the only man who has a son—Kiki. Therefore, as the only "son of a son" of his generation, Kiki will be the successor to his father as head of the ancestry. Kiki's different relatives' claims that he ought to be staying with them were certainly voiced more vigorously because of his particular status within the ancestry. There are no two ways about Kiki's future role. And this he knows and dreads. Because Papan' i Beby has been temporarily substituted for as head of the ancestry by his older sister, it is all the more important for him and for the entire ancestry, that Kiki fulfill his role personally. Papan' and Maman' i Beby always insisted that he must do so, while poor 18-year-old Kiki was horrified and protested loudly that he would not leave Maroantsetra, where he had grown up, to be head of the ancestry in a place far away from home (these discussions happened before he ever left Maroantsetra for his studies). On top of his worries of having to leave his beloved hometown, he was particularly concerned about the anticipated problem of how to deal with "things ancestral." "Just keep your mouth well shut" (*afody tsara vavanao*), his mother instructed him.

Kiki's example not only demonstrates how Adventist and non-Adventist kin continue to rely on each other in ways that are typical of *havana*. But Maman' and Papan' i Beby's determination that Kiki must fulfill his role as head of the ancestry provides powerful evidence that the Adventists, too, like their non-Adventist kin, are absolutely clear about the importance of kinship ties and that they do not wish to jeopardize these any more than their commitment to the church makes inevitable.

A Complete Break with the Past?

Several recent studies of New Churches have argued that one of their key attractions is the possibility they offer to young, aspiring people to shed the weight of kinship and to move out into the (urban) modern world as individuals freed from burdensome traditional obligations, both moral and financial (Maxwell 1998b; Meyer 1998; Simpson 1998, 2003). Such a transformation of one's position in society is achieved by "making a complete break with the past" (Meyer 1998) and by replacing one's kin with a new Christian "spiritual family." To make a complete break with the past means to break with traditional practices, such as "ancestor worship," which many New Churches, among them the Seventh-day Adventists, tell people are of the devil. To make this break complete, it is morally legitimate to also break with those who continue to perform these devilish practices. The break with traditional obligations toward kin, then, is interpreted as a decision for God, and "the church becomes the believer's [new] extended family" (Maxwell 1998: 354).

As the example of Kiki and his parents makes clear, however, nothing could be further from the Malagasy Adventists' intentions than the desire to break with their kin. On the contrary, such a break represents a much dreaded scenario the realization of which they make every effort to avoid. Thus in the case of the Malagasy Adventists, the possibility of breaking away from kin obligations in order to find one's place in the modern world as a free individual does not represent an attraction of the Adventist church. Instead, the break with one's kin is a potential problem the members of the church wish did not exist.

What Exactly Are "Mpiara-Mivavaka"?

It is crystal clear, then, that kin, whether Adventist or not, continue to be kin. What is, however, considerably less clear for the local Adventists is the nature of the relationship between members of the church. The term church members use to express their relationship to fellow Seventh-day Adventists is *mpiara-mivavaka*, which literally means "people who pray together" or "people who go to the same church." If membership of the Adventist church does not in itself imply the loss of one's kin, then *mpiara-mivavaka* are obviously not conceptualized as a substitute for the former. But then, what *is* the relationship between *mpiara-mivavaka*? The answer to this question is anything but clear.

A Little Bit Like Kin

The global Seventh-day Adventist church embraces and advocates an ideology of equality across humankind. With regard to members of the church, it promotes strong ties of mutual support and love between them. Regardless of how one is related by descent, ethnic origin and nationality, skin color or any other features that otherwise serve to divide people into distinctive groups, baptized Seventh-day Adventists are conceptualized as "one big family" and as such are supposed to act with mutual love and in mutual support of each other at all times. The kind of support expected of the members of this family toward all its other members is reminiscent of the moral obligations among *havana*. Ideally, a member of the Adventist church should be able to unexpectedly knock at the door of another Adventist anywhere in the world and be welcomed like a brother or a sister. The reader might suspect that this is little more than empty rhetoric. However, to say so would paint too simple a picture. Although, as we will see later on, the reality of the relations between *mpiara-mivavaka* often does not live up to this ideal, the local Adventists do have certain expectations of other *mpiara-mivavaka*, which are reminiscent of expectations one has of one's kin. Here are some examples:

I mentioned earlier that kin regularly call upon each other to perform jobs that are better done in a large group. *Mpiara-mivavaka* do this as well. The house of Maman' and Papan' i Vangé was almost completely destroyed by the big cyclone. A few days before they were going to collect new palm leaves (which are very big and heavy) in the forest in order to rebuild their house, Vangé, their eldest son, visited all Adventist households in Sahameloka asking to "borrow the strong lads" (*mihindrana góño matanjaka*) to join in the forthcoming expedition. Many strong lads turned up and so the job got done in a day.

Mpiara-mivavaka can also be expected to put each other up, which, again, is normally typical of kin. On one occasion, Maman' and Papan' i Claude took me to Navana, which I had long wanted to see. Navana is a small town, or a big village, by the sea a day's walk from Sahameloka. Neither Papan' nor Maman' i Claude have any kin in Navana, and so upon our arrival, we went straight to the house of an Adventist family and asked to be put up for two nights. We expected to be welcomed and we were. However, we made sure not to impose on our hosts and contributed considerably more rice and fish toward our joint meals than the three of us consumed. Indeed, the sharing of food is a sign of mutual trust in Madagascar, since the danger of what is called *ody gasy*—Malagasy medicine, that is to say poison by witchcraft—is paramount. It was normal for us to bring rice as even kin often do so when visiting each other. However, had we been kin, we would not have been anxious not to be a burden on our hosts. Compare our concern in this situation with the care taken for Kiki by his kin over an entire year, which was provided without complaint by Kiki's kin and accepted by his parents as a matter of course. When we left Navana, we thanked our hosts emphatically. This would not have been necessary, indeed it would have been inappropriate, had we been kin.

Inter-Adventist solidarity is particularly marked in cases of illness. Whenever a member of the church is seriously ill, all *mpiara-mivavaka* are publicly encouraged, at the beginning or the end of a church service, to visit their "brother or sister" and to offer their support, which implies giving a small financial contribution to help toward the costs of medicine. In cases of hospitalization, money is collected in church. When Beby had to spend several days in hospital to have an appendix operation, it was—in the absence of kin—predominantly members of the Adventist church who came to visit her. *Mpiara-mivavaka* took the load off the family when they were keeping the obligatory 24-hour watch over the patient. And it was Maman' i Ominò, a *mpiara-mivavaka* and friend of the family, who stayed with Beby two out of the four nights, resting on a thin mat on the hard cement floor beside Beby's bed.

Mpiara-mivavaka may help each other with work, put each other up and take on the duty of watching over a patient in hospital, all of which are favors typically offered to one's *havana*. Moreover, on rare occasions, the members of the Adventist church publicly act as if they were a distinct kin group. I observed two such cases. On one occasion in Sahameloka the Adventist congregation pooled all their individual contributions to a wedding (rice, money) and handed them over to the groom's family as a group contribution on the part of the village's Adventists. During the festivities, all the different ancestries' contributions were publicly announced ("ancestry X gave this much rice and this much money, ancestry Y this much," and so on), with the Adventist congregation being listed separately. Hence on this occasion, the Adventists represented themselves, and were treated, almost like a separate ancestry.

The second instance I observed that involved something like a public declaration of kinship on the part of the Adventist congregation concerned the tragic death of a young member of the church in Maroantsetra. A 14-year-old boy, who was going to school in the town of Toamasina, died of food poisoning.[6] As soon as the news broke, many church members immediately went to the family's house to offer their support. And even though it was several days before the corpse actually arrived in Maroantsetra, the bereaved family was never without company from the moment the tragedy was heard about to the day of the actual burial. Neighbors, friends, kin and Adventists were all present throughout the many days of keeping the wake. However, it was the members of the church who carried the bulk of the burden of accompanying the family during this time of bereavement. One could even argue that, during these days, the Adventists were claiming the dead body of the boy as theirs, rather than agreeing to hand it over to his (almost entirely non-Adventist) kin. For it was members of the Adventist church who went to the airport to receive the dead boy and his mother, who had flown to Toamasina to bring him home. It was they who rushed forward as the mother stepped out of the airplane and collapsed with grief. It was the Adventist youth group, dressed in their uniforms, who carried the coffin from the airplane. It was they, too, who lifted the boy's dead body out of the coffin when it arrived at the family home and they who put it onto the bed decorated with white cloth, flowers and candles. The entire wake was strongly influenced by the presence of *mpiara-mivavaka*: songs from the Adventist song book were sung, prayers were spoken by the pastor and other members of the church. The Adventists took the lead, while everyone else present followed. The role the Adventist congregation played at the airport and during the wake can be understood as a public declaration of kinship, as it is normally the close kin of a dead person who perform the most important acts on such occasions. On the morning of the burial, a special service was held in the Adventist church before the boy's body was taken to be buried in his father's home village, according to local custom. It remains to be seen what will happen when it is time to exhume him.

But Only a Little Bit

At certain times, and in certain circumstances, the members of the Adventist church act a little bit like kin. But just how far does such "Adventist kinship" go, and can one really speak of kinship?

In English-speaking countries, Seventh-day Adventists refer to each other as "brothers and sisters." In Malagasy, there is no equivalent word to "brother" or "sister," as the terms used to address one's brother or one's sister are also used to refer to one's cousins (even distant ones). It is these kin terms, based on generation, which *mpiara-mivavaka* use to address each other.[7] Moreover, people in Maroantsetra and Sahameloka, as elsewhere in Madagascar, often employ kin terms such as brother/cousin or sister/cousin, child, uncle or aunt not only for real kin, but on the grounds of friendship or in an attempt to create friendship. Almost anyone, except for a complete stranger, can be called a "brother" or a "sister" without such usage implying the kind of reciprocal, supportive relationship ideally characteristic of real kin. Thus, in itself, the use of kin terms among *mpiara-mivavaka* does not imply that they relate to each other as if they were truly kin. Such terms of address merely indicate the existence of some kind of social relationship leaving undetermined the precise nature of the relationship.

Mpiara-mivavaka may sometimes act in ways typical of kin, but do they also consider each other as such? The clearest indicator that they do not is marriage. As mentioned earlier, the people around Maroantsetra, as other Betsimisaraka, follow strongly exogamous marriage rules. No *havana* (kin), whether related through their mothers' or their fathers' sides, can marry each other, if anybody has knowledge of such relatedness. At the same time, the Adventist church encourages its members to marry *mpiara-mivavaka* (fellow Adventists) and many do. The fact that they see no breach of local exogamy rules in marrying *mpiara-mivavaka* shows clearly that they do not consider each other kin. But even if this much is clear there is one more possible type of kinship one needs to consider: that of "artificial kin." In his ethnography of the Merina of highland Madagascar, Bloch distinguishes between genealogical kin, *havana*, and what he calls "artificial kinsmen" (1994a [1971]: 101; 1973: 78). The latter are called *havana mpifankatia*, which one might translate as "kin on the basis of mutual love." These are people who, although not kin to each other by descent, have chosen to enter into such a kin relationship with all the corresponding rights and obligations. There are certain differences between genealogical and "artificial" kin, but these need not concern us here (cf. Bloch 1973).

There is a similar concept of "chosen kin" among the population of the Maroantsetra district, although it is not a very prominent one, and I have little ethnographic data about such relations. "People made into kin" (*ólo atao havana*), as such persons are locally called, are just like proper *havana*, so I was told, apart from the fact that they are buried with their own genealogical kin. Indeed, it can be difficult to establish whether a particular person is another person's "real" or "chosen" kin, as, to all intents and purposes, they behave exactly the same. The act of equating "real" and "chosen" kin also extends to marriage rules, that is, "chosen" kin cannot marry each other either. Intra-Adventist marriages then imply that *mpiara-mivavaka* are not even considered "people made into kin."[8]

Emphasizing the Boundary

Marital practice makes it clear that *mpiara-mivavaka* do not consider each other as kin. Indeed, *mpiara-mivavaka* never refer to each other as *havana*, except, rarely, as "kin before God" (*havana amin' Andriamanitra*). At the same time, they have taken on board the Adventist ethos of reciprocal love and support among *mpiara-mivavaka*, and there is an expectation that, although *mpiara-mivavaka* are not kin, they ought to act almost as if they were. "No, we are not *havana*," they would respond to my questions, "our relationship is one of reciprocal love (*fifankatiavana*). *Havana* often quarrel, but *mpiara-mivavaka* all love each other (*mifankatia sintry jiaby*)." Without wishing to suggest that *mpiara-mivavaka* never act according to the received ideal, such statements struck me as being of a rather abstract nature, because what I observed was not all just love and support among *mpiara-mivavaka*.

The reader will recall Kiki's move to Toamasina and the problem of finding an appropriate home for him. Kiki's example illustrates two things. On the one hand, as I discussed, it shows that kin ties between Adventists and non-Adventists continue to be of central importance. On the other hand, it reveals a lack of support among *mpiara-mivavaka*, or at least a lack of the kind of support one can expect of one's *havana*, such as caring for a son over the course of an entire year. Remember that despite the difficulty in finding a suitable place among kin for Kiki to stay, the possibility of sending him to stay with unrelated members of the church was never even considered. This might have been, one could argue, the case because after all, there were relatives around, and close relatives at that—Papan' i Beby's brother, his nephew, Maman' i Beby's brother—so that there was simply no need to approach *mpiara-mivavaka* for support. However, after I had left Madagascar, Kiki's journey continued. He successfully passed the *bac* in Toamasina and went on to study law, as his parents wrote to tell me, at the university of Fianarantsoa in the southern highlands of Madagascar. Fianarantsoa is hundreds of kilometers away from Toamasina and even further from Maroantsetra, and the family has neither any distant relatives nor any other social contacts in Fianarantsoa. I was curious to find out where Kiki was staying, and so I asked his parents about this in one of my letters to them. Intriguingly, my question was never answered, but Kiki's address read *Cité universitaire*, which meant that he was staying in a hall of residence. Thus even when Kiki was in a far-away place with no kin around, was it not a possibility for Kiki to stay with *mpiara-mivavaka* of whom there would have been many in the town of Fianarantsoa. At the time of writing, Kiki is living in the capital city of Antananarivo. He *rents* a tiny room in the yard of an *unrelated Adventist* family, where he lives and cooks for himself—a scenario unthinkable among kin. In other words, the kind of unquestionable, long-term support we have encountered between kin in Kiki's story is quite absent among *mpiara-mivavaka*.

The reader might say that this is not surprising and that one cannot expect a complete stranger—as Kiki would have been for any Adventist family in Fianarantsoa—to be put up for the foreseeable future, just because one happens to be in the same church. My reply to such an objection would be the following. First, had Kiki had any kin, close or distant, in Fianarantsoa, there would have been no question as to where to send him, namely his *havana*, and it is extremely unlikely that these *havana* would not have put him up, even if perhaps they had never met before. *Havana* support each other not on the basis of personal sympathy, but on the basis of being *havana*, but *mpiara-mivavaka* clearly do not act in this way. Second, though in Fianarantsoa he would have been a stranger for any Adventist family there, in the capital, he actually already knew the people from whom he now rents a room. And third, sometimes, even when *mpiara-mivavaka* know each other, they make a conscious effort not to behave like *havana*, lest the boundary between the two types of relations become blurred. This was brought home to me on a number of rather unpleasant occasions, which were triggered by my activities as a fieldworker.

Six months into fieldwork in Maroantsetra town, I began to make plans to occasionally go off to a number of villages in the nearby countryside for a few days at a time, in order to get to know different Adventist congregations in the district. Unsuspecting of what was to come, I told Maman' and Papan' i Beby my plans. The intensity of their reaction took me by complete surprise.

> You don't know these people from the countryside! They will come and make use of all your things *sans façon, sans façon*! They will even wear your underwear if they don't have any themselves, seriously! If you go and stay with some Adventists in the countryside, they will think they have the right to come here anytime they please and burden us with their problems. Because everyone knows that you are with us and that you are like our daughter.

Between them—and in a very un-Malagasy fashion in many ways—Maman' and Papan' i Beby continued to paint a colorful picture of the potential impositions that the *mpiara-mivavaka* from the countryside that I was planning to get involved with would make, illustrating the reality of the danger with examples of people from the countryside who had come and stayed with people in town for weeks, and even months, without contributing as much as one cup of rice. They were clearly afraid of being pushed into social responsibilities they had no interest in honoring. They were afraid that by staying and eating with other members of the Adventist church, I would create a kind of link between the latter and themselves, a link that had the potential to take on a kin-like quality. During their vibrant exposition as to why they were completely against my plan, Papan' i Beby explained to me that he never stayed with *mpiara-mivavaka*, but always with the village president, when working somewhere in the countryside in his capacity as a hydraulic engineer. The reason was, he emphasized, that he did not wish to create a relationship with *mpiara-mivavaka* who he had not chosen to be friends with, a relationship that would entail mutual social obligations and rights similar to those between kin.

For some time, I did not know what to do. However, a few months later, I decided to move to Sahameloka anyway while continuing to spend a few days in Maroantsetra from time to time, even though

Papan' and Maman' i Beby were not particularly happy with this option either. Unfortunately, the relationship between the two families with whom I lived in Maroantsetra and Sahameloka respectively remained very distant, not to say chilly, right up to the end of my field-work, despite the fact that they were all committed *mpiara-mivavaka*. In the course of the six months during which I primarily lived in Sahameloka, occasionally coming to Maroantsetra, they met on a few occasions. From the very beginning, my family in town made it very clear to my family from Sahameloka—by treating them like distant acquaintances at best—that they tolerated having a relationship with them only for my sake, and only for as long as I was around, and that this would not imply entering into any kin-like relationship with accompanying rights and duties.

There was certainly an aspect of hierarchy informing my host families' attitude toward each other that cannot be ignored. In con-trast to Papan' and Maman' i Beby, Papan' and Maman' i Claude from my family in Sahameloka were not at all disinclined to intensify their relationship to my family in town. And they may have hoped this would happen through my mediation. Their economic and social status—both within the Adventist church and within the larger society—is clearly lower than that of my family in town. They are poor farmers in the countryside rather than state employees in town. And they look up to Papan' i Beby as one of the leading members of the Adventist church in the district. Intensifying their relationship with my family in town would have created potential advantages for them, both material and symbolic. Although this analysis is obviously much too crude the way I present it here, there seems to be an element of truth in sug-gesting that those members of the Adventist church who can poten-tially gain from acquiring certain new quasi-kin emphasize the church's proposition that *mpiara-mivavaka* ought to love and sup-port each other just like kin and that they are "kin before God." In contrast, those members of the church who mainly see the potential for more obligations arising out of a particular relationship are keen to keep the two categories of *havana* and *mpiara-mivavaka* separate.

Uncertainties

The local Seventh-day Adventists are clear about the importance of kin ties and attempt not to jeopardize these more than is inevitable. In contrast, they are not at all clear about the nature of the relationship between *mpiara-mivavaka*. On the one hand, there is no doubt that *mpiara-mivavaka* are not kin. But, on the other hand, the Adventist church tells its members that they ought to love and support each other just as if they were kin. Thus, what exactly is the relationship between people who are not kin, but who ought to act as such? The uncertainty concerning the nature of the relationship between *mpiara-mivavaka* also entails a lack of clarity as to what one can expect of them, and what one owes them, and this in turn leads to inconsistency of behavior between *mpiara-mivavaka*. Sometimes, *mpiara-mivavaka* do act toward each other in ways typical of kin, and indeed, they are expected to; communal work or care for a dead church member serve as examples. At other times, there is not even an expectation that support, comparable to that between kin, be offered by *mpiara-mivavaka*; Kiki staying in a university hall of residence in the distant town of Fianarantsoa illustrates this.

It is precisely because the nature of the relationship between *mpiara-mivavaka* is far from clear, both in theory and in practice, that the boundary between the category of people called *havana* and the category of people called *mpiara-mivavaka* is sometimes emphasized all the more, especially if it is in danger of becoming permeable. This is so in particular in situations when the two sides involved in a relationship between *mpiara-mivavaka* might have different expectations of what that relationship implies. The fact that Papan' and Maman' i Beby gave my family from Sahameloka the cold shoulder must be seen as an attempt on their part to clarify that boundary, a clarification made necessary, from their point of view, precisely because of the fact that the boundary between *mpiara-mivavaka* and kin is insufficiently clear.

However, the very fact that there is scope for the negotiation of the relationship between *mpiara-mivavaka*, highlights the crucial difference between *havana* and *mpiara-mivavaka*. To suggest that kin (*havana*) always love and support each other and that there is never any conflict between them would be to unduly romanticize their relations. Indeed, kin often quarrel and even take each other to court over land issues for example. However, in spite of such disputes, fulfilling one's role as *havana*—as Kiki's example shows—is not a matter of choice, but goes without saying. Recall Maman' and Papan' i Beby's reply to my question as to whether they had informed their kin in Toamasina about Kiki's arrival. "No, that is not necessary, we are family," they said. Although in practice, the intensity of kin relations is flexible, kin are basically obliged to act in certain ways toward each other by virtue of being kin. In contrast, support of the kind typical and expected of kin is, when offered to one's *mpiara-mivavaka*, a voluntary commitment. Many *mpiara-mivavaka* do indeed provide enormous support to each other and act almost as if they were kin; Maman' i Ominò and other church members watching over Beby in hospital are examples. But such support is given voluntarily, and as such, can be withdrawn at any time, unlike one's commitment toward one's kin. What seems to be happening is that the local Adventists are refusing to let church membership interfere with already existing relations, unless that change happens on the basis of their own choice. To make such choices is, however, not easy, because *mpiara-mivavaka* are a new category of people that cannot be subsumed under any existing category of social relations, and because it is not quite clear what exactly *mpiara-mivavaka* are. They are not kin, but neither are they just friends or neighbors. They are *mpiara-mivavaka*. And that relationship implies mutual love and support on the basis of choice, and perhaps a touch of kinship.

The nature of the relationship between *mpiara-mivavaka* is unclear on a conceptual level. This leads to inconsistency in terms of the expectations of, and behavior toward, *mpiara-mivavaka* in everyday life. In contrast, no such uncertainties exist with regard to one's kin. It is less than clear, however, to the members of the church how they should deal, in real life, with being part of two communities that make conflicting demands upon them. Their commitment to the Adventist church stops them from going along with the rest of society, including their kin, in accepting the ancestors as real and invoking them in ritual practice. The strength of kin relations, and one's ability to rely on them, makes them want to minimize the potential damage done to these relations by refusing to ritually care for one's ancestors. Kin ties are one of the few sources of security Malagasy people have. The local Adventists know that they will always be able to rely on their kin, but they cannot be sure that they will always be able to rely on *mpiara-mivavaka*. Particularly at this moment in time, when Adventism is still a relatively recent phenomenon in the area, one simply does not know what will happen and whether in Sahameloka, for example, there will be any Adventists left in ten year's time. Kin, by contrast, do not suddenly disappear.

It is not easy for the local Adventists to steer their way through dilemmas like this, which are caused by their simultaneous commitment to two different "ways of being." And there is no clear blueprint as to how they should lead their life; hence their journey is constantly accompanied by considerable uncertainty. We encountered such uncertainty in Kiki's example, both with regard to finding a home for him in Toamasina, and concerning his and Papan' i Beby's role as head of their ancestry. In both cases, the family acted on the basis of traditional kinship structure, obligations and rights. But loyalty to the principles of the church made Papan' and Maman' i Beby ignore certain kinship rules. They did not send Kiki to stay with Papan' i Beby's brother, as they should have done, but to kin with a more suitable lifestyle. Similarly, although Papan' i Beby is head of the ancestry, he stays away from ancestral rituals, and Kiki is instructed to "keep his mouth well shut" when it comes to such ritual action. Just how people deal with their dual commitment to Adventism and to kinship is different in every case. The scope is wide, as the examples of Maman' i Claude and that of her husband illustrate.

The Nature of Kinship

Maman' i Claude is one of four siblings. Two of these, herself and one of her brothers, are members of the Seventh-day Adventist church. For Maman' i Claude's father (her mother is long dead), this is difficult, because he knows that two of his four children will not perform any ritual work for him after he is dead, instead letting his bones rot in his coffin. Nevertheless, they are still his children, and perhaps he hopes that one day they will come back to ancestral custom. Whatever his thoughts, he often came to Sahameloka to visit his daughter and her family, since he lives in a village just an hour's walk away. Never did I observe any sign of open conflict between them—except when he caught Maman' i Claude working his field on a Tuesday—and both sides made an effort to respect each other's concerns and feelings. When Maman' i Claude's father ate with us, he always waited till we had finished our prayer before starting to eat, though he had never in his life belonged to any church and did not pray himself. Even when we went to see him in his house, he would allow us time for prayer prior to a meal, at which moment Maman' i Claude would pray quietly and quickly. Maman' i Claude, on her part, made sure to always visit her father and all her siblings when in her natal village and to share at least a few bites of rice with each of them. She kept quiet about her church affiliation during these visits and never made the slightest attempt to preach to anybody. This attitude of mutual conciliation was clearly a way of signaling to each other that, despite their disagreement over ancestral rituals, they were, nevertheless, kin. At the same time, it has to be said that there was always a certain tension in the air during these visits that at any time could have developed into conflict, had it not been for the fact that both sides made a constant effort to avoid this happening.

Papan' i Claude is in an entirely different situation. When he became an Adventist, his mother had long been dead, and exhumation and cattle sacrifice had already been performed for her. His father, however, died two years after he had joined the Adventist church and the exhumation was due to take place a few years later. Being the eldest son, Papan' i Claude would have been responsible for the timing and organization of the exhumation of his father, but he refused to have any part in it. When Maman' i Claude told me this story, we were in the middle of a rice field with no one else around for miles. Nevertheless, she whispered as she told me what had happened:

> Papan' i Claude's family knew that he would refuse both to organize, and to attend, his father's exhumation. But on the day of the exhumation, all of his kin gathered next door to us where the ritual meal was going to take place. When everyone had arrived, all the elders of his ancestry [*ny ôlo maventy jiaby*] came to our house, and they took off their hats"—at this point her voice was almost inaudible—"and begged Papan' i Claude to, at least, share a meal of rice with them even if his religion forbade him to accompany them to the tombs. 'This is your father!,' they said to him. Papan' i Claude, however, refused and stayed put inside our house. I knew," Maman' i Claude continued, "I would never have been able to remain firm with all the elders begging us to join them in that way, and so I left and went to Maroantsetra for a couple of days till everything was over. Ever since that time, we are never even invited to any exhumation. And when Papan' i Claude was very ill some time ago, none of his kin came to visit.

Clearly, from the point of view of his non-Adventist kin, Papan' i Claude had gone too far. During the six months that I lived with him and his family, none of his many kin who lived in Sahameloka ever turned up at our house. His dismissal of the elders' plea to at least eat with them was not only a terrible offence, it also amounted, for his kin, to a refusal of kinship. This brings us back to the notion of *fomban-drazana* with its double meaning, which I introduced at the beginning of part III and which I will elaborate on in the final conclusion. From Papan' i Claude's point of view—who at that particular moment acted on the basis of his Adventist commitment—his refusal to have any part in his father's exhumation was merely a refusal to practice *fomban-drazana* as "false religion." But his kin, who do not share this Adventist notion of exhumation as false religion, understood his position as a refusal of *fomban-drazana* in the much broader, ordinary sense of the term, referring to all that which the living generations have learnt from their forebears. In that sense, Papan' i Claude's behavior was a refusal to be part of their community of kin. This is why it was such a terrible offence.

Indeed, kinship is not only enacted and reconfirmed, but also *created*, at exhumations and cattle sacrifice. Among Betsimisaraka, as among other Malagasy people, kinship is not *primarily* constituted by descent. Rather, descent represents a starting point for kinship, a seedling that must be nurtured throughout life. On the one hand, this happens through mutual support between kin in everyday life. On the other hand, the *moral quality of kinship* between the living is constituted by the fact that people have ancestors in common and that they depend on the same ancestors' blessing, with such blessing being secured, among other things, through proper ritual care for them (Bloch 1985; Cole 2001: 157–158).

The fact that the Adventists do not accept the idea that the ancestors have the power to bless their descendants and that they therefore stay away from rituals whose purpose it is to obtain the ancestors' blessing, greatly confuses their non-Adventist kin. Genealogically speaking, Papan' i Claude is still kin to his relatives even when he refuses to take part in rituals such as exhumation, which constitute the moral quality of kinship. Significantly, his kin have not excluded him from the ancestry as a result of his behavior, despite the fact that from their point of view it was extremely shameful. However, Papan' i Claude's non-Adventist kin must become increasingly unclear about the moral quality of the relationship between him and them. If they are morally linked as an ancestry because they depend on the same ancestors' blessing, how is one to interpret Papan' i Claude's rejection of such blessing? How is one to view a person who, in principle, is kin, and who behaved like kin for much of his life, but who has now, at the age of over 40, started to behave as if he were not kin and indeed, as if he wanted to deny kinship? And how is one to react, in concrete terms, to such behavior?

Papan' i Claude himself did certainly not intend to express contempt for kinship through his behavior. Rather, he decided, after a long and difficult period of consideration, to stay away from an event whose performance he, as an Adventist, considered to be wrong. At the same time, he must have been incredibly uncomfortable with what he was doing, and perhaps equally confused as his kin, because he is not only a member of the Adventist church, and his identity is not *solely* defined by that membership. He is also a Malagasy rice farmer who lives in a community, a community that is not ruled by Adventist principles, and as a member of that community, he is deeply committed to a morality that is based on the relations among kin. The Adventist cosmology tells Papan' i Claude that everything he does in life involves a decision to either follow God or else to side with Satan, and it tells him that to perform exhumation is a manifestation of the latter. If that *was* indeed the choice Papan' i Claude was facing in real life, he would be perfectly comfortable with his decision to favor God. However, such a clear dichotomy between God and the devil does not fit the social reality in which he lives his life. That reality is one that is simultaneously influenced by, on the one hand, the Adventist cosmology—which indeed tells him that everything is about just that dichotomy—and, on the other hand, a morality of a completely different order, within which not to exhume one's father's bones is tantamount to rejecting one's kin. The source of Papan' i Claude's uncertainty is the fact that the Adventist cosmology, which he accepts as truthful, suggests to him that at least certain aspects of kinship as conceptualized in the local society are the work of the devil. His tragedy is that he is torn between his commitment to Adventism, and being embedded in, and equally committed to, a way of life, which makes the implementation of some Adventist teachings highly immoral.

The impact of the Adventists' refusal to join their kin on important ritual occasions varies from case to case, depending on a number of aspects such as one's position within one's ancestry. Papan' i Claude's case was certainly made worse by the fact that he was the eldest son of his father. But whatever the exact extent of conflict, a certain tension, which is highlighted when a particular ritual is actually at issue, is present and strains kin relations in almost all the cases I know.[9] And both sides are uncertain how to deal with the situation.

Why are there so many Adventists in Sahameloka?

In chapter 2, I noted that in Sahameloka there is an unusually high number of Seventh-day Adventists, approximately 10 percent of the adult population compared with only 1 percent in the whole of the district. I also pointed out in chapter 1 that most inhabitants of Sahameloka are of slave descent. Because there is a strong tendency in the literature on New Churches to emphasize converts' socioeconomic marginality, making them, according to the theory, particularly receptive to ideologies promising upward mobility in the here and now and eternal bliss thereafter, a possible connection between the high number of Adventists in Sahameloka and, in the majority of cases, their slave descent has to be taken into consideration. In chapter 4, we saw, however, that for a number of reasons, converts' slave descent fails to provide an adequate explanation for the Adventist church's comparative popularity in the village. But then, why are there so many Adventists in Sahameloka? The reason I want to suggest for this fact is to do with the relations between Adventist and non-Adventist kin which, as the examples of Maman' i Claude and Papan' i Claude illustrate, vary dramatically. I do not have enough comparative data from across the district to support my claim statistically, but on the basis of my observations in Sahameloka, I believe that the unusually high number of converts in the village is a result of chain conversion within particular kin groups.

This chapter has shown how difficult it is for both sides to deal with the problem of kin relations between Adventist and non-Adventist people. However, the ethnographic data also illustrates that in many cases, people do find ways of dealing with the situation. Maman' i Claude and her kin are a case in point. Although her father is far from happy with her church affiliation, he has come, perhaps not to accept, but, at least, to tolerate, it. Of his four children, only two are in the Adventist church and therefore only two will not perform ritual work for him once he is dead. The other two, however, will exhume him and do whatever "ancestral work" needs to be done. Hence the actual carrying out of the rituals is not under threat, a fact that non-Adventist villagers have realized since the first people converted to Adventism. Thus while the first converts ran up against almost universal resistance from their kin to their religious commitment, with time it became easier for people who belonged to kin groups in which there were already other Adventists to join the Adventist church themselves. Not that the problem of intra-kin relations was resolved, as this chapter makes abundantly clear. However, in many cases, both sides did at least find ways of handling their relationship. Papan' i Claude's case provides a strong contrast. His relationship to his kin has been so poisoned as a result of the problem surrounding "ancestral work," that for other people within that particular kin group, joining the Adventist church will remain an outstandingly difficult and solitary step to take. In Maman' i Claude's kin group, the relationship between members of the Adventist church and their kin is still incredibly difficult, but at least, there now exist models of how to deal with the situation.

In short, I believe that the unusually high number of Adventists in Sahameloka is due to chain conversion within particular kin groups. I want to emphasize that this is not an explanation of what motivates people to convert to Adventism which, as I explained in the introduction to this book, is not my concern here. Much less is chain conversion an explanation of the nature of people's commitment after initial conversion. Chain conversion might, however, indicate why in some localities it is easier for the church to increase the number of its adherents than it is, at least for the time being, in others.

Toward a New Theory of Kinship?

The Adventists in Sahameloka and Maroantsetra know that kin relations will inevitably be strained, and possibly also jeopardized, because of their absence at rituals performed for the ancestors.

The Adventists wish that this was not the case, they wish that they would be able to be truthful to their religious commitment without harming their relationship to their kin. And they signal their continuing esteem for kinship by being extra careful to fulfill their kin obligations whenever it is possible for them to do so: by keeping ancestral taboo days, by turning up in great numbers at wakes and funerals, by visiting their relatives and showing due respect for their elders and so on.

But the Adventists' desire to combine their commitment to the church with maintaining their ties of kinship has led them, it seems to me, to develop a new theory of kinship. Southall (1986: 417–426) has discussed how, beneath the diversity of kinship systems found among different Malagasy populations, there is an underlying common model of kinship:

> [W]hat seems to be distinctive about all Malagasy kinship systems is not their qualities of cognation or agnation, but their emphasis on kinship and descent status as something achieved gradually and progressively throughout life, and even after death, rather than ascribed and fixed definitively at birth. (1986: 417)

Southall calls this the model of "cumulative kinship" (1986: 417, also compare Astuti 2000). As we have seen, one way by which kinship is gradually achieved, solidified and morally charged, is through the blessing of one's ancestors. The Malagasy notion of kinship is based very much on the continuity between the living and the dead and the relationship between them. The living depend on their ancestors' blessing in order to prosper in life. The ancestors, in turn, need their living descendants to care for them in their tombs and to keep their "ways" alive. Together, living and dead kin form a kin group. I do not wish to suggest that kinship is always, or only, viewed in terms of one's relationship to the dead, but it certainly is at certain important moments, especially when the ancestors are actively invoked and asked to bless their descendants, as happens during exhumation and cattle sacrifice.

The Seventh-day Adventists have no problem with the significance of ancestors as such. On the contrary, like other Malagasy, they hold their ancestors' memory dear and consider it morally right to follow in their footsteps. Their problem lies with the idea that kinship is enacted, reconfirmed and even created through ancestral *blessing*. Thus it might be the case that the Adventists are developing a theory of kinship from which ancestral blessing is removed, one which is almost entirely based on relations between the living only. However, a theory of kinship that involves the conceptual separation between the living and the dead is essentially incompatible with the Malagasy emphasis on the interdependence between dead and living kin. And herein lies the fundamental problem the Malagasy Adventists are confronted with.

Conclusions

In the introduction to this book, I outlined the principal focus of this study of Seventh-day Adventism in Madagascar. The book is primarily concerned with the nature of religious commitment beyond initial conversion and focuses on ordinary church members' experience as practitioners of Adventism in the context of their everyday lives. The conclusion I have come to is that local people's commitment to Adventism is first and foremost nourished by the intellectual pleasure derived from the activity of Bible study. Adventist Bible study is conducted in a participatory, Socratic style, which is based on reflection and dialogue rather than on instruction by a higher authority or the learning by heart of doctrine. I began this book with the image of Papan' i Loricà lost in Bible study for several hours at night, and I propose that it is the joy he derives from the actual process of studying the Bible that explains his commitment, and that of many others, to the Adventist church. For how can one explain the shine in people's eyes when they receive a new edition of the Bible Study Guide, how can one explain Papan' i Claude's concentration when he sits at home on a rainy afternoon trying to make the letters in front of him meaningful, if not by these people's genuine interest in the very process of studying? Enthusiasm and eagerness for Bible study, as we have encountered it throughout the course of this book, are thus not epiphenomena of some other hidden motivation to engage in Adventist practice. Rather the primary attraction of Adventism is the intrinsic worth of the religious activity itself.

The members of the Adventist church enjoy taking part in intellectual discussions, such as the debate between the adherents of evolutionism and the defenders of creationism. However, their intellectual activity within such debates is clearly restricted by the paradigm of literal biblical truth within which they intellectually operate. This paradigm makes it perfectly clear what is right and what is wrong. As I argued in chapter 6, the local Seventh-day Adventists may be compared to the type of scholars whom Thomas Kuhn (1996 [1962]) calls

Normal Scientists (by which he means most scientists at most times). Kuhn likens Normal Scientists to people doing a jigsaw puzzle, because Normal Scientific activity, according to him, is not guided by genuinely open inquiry, but "is directed to the articulation of those phenomena and theories that the paradigm already supplies" (1996: 24). The purpose and the excitement of doing a jigsaw, as well as that of practicing Normal Science and Seventh-day Adventist Bible study, is not to produce a novel outcome, but to discover for oneself how to get to the final result. Kuhn's theory of Normal Science helps us to understand how it is possible for a learning process, which puts so much emphasis on people's active intellectual input, to take place within a fixed paradigm that limits the free play of intellect. I suggest that it is precisely because the core of Adventist religious activity is the *process* of Bible study rather than its result, that the Socratic method and the canonization of knowledge can coexist.

The process of Bible study is not only exciting in its own right, however; the activity of *mianatra* (studying) is also thought to lead to a specific kind of potency: the potency to dis-cover the truth hitherto buried beneath Satan's veil of deception. Once that cover is removed, the truth can emerge in all its clarity. The clarity of the Adventist vision, the *mazava* they are moving toward, is not limited to recognizing the truth of what is happening in the here and now. The clarity the local members of the church approach through Bible study extends to the anticipation of a completely unrestricted view of the truth in paradise. It extends to being able to see, and perceive, everything that has up to that point been inaccessible to the human senses. This anticipation of complete clarity includes seeing God Himself. In sum: the vision, which presents itself to the local church members, when they look at the world through the lens of Adventist cosmology, is amazingly clear.

However, in part III of the book, we encountered several areas of uncertainty that the local Seventh-day Adventists are confronted with, in particular uncertainty of how to act in everyday life—Shall we work on Tuesdays? Who shall we marry? Can we risk buying "powerful land?"—as well as uncertainty concerning the implication of church membership on social relations and on the nature of kinship.

All these uncertainties are triggered by the local Adventists' double vision: with one eye, they see the world through Adventist glasses, with the other through Malagasy glasses. On the one hand, they interpret what they see from an Adventist perspective, yet, on the other hand, they are embedded in a society that is ruled by other principles, especially the notion of kinship, which the Adventists, too, continue to consider the basis of a moral way of life. As a result of being continually torn, one moment to this side, the next moment to the other, they are involved in an endless process of decision making. When outside of a strictly Adventist context, they find themselves on a road that is signposted by both Adventist and non-Adventist signals. And at every turn they take, they encounter a new constellation of conflicting signs that requires them to make a new decision as to where to go.

The Malagasy Adventists are real people and as such, they cannot at any point in life be either just Adventists or just "ordinary" local people. The two visions they embody are always simultaneously present. Just how difficult this situation is and just what kinds of uncertainty it provokes is illustrated particularly forcefully by the two interpretations of what are *fomban-drazana*—literally: the ways of the ancestors—to which I have already drawn attention in various places in this book, and to which I now once again turn.

The Ambiguity of *Fomban-drazana*, or, Who Are We?

We have seen how in Adventist discourse, a novel interpretation of *fomban-drazana* as disembedded "religion" concerned with "things supernatural" is created, and how *fomban-drazana* in this sense is considered by local Adventists the work of the devil. Needless to say, true Christians reject everything associated with *fomban-drazana* as false religion, the epitome of which, in the region of Maroantsetra, are exhumation and cattle sacrifice.

We have also seen that the Adventist definition of *fomban-drazana* differs from the ordinary meaning of *fomban-drazana*, which is much broader and which includes respectful demeanor to elderly people and cultivating rice on the land one has inherited from one's forebears as well as exhumation and other rituals. *Fomban-drazana* in the non-Adventist, ordinary Malagasy sense refers to everything that the living generations have learnt from their ancestors. It is a way of life, which goes far beyond a limited number of identifiable practices. The living follow in the footsteps of their dead kin, and in that sense, to do *fomban-drazana* is to live out what kinship is, to live a type of kinship that is based on the relationship between living and dead kin.

Moreover, following *fomban-drazana* in the sense of following a way of life means, for the local people, to be Malagasy. They are perfectly aware that not all Malagasy people follow exactly the same *fomban-drazana*. For example, they are aware that not everywhere in Madagascar, is Tuesday necessarily a taboo day for work on one's rice fields, as it is for almost all local people, and that not all Malagasy have the same kinds of tombs and mortuary customs. But despite people's awareness of regional differences in what exactly is ancestral custom, there is a marked and explicit sense that all Malagasy people follow their *fomban-drazana* and that this is what makes them Malagasy.[1]

Significantly, the members of the Adventist church are only against *fomban-drazana* in the Adventist sense, that is exhumation, cattle sacrifice, keeping ancestral taboos, and other "manifestations of Satan's power." But they are as wholly in favor of *fomban-drazana* as a way of life that is passed on from one generation to the next, as they are wholly against *fomban-drazana* in the Adventist sense of false religion. As I recounted earlier in this book, the local Adventists consider it a key element of moral behavior, and as such essential, to show respect toward elderly people. They also consider it morally important to honor the memory of one's ancestors. And like everybody else, the Adventists refer to things such as respecting the principle of seniority, or being attached to one's ancestral homeland, as *fomban-drazana* (or alternatively *fomba malagasy* [Malagasy custom]), always emphasizing the moral value of following in the footsteps of one's ancestors.

In short: the local Adventists consider themselves not to be involved in *fomban-drazana* in its sense of false religion, but to be involved in *fomban-drazana* in the sense of a moral way of life. This is reflected in how they talk about themselves in relation to *fomban-drazana* in the Adventist sense, as opposed to *fomban-drazana* in the ordinary Malagasy sense. Whenever they want to distinguish themselves from those who practice exhumation, the local Adventists would state that "The Malagasy do *fomban-drazana*, the Adventists don't," or "The Malagasy believe in the ancestors, the Adventists don't."[2] In such statements, they establish a contrast between themselves and the Malagasy, placing themselves clearly on the non-Malagasy side of things. In such talk, they imagine themselves not to be Malagasy, but instead to be part of another non-Malagasy community, the community of those who do not practice *fomban-drazana*. At the same time, when they talk of the Malagasy following *fomban-drazana* in the sense of the moral way of life they inherited from their forebears, they always include themselves in this category of people. In many circumstances, the Adventists talk with pride about how "*we* Malagasy" follow the ways of the ancestors, by which they mean exactly the same as what non-Adventist Malagasy people understand by *fomban-drazana*: following the ancestors' guidance in daily conduct and in organizing one's life. Maman' i Claude, for example, commented on the way to visit her father and other kin in her natal village after New Year—following a local custom to do so—that "*we* Malagasy respect our elders, this is our *fomban-drazana*."

At this point, it might seem that the Adventists simply have two different concepts, which happen to be referred to by the same term, but which they can neatly distinguish. It might seem that it is entirely clear to them which *fomban-drazana* they are against and which they are in favor of. However, to view the situation thus would be to paint far too simple a picture. First of all, the Adventists are real people and cannot cut themselves into two halves. As Adventists who live in a non-Adventist world, they are constantly confronted with both understandings of what are *fomban-drazana* and, by implication, what it means to reject *fomban-drazana*. With one ear, they hear the rejection of *fomban-drazana* as meaning only the rejection of exhumation and sacrifice and the idea of ancestral power more generally. With the other ear, they hear it to imply the rejection of an entire way of life, which is the basis of kinship and the basis of being Malagasy, and which is deeply moral.

Second, *fomban-drazana* as a moral way of life *cannot be separated* from those practices the Adventist cosmology claims to be of the devil. Because *fomban-drazana* as a way of life is about the relationship between living and dead generations, and that relationship is enacted and created through activities that involve ancestral blessing, which are, therefore, within the framework of Adventist cosmology, of the devil.

Take the example of working the land. One of the most important aspects of honoring the memory of one's forebears is to farm rice on the land one has inherited from them. As we saw earlier working one's ancestral land is not only a matter of sowing and harvesting, but also, in order not to jeopardize the ancestors' blessing, to do so on the proper days and to respect ancestral work day taboos. Thus, the actual farming activities and their timing are inseparable. This inseparability is the source of much uncertainty for those people in villages like Sahameloka who have become members of the Adventist church. Because although they share the concept of honoring the memory of one's forebears by working their land, to accept the possibility of ancestral punishment, in case of transgression of a taboo, is to accept ancestral power. And to acknowledge ancestral power is, within Adventist cosmology, to side with the devil. Therefore, these villagers' commitment to Adventist teachings tells them to ignore such work day taboos. However, they are not only committed Adventists. They are also farmers, who live in a predominantly non-Adventist village among their non-Adventist kin. If they ignore the taboos, which they are subjected to by virtue of belonging to particular ancestries, not only are eyebrows raised, but because of the fact that transgression of taboos may trigger indiscriminate reprisals affecting not only the transgressor, but anybody subject to the particular taboo being ignored, this causes their kin tremendous discomfort and worry. Furthermore, nurturing and maintaining good relations with one's kin is a core aspect of *fomban-drazana* as a way of life, the moral quality of which, as we have seen, the local Adventists continue to accept even after their conversion to Adventism. What this boils down to is a situation in which the Adventists are pushed by their commitment to Adventism to jeopardize the very relations that are the basis of their daily life as villagers and kinsmen, and that they think of as highly moral. The end result of the Adventist, and the kin-focused, morality meeting in the field, as it were, and forming part of one and the same person, is a constant uncertainty on the part of the members of the church, not only in terms of having to decide whether or not to actually go off working on particular days, but also in terms of what exactly it means to work on a Tuesday. Does it mean to defeat the devil, or does it mean to violate a way of life based on the relations between kin? For those who are embedded in the local society and who are, at the same time, committed to Adventism, it means both.

The exact same problem arises for the local Adventists when it comes to exhumation and cattle sacrifice. As I explained in chapter 12, the *moral quality* of kinship is predicated on the fact that kin rely on the same ancestors' blessing. In the context of such a morality, the demonization of ritual practices, which are based on the notion of ancestral blessing, is not only morally wrong, but also doesn't make sense. Because it is, among other aspects, the common ritual care for common ancestors and the blessing thus received collectively, which makes people morally bound kin. Exhumation and sacrifice thus *constitute* kinship, which is the basis of that moral way of life that the living have learnt from their ancestors: *fomban-drazana*. It is because ancestral blessing is *necessarily* part of *fomban-drazana* as a way of life, that practices that involve ancestral blessing—exhumation, sacrifice, keeping ancestral taboos—cannot be separated, or neatly distinguished, from that way of life, as would be the case in an ideal Adventist world. In chapter 12, I told the story of how Papan' i Claude refused to even share a meal of rice with his kin on the occasion of his father's exhumation, and how this resulted in the relations between him and his kin being seriously damaged. It is because he, like all other local Adventists, is committed both to Adventism and to *fomban-drazana* as a way of life, and especially to the principle of kinship, that he must have felt tremendous discomfort at his own decision to stay away from the event. His discomfort stems from the fact that his choice in real life is not between God and Satan—as the Adventist cosmology tells him—but between his commitment to the Adventist morality, within which exhumation is utterly immoral, and his commitment to a morality of a completely different order within which not to care for one's dead kin constitutes a deeply immoral act. Because he is both an

Adventist and a person embedded in the local society, whatever he decides, he will inevitably feel that it is wrong.

This is the real life situation that the local Adventists have to deal and to live with. It is because of the fact that not to perform *fomban-drazana* is to be excluded from social continuity between living and dead generations, and in that sense, to be excluded from society as conceptualized in the local context, that they consider it a *big problem* not to be able to perform particular rituals, rather than a blessing because of the financial advantages resulting from the lack of ritual expenses. The local Adventists often discuss the problem of not being able to perform ritual work for close kin and express a certain envy of the situation of Seventh-day Adventists in other countries who, they presume, do not have this problem, since they do not have *fomban-drazana*. At the same time, they are totally convinced that it would be wrong to exhume dead people. The difficulty of their situation results precisely from the dual understanding of what *fomban-drazana* are that they are constantly confronted with. Because church members are exposed to both understandings of what *fomban-drazana* are, they find themselves in continual oscillation between them. It is this oscillation that must make them sometimes wonder what exactly the church is demanding of them and, as a consequence, who they really are.

We can conclude then, that, in contrast to the clarity of the purely Adventist vision, the situation in real life is extremely ambiguous and difficult to deal with for the local members of the Adventist church. Life before Adventism was certainly not without its own ambiguities and contradictions. But with Adventism, several areas of uncertainty have arrived in the lives of local church members, areas of uncertainty that were unknown to them before: the uncertainty as to how to act in daily life, of what kinship is, and the uncertainty of whether or not they are truly Malagasy people.

In his touching ethnography of the Urapmin of Papua New Guinea who all converted to a charismatic form of Baptism in the late 1970s, Robbins discusses the moral tensions resulting from the fact that the Urapmin live in two, incompatible cultures (2004). On the one hand, they have fully adopted Christian morality which, in Urapmin interpretation, condemns all manifestations of human will as sinful. On the other hand, they continue to live their nonreligious daily lives very largely in traditional terms. In traditional Urapmin morality, persons are defined by the relationships of which they form part, and these relationships are created by human will (for example by the will of two people to get married). Thus in traditional Urapmin culture, human will is only negative when it is seen to have a destructive effect on social relationships. When it is seen as creating or maintaining relationships, it is morally valuable. To live in Urapmin society necessitates the creation of relationships, and to be involved in human relationships inevitably gives expression to one's will. But because in Urapmin Christianity, human will, regardless of what its effects are, is considered sinful, the Urapmin continually find themselves morally wanting. This is their basic predicament of living with two cultures at the same time—traditional Urapmin culture, and Baptist Christianity—and this is why they are deeply troubled, troubled about the sinful nature of their own existence.

The Malagasy Adventists are also confronted with fundamental contradictions between what one might call traditional morality based on the communication between living and dead kin, and Seventh-day Adventist morality that denies the very existence of such communication. The cases of the Urapmin and that of the Malagasy Adventists are different in many respects; but they are similar in that both groups of people have to find ways of living with two fundamentally contradictory moralities. Yet on top of that, the Adventists in Maroantsetra and Sahameloka also face another problem that the Urapmin are spared: the problem of living in a non-Adventist social world. And in many ways, this is their biggest problem in life.

A Paradox

When one thinks back on the entire ethnography presented in this book, one notices a paradox. The Adventist construction of *fomban-drazana* as false religion only refers to practices that are concerned with "supernatural" entities in the sense of entities that are invisible and not straightforwardly of this earth. The basis of this novel, specifically Adventist, definition of what *fomban-drazana* are is the conceptual separation of things visible, on the one hand, and things invisible, on the other, between the empirical world and a realm "beyond," which is essentially different. By introducing a conceptual divide between phenomena that are visible to the eye and others that are not, and by thereby representing such practices as exhumation and cattle sacrifice as a separate, "religious" matter concerned with the "supernatural," the Adventists Christianize *fomban-drazana*. In the ordinary Malagasy view of things, too, of course, there is a difference between the visible and the invisible. The difference is precisely that: some phenomena or entities are visible, others are not. This difference, however, is not essentialized: elders and ancestors, for example, are not thought to be of a fundamentally different nature. The criterion of visibility does not, in the ordinary Malagasy view, create a clear separation between the "natural" and the "supernatural" world. In contrast, the Adventist construction of *fomban-drazana* as false religion essentializes the difference between the visible and the invisible.

However, when it comes to what *Adventism* is all about—which is to understand God's truth through the process of Bible study, to travel the road to clarity—the whole point is that there is *no* conceptual separation between the empirically accessible, visible world of the here and now and the intrinsically unknowable hereafter. Obviously, there is a difference between a person sitting on a chair and God sitting on His golden throne in paradise, for example. First of all, God is not human, He is God. But apart from the divine nature of God, the difference is precisely the fact that the person in the here and now is visible while God is not—at least not yet! But it is the local Adventists' "belief/trust" (*finoana*) that God will be visible (as discussed in detail in chapter 10). In contrast to the Adventists' construction of *fomban-drazana* as false religion, Adventism itself is not disembedded, because within Adventist cosmology, "supernatural," invisible phenomena and entities are nothing intrinsically special. In this sense, the Adventists' concept of the "religion" they have embraced is very much in tune with the way other Malagasy think about the relationship between this and "another" world, two worlds that are perceived as basically one and the same, only separated by a curtain hindering visibility.

To summarize: the local Adventists are engaged in a double process that involves a fundamental contradiction. In their construction of *fomban-drazana* as false religion, they introduce the typically modern Christian distinction between this and another world into the concept *fomban-drazana*, which in the ordinary Malagasy sense contains no such distinction. However, paradoxically, their understanding of the Adventist "religion" is radically different to modern mainstream Christianity precisely because that distinction is removed.

Toward an Anthropology of Discontinuity

I have argued that the principal attraction of Seventh-day Adventism for its practitioners in Maroantsetra and Sahameloka is the joy of the intellectual inquiry involved in Bible study. This conclusion necessitates clarification, however.

In the introduction to this book, I briefly summarized the two basic approaches to conversion we find in the related literature: a utilitarian approach, which explains conversion primarily in terms of worldly advantages; and an intellectualist approach, which holds that people convert to Christianity because they see it to offer satisfactory answers to questions of meaning. Can the present study be grouped with either of these approaches?

First of all, while both the utilitarian and the intellectualist approach are *primarily* explanations of initial conversion, this book is concerned with what Seventh-day Adventism has come to mean to people years after they converted. In that sense, it bears little similarity to either of the above approaches.

Some authors have criticized the intellectualist approach on the grounds that it cannot possibly explain initial conversion, simply because most people, at the moment when they convert, have at best a very partial understanding of the worldview the new religion offers, and therefore cannot be attracted by that world view, as the intellectual explanation holds (see Hefner 1993b: 118–122; Robbins 2004: 86–87). If, however, one uses the intellectualist approach to explain the significance of a religion to people after their initial conversion, as Robbins does in his account of Urapmin Christianity (2004), then my findings bear a certain, though clearly limited, affinity to the intellectualist approach. I entitled the book "The road to clarity" because this title captures both the road of Bible study and the clarity, which this road is thought to lead to. It is the latter aspect—the *mazava* envisaged by local Adventists, the anticipation of seeing God sitting on His golden throne in paradise—that may be classified an intellectualist explanation, for it is based on the satisfaction the Adventist worldview offers.

However, I wish to emphasize once again that the core attraction of Adventism for people in Maroantsetra and Sahameloka is not the answers it offers, but the very activity of Bible study and intellectual inquiry. Thus despite the prominence of the word "intellectual" throughout the text, my argument is not simply another example of an intellectualist explanation, because Bible study is *not a means to an end*, but an exciting and attractive activity in and of itself.

* * *

This conclusion does not square well with one of the fundamental assertions of modern social theory, namely the idea that a phenomenon such as Seventh-day Adventism must, beneath the surface of global similarity, be essentially and fundamentally different depending on the cultural and social context in which it occurs, and that therefore such a phenomenon has to be explained by reference to that particular cultural context. My findings do not support this widely held view and therefore invite a brief discussion of it.

Since the end of the colonial period, anthropology has been moving toward a theoretical position that emphasizes the agency of once colonized peoples. At least since the beginning of the 1980s, anthropologists have paid much attention to how local people actively shape their own worlds rather than being "ruled" by a particular cultural system, indigenous or imported (Ortner 1984). The emphasis on agency has been highlighted particularly with regard to the relationship between the "West" and the "Rest." Confronted with a widespread outcry concerning the dangers of globalization and especially the loss of cultural heritage, anthropologists have considered it their duty to show the world that modernization and globalization do not, because of human agency involved in the process, equal homogenization and the eradication of cultural difference. On the contrary, it has been demonstrated in numerous case studies that people in the Third World are not passive victims of cultural imperialism, but active agents who control the impact of the outside world upon their culture and lives. This focus on agency continues to inform contemporary social anthropological theory, as exemplified by three recent ethnographies of Malagasy communities. Cole (2001) focuses on local people's active role in modeling the past to the needs of the present, explaining how these people thereby shape social memory; Lambek (2002) examines how, through spirit possession and ritual practices, people create themselves as historical subjects; and Emoff (2002) analyzes music and instruments used in spirit possession with regard to local people's creative appropriation of European musical input.

The general recognition of subjects' agency has been particularly pronounced and important in postcolonial studies of world religions, especially Islam and Christianity (cf. Jean Comaroff 1985; Jean and John Comaroff 1991, 1997). In response to an earlier focus on conversion as an expression of foreign domination and the loss of indigenous religious traditions, analysts now stress how, far from being passive recipients of incoming religions, converts absorb these in many creative ways and in the process change and modify them so as to make them compatible with locally salient cultural ideas (Barker 1990a; Maxwell 2001: 503; see also Engelke 2003: 300). It has been argued that the criterion of compatibility between local tradition and incoming religion explains why in some cases, local people do convert to Christianity, and why in other circumstances, they do not (see, e.g., the contributions in Hefner 1993). The process of "indigenisation" (Barker 1990a: 9, 1990b: 260), whereby the foreign is rearticulated in local terms—a key focus in many recent studies of Christianity—may even happen to such an extent that what is being embraced in the name of Christianity is hardly recognizable as such at all (see Rafael 1993). "Having refuted the myth of the Christian monolith," many analysts now stress "cultural particularism" instead, "so thoroughly deconstructing Christianity as to conclude that it is really no more than a congeries of local traditions" (Hefner 1993a: 5).[3]

As with research on Christianity in general, contemporary studies of New Churches are characterized by a marked interest in the process of indigenization, whereby the foreign is transformed into "new wine in old wineskins" (Sundkler 1961 [1948]). Such an approach stresses cultural continuity in spite of the introduction of fundamentally new and different systems of meaning, such as the arrival of Seventh-day Adventism in Madagascar, within a local culture. Let me give a little known, but representative, example of studies in this tradition stressing cultural continuity. In his analysis of alcohol consumption and abstinence among the Puruhu of Ecuador, Swanson (1994) argues that the arrival of American evangelicalism only produced superficial similarities between American and Puruhu teetotalers, and that beneath the surface, the motivation to not drink revealed as deep a cultural difference as exists between non-evangelical US-Americans and Puruhu people.

However, analyses of New Churches also emphasize the opposite, namely that converts to New Churches often "make a complete break with the past" (Meyer 1998). These two aspects might seem contradictory at first, but they are easily reconciled when one realizes that the break with the past is said to be localized at the level of the *involved actors'* imagination (these people consider themselves to become completely new persons, especially in Born-Again contexts), while the claim to continuity with traditional cultural concepts is a claim made by *analysts* of such churches.

The focus on continuity dominates contemporary studies of intercultural contact and reflects a concern in anthropology, and the social sciences more generally, to stress cultural particularism, that is "the inability of people to view the world except through their received categories" (Robbins 2003b: 221). If I were to follow this school of thought, I would have to emphasize that Seventh-day Adventism in Madagascar must necessarily be an essentially different phenomenon to Seventh-day Adventism in, say, South America, Europe, the United States or Papua New Guinea. Consequently, Adventism in Madagascar would have to be analyzed and interpreted primarily through the lens of already existing cultural notions, and its attraction would have to be explained by reference to the specific social and cultural context in which it presently occurs.

However, the conclusion I have come to—that the core of the attraction of Seventh-day Adventism for people in Maroantsetra and Sahameloka is the intellectual excitement it offers—does not square well with the dominant social scientific concern with cultural particularism. To be sure, there are significant points of contact between Adventism and locally prevalent concepts and practices, such as the importance of work day taboos or the high esteem of the written word or the emphasis put on the activity of *mianatra* (studying). Following Meyer's lead (1999), one could also argue that the Adventists, rather than giving up the concept of ancestral power, merely add an extra twist, turning ancestral into Satanic power. Such interpretations and other similar ones cannot be dismissed. At the same time, the existence of specific points of contact between "the new" and "the old" does not imply that the new is but "new wine in old wineskins," neither on the conceptual nor on the practical level.

First of all, to one-sidedly highlight continuities between Adventism and local tradition would be to fail to acknowledge the radical nature of the Adventists' position within Malagasy society and the fundamental challenge they pose to traditional practice. It would be to fail to recognize what Papan' i Claude did when he refused to eat with his kin at his father's exhumation. Thus instead of joining the chorus of "continuity theory," this book is a contribution to the much needed development of an emergent "anthropology of discontinuity" (Robbins 2003b: 222).[4]

Second, to focus one's attention too much on the continuity between the old and the new would be to lose sight of what is the central concern of this book: the experience and intrinsic worth of Adventist religious activity in itself. That experience, which is characterized by the excitement of Bible study and the desire for intellectual comprehension, cannot be explained satisfactorily by reference to the particular social and cultural context in which it occurs. When trying to understand the nature of religious commitment, we have to allow for human motivations that may not be explicable by specific cultural contexts. In *The Savage Mind*, Lévi-Strauss suggests that universal "intellectual requirements" (1972: 9) are the foundation of all culture. Perhaps the pleasure the Malagasy Adventists find in the intellectual stimulation and satisfaction that Bible study offers them is an expression of the human "desire for knowledge for its own sake" (1972: 14).

Notes

Introduction

1. Note that this usage of the term "intellectualist" differs from the meaning of the same term in Maurice Bloch's preface to this book.
2. Heirich 1977: 654, Snow & Machalek 1983: 261–264, Meyer 1998: 320.
3. See the contributions in the edited volumes by Caplan (1987), Barker (1990), Hefner (1993), Marty & Appleby (1991–1995). See also Rambo's synthetic work on conversion studies exploring "the complex, multifaceted experiences *culminating* in conversion" (1993, emphasis added).
4. Among these are the five vast volumes edited by Marty and Appleby on Christian, Islamic, Jewish and other types of religious "fundamentalism" (1991–1995), Martin (1990) and Stoll (1990) on evangelicalism in Latin America, Gifford (1998) and Meyer (1999) on Pentecostalism in Africa, to name only some of the best known in a sea of publications.
5. Although I fully agree with Robbins's general emphasis on the necessity to distinguish between conversion and long-term commitment, I am not entirely convinced by the details of his two-stage model of conversion. What fails to convince me is the rigidity of the model and Robbins's suggestion that initial conversion *always* happens for (broadly under-stood) utilitarian motives. It also seems to me that there is no reason to assume that these motives are necessarily dropped at a later time.
6. For a critique of such an approach focused on defining the social profile of potential converts, see Harding's famous article on how she herself became, temporarily, "convicted by the holy spirit" (1987).
7. This is true, for example, of most of Susan Harding's excellent work on North American Baptists (especially 1991, 1992, 1994, 2000), Stoll's study of "neo-Pentecostalism" in Guatemala (1994), Gifford (1998) and Maxwell (2001) on Pentecostalism in Africa, Peacock and Pettyjohn's comparison of different leaders' life narratives (1995), as well as of a critical study of fundamentalism by the theologian Percy (1996).
8. See also Josephides on Seventh-day Adventism in Papua New Guinea (1982, unpublished Ph.D. thesis), Swanson on Evangelical Christianity in Ecuador (1994), Malley on Evangelical Biblicism in the United States (2004).

9. Although Simpson's conclusions are strikingly similar to Meyer's well-known point concerning "the complete break with the past" (1998), he does not mention her work once (both authors argue that embracing "fundamentalist" Christianity enables people to shed off what they consider their "ignorant, African past of the village" and, having been freed from that past, to embrace modernity as newly fashioned, modern Christian selves).

1 People in Search of a Living

1. This article, which was originally given as a paper at a conference in Madagascar in 1999, is reproduced (with very few changes) as chapter 2 in Larson, P.M. 2000b: 61–64.
2. For details see Grandidier, G. 1898, Decary 1935: 6–7, Deschamps 1949: 215–223, Esoavelomandroso, M. 1979: 41–48, Sylla 1985, Mangalaza 1994: chapter 2, Cole 2001: 37–39.
3. Grandidier, A. 1905: 30–41, 1907: 278–285, 1913: 52–54, Razoharinoro-Randriamboavonjy 2000.
4. Grandidier, A. 1907: 242–247, 278–285, 327–330; 1913: 52–54; Drouhard 1926, Filliot 1974: 130–132, Vérin 1986: 103–104, Ellis & Randrianja 2000: 56–58, 72–73, Larson, P.M. 2000a: 132–134, 140, Razoharinoro-Randriamboavonjy 2000: 19–21, 24, 25.

The trade in slaves from Madagascar's east coast became particularly intensified with the booming of the colonial economies in the nearby Mascarene islands (Mauritius, La Réunion) between 1770 and 1830. These lacked an indigenous population, and therefore relied on Madagascar both for labor and food in exchange for various European goods and money. Antongil Bay was one of several locations along the east coast where Malagasy and Europeans engaged in such trade (Filliot 1974: 130–132, Esoavelomandroso, M. 1979: 202–203, Larson, P.M. 2000a, Razoharinoro-Randriamboavonjy 2000). In the seventeenth and the eighteenth centuries, Antongil Bay was also a major refuge for pirates who were operating in the Indian Ocean (Grey 1933: 50–70, Decary 1935: 7–15, Deschamps 1949: 131).
5. See Deschamps 1949: 224–229, Deschamps 1960: 107–108, Petit 1967: 32, Filliot 1974: 153–158, Fanony 1975: 81, Vérin 1986: 122–130. According to the historical sources cited in Vérin (1986: 122–130), especially Froberville (1845), the Malagasy fleet—which consisted of groups from the east and the west coast of the island cooperating in a joint endeavor—was up to 18,000 men strong crossing the sea in as many as 500 massive outrigger canoes at a time. Upon their arrival in the Comoro Islands and on the eastern African shore, they captured great numbers of slaves whom they later sold to European traders. These raids are reported to have been disastrous for the invaded towns and villages. Although Antongil Bay did not play a central role in these expeditions, its population was clearly involved in them. Fanony studying

his home village a hundred kilometers south of Maroantsetra collected oral history confirming such slave raids to the Comoro islands and even east Africa (Fanony 1975: 80–81).

6. See Shepherd 1980, Campbell 1984, Mosca 2000, Larson, P. M. 2000a.

7. See Bloch 1980, Shepherd 1980, Feeley-Harnik 1982, Ellis, S. 1985, Domenichini-Ramiaramanana 1999.

8. The Zafindrabay were probably a sub-group of the Zafinifotsy dynasty (Lambek 2002: 78), one of a number of powerful Sakalava kingdoms, which emerged in western Madagascar in the seventeenth and the eighteenth centuries.

9. For details on the Zafindrabay in the Maroantsetra area see Petit 1966, 1967, also Pont 1930.

10. Pont 1930 also makes this point. Feeley-Harnik (1991: 262) encountered almost identical collective memories concerning a Zafinifotsy ruler among her informants in Analalava which is very close to the region where the Zafindrabay probably originated from (the Sambirano river to the south of Ambanja [Petit 1966: 29]).

11. In the 1770s, a bizarre figure turned up in Maroantsetra: Baron de Benyowsky, a Hungarian count of Polish origin who fantasized about gaining power over large parts of Madagascar in the name of the French king; Maroantsetra was the centre of his imaginary power. His importance, however, was more a product of his imagination than reality, and his memory has sunk into oblivion even among the most educated local people (see Benyowsky 1772, 1904, Ellis, W. 1848: 64–92, Simyan 1933, Sicard 1981).

12. See Dandouau and Chapus 1936: 87–93, Petit 1967: 34–35, Esoavelomandroso, M. 1979: 48–54.

13. The following information is based on various types of reports by colonial administrators in Maroantsetra which are kept in the colonial archives in Aix-en-Provence (Centre des archives d'outre-mer, CAOM). The relevant documents are: MAD ggm 2D/150 (1901–1906), 2D/151 (1917–1930), 2D/154 (1905–1953), 6(14)D6 (1903–1916).

14. See CAOM ggm 2D/154, Tronchon 1986: 46, 50, 64. Rabemananjara left his home village at the age of fourteen to study in Madagascar's capital (for a sketch of his biography see Tronchon 1986: 211–212).

15. See Cachin 1867; Monographies de la Sous-Préfécture de Maroantsetra 1950–1970, Archives Nationales, Antananarivo.

16. Unpublished statistics provided by the local Ministry of Population.

17. 95.5% of the district population is registered as Betsimisaraka, the "ethnic group" which occupies much of the east coast including the district of Maroantsetra (unpublished statistics provided by the Ministry of Population in Maroantsetra for 1997). Unfortunately, there were no separate statistics available concerning Maroantsetra town only, or detailing the number of Antimaroa, that is Betsimisaraka from the district of Maroantsetra. Thus some of the people registered as Betsimisaraka may be migrants from other places along the east coast.

18. In 1997 the migrant groups were, in numerically descending order: a large number of Tsimihety from nearby areas (4,600 out of a total of 6,700 migrants), and much smaller numbers of Antaimoro, Sainte-Mariens, Merina, Betsileo, Makoa, Malagasy-Indians, Malagasy-Chinese, Comorians and French. The Malagasy-Indians have been present in the area since 1902, the Malagasy-Chinese since 1908 (Petit 1964: 44). The strong presence of the Tsimihety has been noted since at least 1923 (Poirier 1923). The following other migrant groups were also already present in 1923: Merina, Antaimoro, Makoa, Sihanaka, Saint-Mariens, Anjouanais (Poirier 1923: 145).

19. In 1997, 94 Malagasy-Indians lived in the district of Maroantsetra, 46 Malagasy-Chinese, 382 Merina and 16 French people. Almost all of these lived in town.

20. To be correct, an eighth one has recently been founded by a man who split from his ancestry because of a disagreement over family property. This newly created ancestry, however, only consists of a handful of people who live around one small yard.

21. Some of the younger couples who have founded new households in the last few years had to move away from the traditional locality of their ancestry within the village due to lack of space to build new houses there. They now live in a newly settled area on the outskirts of the village called "The *second* new settlement" (Antanambao faharoa) where members of the village's different ancestries mix, but where, at the same time, an ancestry-based settlement pattern is developing.

22. Like other Betsimisaraka (Cole 2001: 93) and other Malagasy groups (Astuti 1995), people in the area of Maroantsetra say that everyone has "eight ancestors" (*valo razana*), four on one's mother's side, four on one's father's.

23. Cole's informants used the expression "The father's foot is stronger (*tongo-dray mahery*)" (Cole 2001: 71).

24. According to Petit (1967: 29, 37), Sahameloka already existed as a village during Zafindrabay times. Unfortunately, Petit does not tell us how he obtained the information he provides. However, it contradicts the oral history I was able to gather in Sahameloka.

25. On the expression *mitady* (present form of *nitady*) in talk of migration see Feeley-Harnik 1991: 243.

26. *Ólo talôha mangalatra zaza, zaza angalariñy eto ambidy amin'ólo any. Fandrinesako azy nangalariñ' ólo i razam-benay akao io, nambidin' ólo akao. Izy tônga teo dia teo fô, tômbo teo, namelon-teña teo izy, tamaña teo izy. Fô tany niavian' izy io any tsy haiky eky ay! Avy lavitry [. . .] Ambidy any Nandrasana, ólo tao no nividy azy.*

27. See Feeley-Harnik 1982: 37 on the Malagasy expression *very* (lost) as referring to slavery.

28. Brown (2004) reports an even more frank and seemingly unproblematic admission of slave ancestry from the other side of the Masoala peninsula.

29. I don't find the "hygiene explanation" convincing though, because after someone's remains have been exhumed and put to rest inside a stone sarcophagus, there is no more danger of pollution. The permission to take the ancestors back to the villages in the forest is, it seems to me, more likely to do with the change of political regime that was occurring in Madagascar at the time.
30. Bloch 1994b, Rasolofomanantsoa 1997, Graeber 1997, Evers 1999, 2002, Rabearimanana 2000.
31. Freeman's ethnography of the northern Betsileo confirms the general situation descendants of slaves find themselves in (2001: 117, 128–130, 143, 159–161).
32. It is interesting to note that, already in the 1930s, Zafindrabay sarcophagi and those of "ordinary" ancestries looked exactly the same (Pont 1930, Decary 1939).

2 Christianity and Seventh-Day Adventism in Madagascar

1. For details on the history of Christianity in Madagascar in the nineteenth century see Ellis, W. 1848, Lovett 1899, Raison-Jourde 1991, Hübsch 1993.
2. For details see in particular Raison-Jourde 1991, 1995, Hübsch 1993.
3. http://news.bbc.co.uk/1/hi/world/africa/1866530.stm
4. For analyses of the political crisis, see *Politique Africaine*, No. 86, June 2002.
5. Lupo 1985, Raison-Jourde 1991: 668–669, Hübsch 1993a: 499.
6. See LMS reports 1901–1930, Hardyman 1948, Lupo 1985, on the Anglicans: Razafiarivony 1999.
7. Ellis, W. 1848: 132, 143, LMS report 1882: 91–92.
8. But see Lupo 1997 for an overview of Christianity in the southwestern province of Tulear.
9. Of the national population, 51% are Christians. The Protestant and Lutheran church together have 5 million members, the Catholic church 3 million members; 400,000 people are Anglicans (Jacquier Dubourdieu 2002: 72).
10. See, e.g., Bloch 1994b, 1995b, Emoff 2002.
11. In the introduction to the above mentioned special issues of JRA, Karen Middleton (who works in the deep south of the country where Christianity is indeed not relevant) laments the absence of contributions on both Christianity and Islam. She goes on to stress that "The case of Islam is particularly intriguing, for while Islam remains overt religious practice only in some regions and some communities [in the northwest and southeast of Madagascar], Islamic culture taken more broadly has had a lasting and pervasive historical impact throughout the island" (1999b: 236). It seems strange to me that Christianity should be less intriguing, as it is more widely present as a practiced religion than Islam.

12. Perhaps it is to be understood as a parallel development that anthropology's main contribution to the study of Christianity in Oceania has been detailed ethnographic research about millenarian movements, and especially cargo cults (see Barker 1990a: 8, Forman 1990: 27).

13. Meyer (1999: 231) notes that some AICs are moving in the direction of the New Churches in terms of worship and doctrine.

14. Meyer also notes for Ghana that in the 1970s, the AICs' syncretism swapped over to some of the mission churches who began to integrate into their church services traditional elements such as African music, drumming and dancing. This may be one reason why those who do not appreciate such syncretism leave the mainline churches in order to join one of the New Churches where the Africanization of Christianity is taboo (Meyer 1999: 122–28).

15. See *Madagascar, Églises instituées et Nouveaux Groupements Religieux.* Antananarivo: Institut Catholique de Madagascar. Collection ISTA, no. 7.

16. Schoffeleers 1985, van Dijk 1997, special issue of Journal of Religion in Africa 1998, vol. 28 (3), Meyer 1999, Simpson 1998, 2003 (for a review of this literature see Robbins 2003b).

17. For details on his life and prophecies, see Knight 1993 (in particular chapters 2 and 3), Vance 1999: 14–22.

18. This date was the result of complicated calculations based on the Book of Daniel and the Book of Revelation (for details see Hoekema 1963: 90–94, Nyaundi 1997: 15–19, Vance 1999: 18–27).

19. On Ellen G. White see Hoekema 1963: 96–98, Knight 1993: 300–303, Vance 1999: 22–25, 42–44. Several publications have been devoted to her life and work, among them Numbers 1976 on her work as a health reformer. For a bibliography of her voluminous writings, see Hoekema 1963: 424–425.

20. For the development of this doctrine, see Hoekema 1963: 95–96.

21. Statistical information is available on the website of the international Seventh-day Adventist church. See http://www.adventist.org

22. Steley 1990 on the whole Pacific region. On Papua New Guinea: Josephides 1982, Chowning 1990, Jebens 1995, Westermark 1998. On Pacific Islands: Ross 1978, Miyazaki 2000.

23. A notable exception to the dominant utilitarian interpretations is Lewellen's study of Seventh-day Adventism in Peru (1979).

24. For details on the mission in Africa see Pfeiffer 1985, Owusu-Mensa 1993, Nyaundi 1997.

25. The number of Adventists in eastern Africa in 2003 in numerically descending order: Rwanda: 4.7% (the high number of Adventists does not seem to be related to the genocide of 1994), Zambia: 4%, Zimbabwe: 3%, Malawi: 2%, Angola: 1.8%, Kenya: 1.6%, Botswana: 1.4%, Burundi: 1%.

26. In a recent monograph of a Catholic mission school in Zambia—where, however, the majority of the students are not Catholics, but belong to various "fundamentalist" groups, including the Seventh-day Adventist

church—Simpson argues that students come to the school because of its reputation for outstanding exam results (2003, also 1998). A good education is thought to turn these, mainly male, students into modern, civilized gentlemen. Freed from their ignorant African past of the villages they can now succeed in modern, urban Zambia. Embracing "fundamentalism" is thought to perfect this process. Submission to the Catholic Brothers' rigid discipline is accepted by the students of all religious affiliations in view of the promised transformation of each individual's personality and the improved chances of success in postcolonial Zambia. Yet, many of the students also try to escape "the panoptic gaze" of this "total institution" by becoming involved in the activities of the "counter-Christianities,"—the Born Agains and the Adventists,—which take place away from the Brothers' gaze within the school compound. This is once again an argument, which suggests that people embrace (fundamentalist) Christianity because of expectations of social and material upward mobility. Poewe (1978) provides a comparison between Seventh-day Adventists and Jehovah's Witnesses. Dixon-Fyle (1978) documents the Zambian Adventists' significant involvement in, and contribution to, anticolonial consciousness and protest. Besides this general scarcity of social scientific studies on Seventh-day Adventism in Africa, there are a number of publications by members of the Seventh-day Adventist church documenting Adventist history in particular African countries that provide much useful information (see Pfeiffer 1985 on the contributions of the Adventist church to the development of several east African countries, Owusa-Mensa 1993 on the history of Adventism among the Akan people of Ghana, Nyaundi 1997 for an analysis of Kenyan Adventism, and Höschele 2004 on the history of Seventh-day Adventism in Tanzania).

27. According to my informants, one is allowed, for example, to wash a sick person's sheets if necessary, to buy medicine and even to miss a Sabbath service in order to visit a friend in hospital.

28. Rabearimanana 1993: 389, Centre des archives d'outre-mer (CAOM), Sous-série Affaires Politiques, MAD ggm 6(4)D51.

29. Cf. Gerber 1950: 182, Rabearimanana 1993: 389.

30. For the early history of Seventh-day Adventism in Madagascar, see Gerber 1950: 182–184.

31. Seventh-day Adventist schools enjoy a very good reputation, and not just among Adventists. One Muslim family from Maroantsetra sent their children to the Adventist school in Antananarivo, because of its good academic reputation and because of the conveniently overlapping Adventist and Muslim dietary taboos (alcohol, pork).

32. Centre des archives d'outre-mer (CAOM), Sous-série Affaires Politiques, MAD ggm 6(4)D51; 6(4)D58.

33. Centre des archives d'outre-mer (CAOM), Sous-série Affaires Politiques, MAD ggm 6(4)D48. What is kept in the colonial archives is unlikely to be the complete survey. In particular the information on

the central province around the capital is very fragmentary. The figures for the central province of Imerina are not detailed in the reports of any of the missions. The LMS, the French Protestants, and the Anglicans, however, state their overall number of members including Imerina. In this survey, the LMS claimed a total of 203,176 converts, the French Protestants (MPF) 229,356, the Anglicans 25,000. The Catholics claimed 147,258 (not including Imerina) and the Norwegian Lutherans (who mainly worked in the south of the country) 63,833.

34. It is unclear exactly how many Adventists there were. The colonial statistics report 610 members, a number which, however, does not include the central province on which there is no information. Gerber, an Adventist himself, notes 466 church members for the whole country in 1940 (1950: 184).

35. *Rakelimalaza* is a famous talisman in central Madagascar where it has great symbolic and political significance (see Ellis, S. 1985).

36. http://www.adventistyearbook.org

37. 33,000 live in the central and eastern provinces of Antananarivo and Toamasina ("Central Malagasy Conference"), 29,000 belong to the "North Malagasy Mission" (including the provinces of Mahajanga and Antsiranana), while only 11,000 live in the provinces of Toliara and Fort-Dauphin in the south.

38. *Tantara ny nidiran'ny finoana katolika teto Maroantsetra* (The history of the arrival of the Catholic faith here in Maroantsetra).

39. Centre des archives d'outre-mer (CAOM), Sous-série Rapports périodiques des circonscriptions administratives, MAD ggm 2D 150. Quote from 1906.

40. The Protestants built their first church in Maroantsetra in 1913 (Monografie de la Sous-Préfécture de Maroantsetra 1953), and the LMS Ten Years' Report of 1911–1920 mentions the presence of two of its missionaries in town.

41. Monografies de la Sous-Préfécture de Maroantsetra 1950–1970.

42. Unpublished statistics provided by the Ministry of Population in Maroantsetra. No statistics are available between 1970 and 1997.

43. The first Anglican church in Maroantsetra was built in 1929, but the number of Anglicans has always remained very small. In 1997, there were half as many registered Anglicans as Seventh-day Adventists, but in contrast to the latter, the Anglicans were hardly noticeable in town (Monographies de la Sous-Préfécture de Maroantsetra, 1953; and unpublished statistics provided by the local Ministry of Population).

44. Jesosy Mamonjy (see Walsh 2002 on Jesosy Mamonjy in another area of Madagascar), Fiangonana Pantekôtista and Ara-Pilazantsara.

45. The Ara-Pilazantsara started to work in Maroantsetra in 1983 and at the time of fieldwork had 700 members in the district (personal communication with the local pastor of Ara-Pilazantsara, who, however, tended to exaggerate the impact of his church). The Jehovah's

Witnesses arrived in 1988 and numbered only 60 members (personal communication with the elder of Jehovah's Witnesses [there was no pastor]). I am not certain of the exact date of arrival of Jesosy Mamonjy and the Fiangonana Pantekôtista. But Jesosy Mamonjy, an offshoot of the biggest international Pentecostal organization, the Assembly of God, only began to work in Madagascar in the early 1960s (Jacquier Dubourdieu 1997), the Fiangonana Pantekôtista in 1970 (Ramino 1993: 422). Their membership numbers probably lie somewhere in between the mere 60 of the Jehovah's Witnesses and the alleged 700 of Ara-Pilazantsara. The Seventh-day Adventist church is the only one of these five New Churches whose membership was recorded in the 1998 statistics of the local Ministry of Population.

46. In the Toamasina region, including the port of Toamasina, 208 out of 253 Adventists were Merina; in Maroantsetra, the highlanders numbered just 65 out of a total of 177 local Adventists.

47. In 1998, 107 people were baptized as Seventh-day Adventists, and in 1999 at least 250.

48. *Faneva Advantista* 1999:17–18, and personal communication with the pastor in Maroantsetra.

49. http://www.pcusa.org/missionconnections/letters/turkd_0203.htm. Also see Jacquier Dubourdieu 2002: 70–71. For a photograph of *mpiandry* consult http://www.thelutheran.org/0205/page47.html

3   International and Local Structure of the Adventist Church

1. For details see Vance 1999, chapter 3. Or consult the website of the General Conference of Seventh-day Adventists (http://www.Adventist.org/worldchurch).

2. The district of Maroantsetra counts 47 Adventist congregations including such informal groups.

3. Since I am not a baptized member of the Adventist church, I was not allowed to attend these meetings. Thus the information given here is based on what I have been told. See also Vance 1999: 59–60.

4. The strong participation of lay people has been noted by many writers on different religious movements classified as "fundamentalist" (see e.g. Martin 1990: 292, Maxwell 1998a: 257, Corten 1999: 25, 127, 135). Concerning Seventh-day Adventism: Hoekema 1963: 5, Kessler 1967: 226, 242, Josephides 1982: 145–154, Westermark 1998: 56.

5. The decision as to who is going to lead on a particular day depends on people volunteering and the pastor or the committee selecting people and assigning them particular duties such as to read a passage from the Bible.

6. While in Sahameloka people felt that a lay leader ought to be a married person (*ôlo mitôndra trano*, literally: a person who has their own household), this was not the case in Maroantsetra, where there were unmarried lay leaders.
7. Because of the sensitivity of the question of slave descent, Rakoto is a pseudonym.
8. See e.g. Coleman 1992: 75, Marty 1992: 20, Percy 1996: 166.
9. Whenever I taped conversations from which I quote, I provide the transcriptions in Malagasy. Where there is no transcription, the quotations are based on my fieldnotes.
10. *Ny andro Alahady, raha zahana amin' ny baiboly akô, raha foronin' olombelona fô ny andro Alahady fô tsy Andriamanitra namoro azy. Amin' ny boky akô, hita fô, Sabata hatrany hatrany ny andron' ny Tompo hoy izy, fa zahay no nañôvana ny Alahady misolo ny Sabata. Nañôvan-jare Monsenera sonia tamin' ny taono trois cents vingt et un.*
11. This does not rule out the possibility of the global or regional headquarters of the Seventh-day Adventist church issuing a particular opinion or guideline on any given issue.

4 Profiles

1. Pfeiffer tells us that Seventh-day Adventists all over Africa are predominantly young (1985: 9). Gifford (1994: 516) has noted the same with regard to New Churches in Africa.
2. In what follows and for the rest of this book, I will use teknonyms to refer to people. In the area of Maroantsetra, as elsewhere in Madagascar, the use of teknonyms is common practice. There is no local rule as to which child a teknonym should refer to, whether, for example, it should refer to a boy or a girl, or to the youngest or the oldest child. Indeed, often one person is called by different teknonyms. Thus Papan' i Beby—Beby's dad—is sometimes called Papan' i Kiki—Kiki's dad—depending on who is addressing him.
3. Boys and girls inherit equally. If, for example, Mazava marries somebody from a nearby village, as indeed is likely, she and her own family will work the fields she inherited from her parents themselves. If she moves to a place beyond walking distance to Sahameloka, one of her brothers will cultivate her land and they will work out a sharecropping arrangement.
4. These names are pseudonyms.
5. Since his patrilineal ancestry originates from elsewhere, the tomb is located within the "burial ground of immigrants/guests" (*ny fasam-bahiny*) in Maroantsetra from where many ancestors' bones are taken back to their place of origin (*tanindrazana*) after exhumation.
6. *Hivavaka ndreky izaho hoy izaho, ake mizaha ny fandehany; izy ka mbôla tahaka ny teo koa izy, zaho mandandaña enin' ahy, midôko fô. Fa izy ka hitako misy fiovany ny anahy, zaho manaraka ity fô.*

5 Bible Study

1. I quote: "The adult Sabbath School Bible Study Guide is prepared by the Sabbath School/Personal Ministries department of the General Conference of Seventh-day Adventists. The preparation of the guides is under the general direction of a world-wide Sabbath School Manuscript Evaluation Committee, the members of which serve as consulting editors. The published guide reflects the input of the committee and thus does not solely or necessarily represent the intent of the authors" (see any Bible Study Guide, contents page).

2. These and more examples to follow are taken from the Adult Sabbath School Bible Study Guide of October–December 1999.

3. All bold and italic passages in the original.

4. Seventh-day Adventists around the globe use a variety of Bible versions. Church members in Madagascar use the standard Protestant Bible.

5. Strictly speaking, Friday evening is already part of the Sabbath since for Seventh-day Adventists, the day ends with the sunset. But in order to avoid confusion, I will use the term Sabbath to refer to Saturdays in what follows.

6. Different *moniteurs* are chosen every week in the course of a meeting of the local church committee on Friday evening. Any adult member can act as *moniteur*.

7. Compare Robbins 1998 for a strikingly similar claim among Baptists in Papua New Guinea.

8. The following extract is based on a transcription focusing on content rather than linguistic professionality.

9. The style of discussion bears a certain resemblance to traditional oratory styles for which the Malagasy are famous (see Bloch 1975, Keenan 1975, Cole 2001: 181–185).

10. At one point during my stay in Maroantsetra, Kiki refused to eat bread on the Sabbath (which I tended to buy every morning for the whole family for breakfast) because it had been *bought*, i.e., it had involved the handling of money. The rest of the family laughed and called him a *fondamentaliste* and warned him of the danger of fanaticism. A few months later, during which time everyone had been eating bread on Saturday mornings except for Kiki, his mother and father suddenly came to the conclusion that Kiki was in fact right and from then on, nobody ate any bread on the Sabbath anymore.

11. *Mianatra* also means to imitate or copy ("apprendre, étudier, imiter, contrefaire," Abinal & Malzac 1993: 37). When Beby, for example, copies biblical verses in her notebook decorating the page with flowers, she might *mianatra* in the sense of copying. However, in the great majority of situations it is the aspect of study in the sense of intellectual engagement that is being emphasized.

12. See Levine 1995: 162 on Latin America; Gifford 1998: 78, 169 and Meyer 1999: 135–136 on Africa, Miyazaki 2000: 34–35 on Fiji.

6 Knowledge of the Bible and Scientific Inquiry

1. In his recent publication about the nature of Evangelical Biblicism among the members of a Baptist church in the United States, Malley distinguishes between "belief traditions" and "interpretive traditions." The crucial difference between them is that, while a belief tradition emphasizes the importance of *believing* certain propositions, in the interpretive tradition, beliefs must be *justified by reference to a sacred text* (Malley 2004: 79–80). As my informants' contempt for local Catholics and Protestants who "just believe" makes clear, Seventh-day Adventism, like other forms of "fundamentalist" or "evangelical" Christianity, belongs to the interpretive tradition.

2. *Talôha zeny nivavaka tamin' ny FJKM tao zaho. Tsy dia lasa nahomby tsara be le fianarana nataoko tamin' ny le Soratra Masina . . . tamin'ny FJKM tao. Hitako tsara be fô tamin'ny Advantista, tena . . . nañambara tsara be mikasika an' Andriamanitra. Zeny le tena nahatafiditra zaho tamin' ny Advantista. Tena le ampy tsara be le fianarana! Tena le mianatra! Rehefa nandeha tatô, mianatra (drawn out and hightened to stress) tatô eh! Satria hianatra ny tenin' Andriamanitra, hianatra ny momban' Andriamanitra, zeny le dikany andehanana am-piangonana.*

3. *Rehefa mandinika Soratra Masina aty izaho, isaka mahita ny teny tsy fantatro . . . , satria misy teny tsy fantatro izy reo ao nazavaina na . . . Ôhatra, mikasika ny Sabata tsy fantatro, tamin' izaho mbóla Protestanta. Rehefa nanontany le pastera Protestanta izaho, misy intelo vao izy nanapa-kevitra fô: "Mandehana amin'ny Advantista ianao fa ry zareo mahay manazava ny momba ity," hoy izy. Indray andro, nandeha izahay, nahita ny pastera Advantista zahay. Nametraka fanontaniana maro maro ao amin'ny Soratra Masina izahay. Misy 15 fanontaniana napetranay tamin'azy. Dia voavaliny ara-tSoratra Masina!*

4. *Izahay voalohany zeny, Katolika. Kanefa, amin' ny Katolika akao, tsy fatra-pandinika baiboly loatra, milaza fô "Marina ny fivavahana Katolika." Zeny fô.*

5. An interesting topic for further research would be the local Adventists' perception of what exactly the Bible is, with regard to such issues as translation (for a detailed analysis of this question, see Malley 2004: chapter 2).

6. It has long been recognized that "fundamentalists" are not opposed to science, but rather attempt to validate religious truth on scientific grounds (Caplan 1987a: 11–12, Marty & Appleby 1992: 31–33, Mendelsohn 1993, Moore 1993, Tibi 1993. For an excellent account of Creation Science, see Numbers 1992. Numbers himself is a scientist with a Seventh-day Adventist background and upbringing, who later denounced Adventism. He is nevertheless wary of the science/religion dichotomy and continues to take the creationist argument seriously.) However, existing research on the incorporation of science into fundamentalist religions (through the use of high tech media for instance) has focused entirely on the level of leadership and public rhetoric.

7. The use of imported concepts such as *la nature* is interesting with regard to questions of globalization through Adventism. At the same time though, one must not assume that what the pastor meant necessarily corresponds to the concept of nature as expressed in the French term *la nature*.

8. Price was the chief Creationist authority in the famous Scopes (Monkey) Trial (Spuhler 1985: 108) which dealt with the "evolution versus creation" debate in the United States in the 1920s (for details see Larson, E. J. 1997, also Harding 1991). For an overview of creationist history and theory see Numbers 1992, Noll 1994; for an interesting contribution discussing, from a cognitive point of view, the reasons why creationism is so successful, see Evans 2000.

9. Overlaps of doctrine include the Second Coming of Christ and the end of death in paradise, the prominence of the fight between God and Satan and the rejection of ancestral ritual.

10. I thank Brian Malley for clarifying this part of his argument to me (personal communication).

11. This, of course, links up with a long discussion in social anthropology about the relationship between "science" and "religion."

12. Ever since the Great Disappointment of 1844, the global Seventh-day Adventist church has been careful not to give any specific date for Christ's return.

13. Those readers familiar with Malagasy history might feel that the issue of having to run and hide in the forest has to be analyzed in connection to what happened during the anticolonial insurrection in 1947, when thousands of Malagasy villagers did indeed have to run and hide in the forest (see Bloch 1995b, Cole 2001). However, the area of Maroantsetra was not directly involved in the uprising and the local population, fortunately, did not undergo the experience of having to hide in the forest for months and sometimes years as was the case elsewhere.

7 Text and Learning

1. For details see Bloch 1968 (reprinted in Bloch 1998: 131–151), Munthe 1982, Dez 1983, Rajaonarison 1994.

2. For good photographs of *Sorabe*, see Mack 1986: 35, 65.

3. Their wages consisted of a certain percentage of the retail price of the books they sold. Although a bookseller employed by the Seventh-day Adventist church is not supposed to do any other work, this rule was broken by most local booksellers simply because the job was not normally lucrative enough, especially considering that there were 12 Adventist booksellers in Maroantsetra, which was far too many in a town of its size. When they ran out of business in Maroantsetra, therefore, some of them sometimes traveled to other nearby towns to try their luck there.

4. Most of the books the Adventists sold cost around £10–18. In comparison: a civil servant or a teacher had a monthly salary of about £40.

5. Adventist booksellers are sometimes called to Madagascar's capital for instructions regarding the content of the books they sell, so that they can extol their virtues without actually having read them.

6. The Bible cost £40 with the bookseller receiving £7 of this.

7. According to UNICEF statistics available on line, about 50% of men and 44% of women are literate in Madagascar. 16% of both sexes take secondary education.

8. There were no statistics available on local levels of literacy.

9. Compare Bloch (1993b: 91–94) for a description of a day at school with Zafimaniry children.

10. But compare Lave 1988 (also Bloch 1993b) for a discussion of how poor school knowledge exists side by side with elaborate knowledge in things such as mathematical calculation outside the context of the school.

11. In certain very isolated areas, one might hear people refer to other Malagasy, in particular the Merina, as *vazaha* (Maurice Bloch, personal communication). In the area of Maroantsetra though, this is not the case.

12. Poewe 1978: 309, 316, Pfeiffer 1985, Chowning 1990: 35–36, Martin 1990: 75–76, 87, 207, Nyaundi 1997: 78–84, 248, Westermark 1998: 60 and footnote 17. In Lewellen's analysis of Adventism in the Lake Titicaca region, access to education also plays a pivotal role (1978, 1979). But in contrast to the rest of the literature, he does not suggest that people value education primarily for instrumental reasons.

13. There are exceptions to this, like my host family in Maroantsetra for whom the education of their children has always been, and still is, their primary concern. They are prepared to make significant financial sacrifices in order to send both their son and their daughter to good schools outside of Maroantsetra.

14. It may seem to an outside observer that the kind of scientific knowledge I discussed in chapter 6—knowledge of particular fossil finds, astronomical data—is typical school knowledge. However, from the perspective of Adventist practitioners, who see themselves involved in a process of discovering truth, knowledge of fossil finds is not merely information about geology, but it is primarily thought of as proof within a process of critical investigation.

15. Dictionary entries read: mahay = "savoir, connaître; pouvoir, pouvoir faire, être capable, être compétent, fréquenter, savoir gouverner, savoir conduire" (Abinal & Malzac 1993: 205). Or: mahay = "savoir, connaître, compétent" (Rajaonarimanana 1995: 132).

16. See Freeman 2001 for a beautifully written discussion of the difference, yet also intimate interrelatedness, of *fahaizana* (outsiders' knowledge), on the one hand, and *fomba* (ancestral tradition), on the other, among the northern Betsileo.

17. For the same phenomenon in other parts of Madagascar, compare Bloch 1994a [1971]: 30–32, Cole 2001: 221–222, Freeman 2001: 211–215.

18. *Tsaboin' ny olombelona? Tsaboin' i Zanahary, tsy zeny?*

8   The Great Controversy

1. When the Seventh-day Adventists in Maroantsetra and Sahameloka speak of God, they use the expressions Andriamanitra, Zanahary and Jehovah interchangeably.

2. This was one of two mass baptisms that happened during my stay in Madagascar. Normally, only between two and perhaps 15 people would be baptized at any one time.

3. Baptism is the only time when the creed is spoken by church members; the creed is not part of a normal Seventh-day Adventist church service.

4. Denise's baptism involved the only two instances of exorcism I witnessed among the local Adventists. In contrast to the Revival movement within the Lutheran and the Protestant churches in Madagascar (*Fifohazana*) and to the praxis among Pentecostal groups, exorcism is not normally part of Adventist religious activities.

5. *Fa sekren' Andriamanitra jiaby hainy. Tsy mihinana ôraña Advantista, tsy mihinana fôza Advantista. Nalain' i Satana anie izy io e! Nalainy le raha satria, ny antony nangalany azy dia tsotra: Fantany zeny, le raha mbô mifanarakaraka amin' Andriamanitra kôa, mbô nalainy izy io, nataony. Matetika anie misy ôlo takatra maladie de foie, tsy mahazo mihinana inona izy, hoy i doketera? Tsy mahazo mihinana fôza izy, tsy mahazo mihinana ôraña izy, satria mampitombo ny aretiny. Fantatr' i Satana kôa raha zay! Fa tsy mahasoa ainantsika, ino? Ny fôza ndraiky ny ôraña. Tsy mahasoa, tsy mahatsara antsika, dia tsy azo hohanina. Ary zeny mahatônga ôlo tena mino azy, mino azy tan-teraka! Ary le fôza sy ny ôraña efa fantatr' i Satana fô, izy tany an-danitra, dia tsy azo hohanina.*

6. *Ataovy tsipiky tranon' andre, tsipihiny i le tranon' azy. Tamin' ny zanak' Israely niboaka avy tany Ejypta, ino ny zavatra nitranga? Ataovy mariky, ny tranonare. Satria nihinana ondry zeny zareo, dia koa lafa lany, hoy izy, ataovy mariky, isaka varavaranan' andre, mbô tsy hidirana reo. Satria handeha hamono ôlo zeny zareo tamin' io andro io. Hamono le talañolon-draha jiaby amin' ny tanàna io. Karahan' izeny koa. Ny anazy mañano marika amin' ny anazy. Mbôra, izy koa efa mandalo akeo ny anjelin' azy, mahita fa ity ny anahy. Ka lafa nan-dalo teto ny anjelin' Andriamanitry, nanakory? Hitan' le mariky ny zanak' Israely.*

7. The Adventist concept of God as a man contrasts with the indigenous Malagasy notion of a creator-force called *Zanahary*, who is perceived to be both female and male. The Adventist concept of the morality of

God and the immorality of Satan also stands in contrast to the concept of *Zanahary* in that *Zanahary* is "not associated with a moral purpose" (Bloch 1995a: 67).

8. The Adventist conceptualization of God and Satan as (im)moral persons corresponds well with Boyer's theory of the naturalness of religion (1994). According to Boyer, religious entities are basically like humans in that they are guided by human intentions—in that sense they are not bizarre, but perfectly natural. However, they are not entirely like humans, because they have certain superhuman abilities such as being everywhere at the same time (putting mildew on my book and making the clove price grow and . . .) or being omniscient.

9. *Karaha ôlo torana zaho, karaha ôlo nandry. . . . nifôha. Izy mbôla mandry afindra amin' ny toeran-kafa, tonga eo izy sao mifôha.*

9   The Construction and Rejection of Ancestral Religion

1. See, e.g., Bloch 1994a [1971], Fanony 1975, Feeley-Harnik 1991, Astuti 1995, Graeber 1995, Middleton 1999a, Cole 2001, Evers 2002, Lambek 2002.

2. Feeley-Harnik (1984), however, has argued that the preoccupation of the Sakalava of western Madagascar with their ancestors may in fact be a rather recent phenomenon (only going back some 150 years) that developed as a reaction against Merina rule and, later on, colonial policies. Feeley-Harnik suggests that the only way the Sakalava kings were able to survive in the face of the loss of their political power as living rulers, was by going "underground," as it were, and ruling their subjects as ancestors. See also Woolley 2002 for a study, which emphasizes that not everywhere in Madagascar are the ancestors the *only* fertility-creating power.

3. In the local dialect, exhumation is called *fañôkoaraña, tsaboraha* or *tsaboasa. Fanôkoaraña* is derived from the word *akarina*, which means to bring up something (the ancestral bones in this case), *tsaboraha* literally means "to perform things," *tsaboasa* "to perform work."

4. *Hazovato* can be made of either wood (*hazo*) or cement (*vato* = stone) with the choice between these materials largely depending on a family's financial means. Most *hazovato* are small and contain the bones of only one or two ancestors. Some, however, are so large that it takes some 30 men to lift their lid. In these cases, the ancestral bones of women are piled up on top of each other on one side, those of men on the other. The two piles are separated by a cement wall running the whole length along the middle.

5. The translation in the Protestant Bible that the Malagasy Adventists use is: *Fa fantatry ny velona fa ho faty izy; fa ny maty kosa tsy mba mahalala na inona na inona, ary tsy manana valimpitia intsony izy; fa hadino ny fahatsiarovana azy. Na ny fitiavany, na ny fankahalany,*

na ny fialonany, dia samy efa levona ela sady tsy manana anjara intsony mandrakizay amin' izay atao aty ambanin' ny masoandro izy.

6. *Tamin' ny zeny, nifandray tañana. Nangatsiaka (drawn out to stress) tañan' anazy! Izy tsy nahazo zahany, satria andro maiziny, tsy azo atao raha ôhatra mazava le andro, andro ho aliny, andro maiziny, zay mañantso azy. Afaka fandray mañano io (gesture). Fô izy mangatsiaka (drawn out) le tañan' anazy![. . .]Ie, reny, ie! Tamin' ny zeny, toaka zeny, alefa mañano io (gesture), apetraka, mañano io iny (gesture). Reny izy malaka azy. Reny izy "cho! cho! cho! cho!." Izy migiaka toaka io. Ia, reny izy migiaka toaka io. Izy avy akeo, raha ôhatra lasa izy iny, mahita i cho, cho-be' anazy, hôatr' i . . . (gesture) fôña lany. Fô le tavela amin' ny zeny, tsy mahery, lasa le fofon' ny toaka le mampahery azy.*

7. *Ny tenin' Andriamanitra hoe, tsy le razana miteny, fô le devoly misandoko le Andriamanitra izy miteny. Le devoly rehefa naidina ambony ny tany aty, io mbô haka voninahitry manôkana, hisolo Andriamanitra. Ke raha ôhatra tsy mino zeny anteña, milaza fô, le razana maty miteny. Fa raha mino ny tenin' Andriamanitra anteña hoe, i le devoly izy malaka le feo le ôlo. Zeny arakaraka ny fahaizako azy. Ke rehefa nodinihiko ny Soratra Masina, marina izeny, hoy izaho. Ny maty, hoy izaho, tokony tsy afaka hiteny. Fô le devoly, rafin' Andriamanitra avy tany mbô halaka voninahitra manôkana izy, malaka safidy tendan' ôlo jiaby, ary izy mahefa mankarary le ôlo. Rehefa marary le ôlo, voafitaka amin' zeny, le ôlo hoe, milaza fa, manankery ny razana e! Kanefa izy avy akeo manome aomby azy, izy nankarary iny, ambelany ke sitrana le ôlo. Ke milaza anteña fô, eh, misy antony tatô ny razana fô, i tsaboraha ka vita koa, naivana e! Zeny le fihevitran' le olom-belona. Sitrana, satria i devoly nanery anteña iny nankarary le ôlo. Ke izy koa nahazo ny aombin' azy izy, tsy hitany le ôlo, fa ambelany, satria nanaraka azy.*

8. See in particular Meyer 1999, but also Taussig 1980, Harding 1994: 62, Lehmann 1996: 139–142. Regarding Seventh-day Adventism, see Josephides 1982: 141–142, Chowning 1990: 49, 53, Westermark 1998.

9. *Mino* stems from the linguistic root *ino*, which means: the action of agreeing, of submitting unconditionally, of declaring oneself convinced and persuaded; of believing, of accepting the verities of faith (my translation of: "Action d'acquiescer, de se soumettre sans réserve, de se déclarer convaincu et persuadé; de croire, d'admettre les vérités de la foi" [Abinal & Malzac 1993: 281]).

10 Clarity

1. *Mazava* stems from the root *zava*, which denotes light, clarity, transparence, purity ("lumière, clarté, transparence, netteté"; Abinal & Malzac 1993: 869).

2. This is also how the purpose of the millennium is described in Adventist publications. It is interesting that this point in the official doctrine is well known among local Adventists, while other aspects have failed to attract attention.
3. E.g., Worsley 1970: 22, Bozeman 1997: 140, Robbins and Palmer 1997: 9.
4. See Spuhler 1985, Caplan 1987a: 11–12, Mendelsohn 1993, Moore 1993, Tibi 1993.
5. The verb *mino* and the related noun *finoana* stem from the linguistic root *ino*: "Action d'acquiescer, de se soumettre sans réserve, de se déclarer convaincu et persuadé; de croire, d'admettre les vérités de la foi" (Abinal & Malzac 1993: 281).

11 Making Choices

1. The importance of economic benefit is stressed by Ross (1978: 195), Steley (1990: 124–129), Stoll (1990: 103) and Westermark (1998: 56, 61–62).
2. See Cole (2001: 109–113) on keeping *fady* as a performative act of remembering one's ancestors.
3. In Sahameloka and Maroantsetra, many people do not know exactly how old they are. The birth of a child is not usually remembered with reference to a calender year, but to particular events ("she was born when we drained the lake") or other people's life stages ("he was born when his brother could already walk"). Thus baptism is often based on an estimation of someone's age. In any case, the globally relevant Church Manual does not clearly stipulate any particular age.
4. The Adventist church has its own wedding ceremony, which, however, is very unspectacular involving little more than the pastor's blessing of the couple.
5. On the social significance of land in Madagascar see Bloch 1994a [1971], Cole 1997: 411, Evers 2002, Woolley 2002.
6. In the area of Maroantsetra, children who do not have any teeth yet are not considered full persons, and if they die are disposed of with the minimum of attention (on Malagasy personhood, cf. Bloch 1993a). In the past, such "water children" (*zaza rano*) used to be wrapped in cloth and then left exposed to the elements at the top of a tree at some distance from human habitation. However, some years ago, this practice was made illegal by the Malagasy government, so that nowadays, "water children" are buried, but with no ceremony and without a coffin, and with no intention of exhuming their bones later on. While news of the death of a "full person" spreads very rapidly causing everyone to rush home in order to quickly visit the bereaved family, the death of a "water child" is often discovered by those outside the immediate family only after it has been buried.

12 Kinship

1. In his analysis of their aggressive behavior, Walsh focuses on the salvationist *ethos* of Jesus Saves Christians. My hunch, however, is that their conduct had a lot to do with the fact that these people were migrants and complete strangers to the place and the people they offended so badly. Jesus Saves Christians are also present in Maroantsetra, but I never heard of them violating local rules of social conduct.

2. Other studies of Seventh-day Adventism convey an extremely varied picture concerning the social integration, and segregation, respectively, of Adventists around the world. While some studies speak of the spatial segregation of Seventh-day Adventists (Ross 1978: 196 [Solomon Islands], Chowning 1990: 38 [Papua New Guinea], Nyaundi 1997: 251 [Kenya]), which, I assume, implies at least a certain degree of social segregation as well, Westermark (1987: 117 [Papua New Guinea]) emphasizes that "church members do not live in isolation from non-Christians or the members of other churches." Lewellen's work on Adventists in Peru in the 1970s (1978, 1979) suggests a similar pattern. Josephides's account (1982) concerns a context in Papua New Guinea in which almost the entire community has converted to Seventh-day Adventism. In such a situation, many problems on the social level do, of course, not arise.

3. The Malagasy version reads: *Raha misy manaraka Ahy ka tsy manka-hala ny rainy sy ny reniny sy ny vadiny sy ny zanany sy ny rahalahiny sy ny anabaviny, eny, ary ny ainy koa aza, dia tsy azo ekena ho mpianatro izy.*

4. On one occasion, the brother-in-law of the Adventist pastor in Maroantsetra went to Toamasina for a couple of months. Not only is he the brother-in-law of a still practicing pastor, but he is also the son of a retired Adventist pastor. Nevertheless, he stayed with distant non-Adventist kin rather than, say, another pastor in town.

5. Ritual practices relating to the ancestors are somewhat different in the region where Maman' and Papan' i Beby come from to those performed in Maroantsetra. In particular, exhumation is not practiced.

6. This incident was not linked to witchcraft by anybody. Eating out in a restaurant, he had been served a poisonous tuber, which grows among potatoes, and which is apparently almost indistinguishable from them.

7. The terms of address among Adventists are *rahalahy, rahavavy, anadahy, anabavy*. *Raha* indicates that the persons concerned are of the same sex, *ana* indicates the opposite (*rahalahy* = brother of a male EGO, *anadahy* = brother of a female EGO, *rahavavy* = sister of a female EGO, *anabavy* = sister of a male EGO).

8. Among the Merina, who in contrast to the Betsimisaraka, form strongly endogamous groups, "artificial" kin marry each other, which in their case is a confirmation that their relationship is indeed one of kinship and, at the same time, has the effect of turning "artificial kin" into real *havana*, from the next generation onward.

9. The only exception I am familiar with is the case of Papan' i Fredel in Sahameloka. Since he was a heavy drinker before joining the church and would have ruined his family had he gone on wasting the little money they had on drink, his non-Adventist relatives were clearly in favor of his church affiliation because he mastered alcoholism as a result.

Conclusions

1. The issue here is not how this sense of national unity came about historically. The point I want to make is simply that, at least in the area of Maroantsetra, such a sense of national unity does exist—despite the strongly felt antagonism between highlanders and *côtiers*—and that it is based on the notion that all Malagasy follow their own *fomban-drazana*.

2. *Mañano fomban-drazana ny Malagasy, tsy mañano fomban-drazana ny Advantista. Mino ny razana ny Malagasy, tsy mino ny razana ny Advantista.*

3. Although in his introduction to the volume "Conversion to Christianity" (Hefner 1993a), Hefner warns against the pendulum swinging too much to the particularist side (see quote), the contributions to the volume almost invariably emphasize the aspect of compatibility and indigenization.

4. One of Robbins's (2004) key points is that the *initial* attraction of a new religion—the first stage of conversion—is indeed always related to a specific cultural context and specific desires within that context (this is the sense in which he uses the word "utilitarian"). However, as this study of Seventh-day Adventism in Madagascar examines *post-conversion* commitment (Robbins's second stage of conversion), our respective approaches are not contradictory.

Bibliography

Abinal & Malzac 1993 (1888). *Dictionnaire Malgache-Francais*. Fianarantsoa [Ambozontany].

Ammerman, N. T. 1994. Accounting for Christian Fundamentalisms: Social dynamics and rhetorical strategies. In: M. E. Marty & R. S. Appleby (eds.) *Accounting for Fundamentalisms* (The Fundamentalism Project, volume 4). Chicago and London: The University of Chicago Press.

Asad, T. 1993. The construction of religion as an anthropological category. In: *Genealogies of Religion. Discipline and Reasons of Power in Christianity and Islam*. Baltimore and London: The Johns Hopkins University Press.

Astuti, R. 1995. *People of the Sea. Identity and Descent among the Vezo of Madagascar*. Cambridge: Cambridge University Press.

——— 2000. Kindreds and descent groups: New perspectives from Madagascar. In: J. Carsten (ed.) *Cultures of Relatedness. New Approaches to the Study of Kinship*. Cambridge: Cambridge University Press.

Ault, J. 1987. Family and fundamentalism: The Shawmut Baptist Church. In: J. Obelkevich, L. Roper, & R. Samuel (eds.) *Disciplines of Faith. Studies in Religion, Politics and Patriarchy*. London and New York: Routledge & Kegan Paul.

Barker, J. (ed.) 1990. *Christianity in Oceania. Ethnographic Perspectives*. ASAO Monograph no. 12. Lanham, New York, London: University Press of America.

Barker, J. 1990a. Introduction: Ethnographic perspectives on Christianity in Oceanic Societies. In: J. Barker (ed.) *Christianity in Oceania. Ethnographic Perspectives*. ASAO Monograph no. 12. Lanham, New York, London: University Press of America.

——— 1990b. Afterword. In: J. Barker (ed.) *Christianity in Oceania. Ethnographic Perspectives*. ASAO Monograph no. 12. Lanham, New York, London: University Press of America.

Benyowsky, M. A. 1772. *Protocolle du Regiment des Volontaires de Benyowsky*. British Library ADD (manuscripts) 188844.

——— 1904. *Memoirs and Travels of Mauritius Augustus Benyowsky*. London: Kegan Paul.

Bloch, M. 1968. Astrology and writing in Madagascar. In: J. Goody (ed.) *Literacy in Traditional Society*. Cambridge: Cambridge University Press.

——— 1971. The implications of marriage rules and descent: Categories for Merina social structures. *American Anthropologist*, 73 (1):164–178.

——— 1973. The long term and the short term: The economic and political significance of the morality of kinship. In: J. Goody (ed.) *The Character of Kinship*. Cambridge: Cambridge University Press.

——— 1975. Introduction. In: M. Bloch (ed.) *Political Language and Oratory in Traditional Society*. London, New York, San Francisco: Academic Press.

——— 1980. Modes of production and slavery in Madagascar: Two case studies. In: J. Watson (ed.) *Asian and African Systems of Slavery*. Oxford: Blackwell.

——— 1985. Questions historiques concernant la parenté sur la côte est. *Omaly sy Anio*, 21–22: 49–56.

——— 1986. *From Blessing to Violence. History and Ideology in the Circumcision Ritual of the Merina of Madagascar*. Cambridge: Cambridge University Press.

——— 1987. Descent and sources of contradiction in representations of women and kinship. In: J. F. Collier & S. J. Yanagisako (eds.) *Gender and Kinship. Essays Towards a Unified Analysis*. Stanford: Stanford University Press.

——— 1989a. *Ritual, History and Power. Selected Papers in Anthropology*. LSE Monographs on Social Anthropology no. 58. London: The Athlone Press.

——— 1989b. Literacy and enlightenment. In: K. Schousboe & M. T. Larsen (eds.) *Literacy and Society*. Copenhagen: Akademisk Forlag.

——— 1992. What goes without saying. The conceptualization of Zafimaniry society. In: A. Kuper (ed.) *Conceptualizing Society*. London: Routledge and Kegan Paul.

——— 1993a. Zafimaniry birth and kinship theory. *Social Anthropology* 1 (1B): 119–132.

——— 1993b. The uses of schooling and literacy in a Zafimaniry village. In: B. Street (ed.) *Cross-cultural Approaches to Literacy*. Cambridge Studies in Oral and Literate Culture. Cambridge: Cambridge University Press.

——— 1994a (1971). *Placing the Dead. Tombs, Ancestral Villages, and Kinship Organization in Madagascar*. Prospect Heights, Illinois: Waveland Press.

——— 1994b. The slaves, the king, and Mary in the slums of Antananarivo. In: N. Thomas & C. Humphrey (eds.) *Shamanism, History, and the State*. Ann Arbor: The University of Michigan Press.

——— 1995a. People into places: Zafimaniry concepts of clarity. In: E. Hirsch & M. O'Hanlon (eds.) *The Anthropology of Landscape. Perspectives on Place and Space*. Oxford: Clarendon Press.

——— 1995b. The resurrection of the house amongst the Zafimaniry of Madagascar. In: J. Carsten & S. Hugh-Jones (eds.) *About the House. Lévi-Strauss and Beyond*. Cambridge: Cambridge University Press.

——— 1998. *How We Think They Think. Anthropological Approaches to Cognition, Memory, and Literacy*. Boulder (Colorado): Westview Press.

Bloch, M. 2002. Are religious beliefs counter-intuitive? In: N. Frankenberry (ed.) *Radical Interpretations of Religion*. Cambridge: Cambridge University Press.

Boyer, P. 1994. *The Naturalness of Religious Ideas: A Cognitive Theory of Religion*. Berkeley: University of California Press.

Bozeman, J. M. 1997. Technological millenarianism in the United States. In: T. Robbins & S. Palmer (eds.) *Millennium, Messiahs, and Mayhem. Contemporary Apocalyptic Movements*. London and New York: Routledge.

Brown, M. 2004. Reclaiming lost ancestors and acknowledging slave descent: insights from Madagascar. *Comparative Studies of Society and History*, 46 (3): 616–645.

Bruce, S. 2000. *Fundamentalism*. Cambridge: Polity Press.

Cachin, M. 1867. Journal d'exploration du district de Marantsetra. In: Baron de Richemont, *Documents sur la Compagnie de Madagascar*. Paris.

Campbell, G. 1984. Madagascar and the slave trade (1810–1895). *Omaly sy Anio*, 17–20 (1983–1984): 279–309.

Caplan, L. (ed.) 1987. *Studies in Religious Fundamentalism*. Basingstoke: Macmillan.

Caplan, L. 1987a. Introduction. In: L. Caplan (ed.) *Studies in Religious Fundamentalism*. Basingstoke: Macmillan.

Chowning, A. 1990. God and ghosts in Kove. In: J. Barker (ed.) *Christianity in Oceania. Ethnographic Perspectives*. ASAO Monograph no. 12. Lanham, New York, London: University Press of America.

Cole, J. 1997. Sacrifice, narratives and experience in east Madagascar. *Journal of Religion in Africa*, 27 (4): 401–425.

——— 1998. The work of memory in Madagascar. *American Ethnologist*, 25 (4): 610–633.

——— 2001. *Forget Colonialism? Sacrifice and the Art of Memory in Madagascar*. Berkeley, Los Angeles, London: University of California Press.

Coleman, J. 1992. Catholic integralism as a fundamentalism. In: L. Kaplan, (ed.) *Fundamentalism in Comparative Perspective*. Amherst: The University of Massachusetts Press.

Comaroff, J. 1985. *Body of Power, Spirit of Resistance. The Culture and History of a South African People*. Chicago and London: The University of Chicago Press.

Comaroff, J. & Comaroff, J. 1991. *Of Revelation and Revolution, vol. 1. Christianity, Colonialism, and Consciousness in South Africa*. Chicago and London: The University of Chicago Press.

——— 1997. *Of Revelation and Revolution, vol. 2. Dialectics of Modernity on a South African Frontier*. Chicago and London: The University of Chicago Press.

Corten, A. 1999. *Pentecostalism in Brazil: Emotion of the Poor and Theological Romanticism*. Basingstoke: Macmillan, New York: St. Martin's Press.

Dandouau, A. & Chapus, G. S. 1936. Histoire des tribus de Madagascar. In: *Bulletin Officiel de la Direction de l'Enseignement*. Tananarive: Imprimerie Officielle.

Decary, R. 1935. *La piraterie à Madagascar. Contribution à l'étude du passé malgache.* Tananarive.

—— 1939. Sépultures chez les Betsimisaraka du Nord (Madagascar). In: *Bulletin de la Société d'Anthropologie de Paris,* 47–50.

Deschamps, H. 1949. *Les pirates à Madagascar.* Paris: Berger-Levrault.

—— 1959. *Les migrations intérieures passées et présentes à Madagascar.* Paris: Éditions Berger-Levrault.

—— 1960. *Histoire de Madagascar.* Paris: Éditions Berger-Levrault.

Dez, J. 1983. Le temps et le pouvoir. L'usage du calendrier divinatoire antaimoro. In: F. Raison-Jourde (ed.) *Les souverains de Madagascar.* Paris: Karthala.

Dixon-Fyle, M. 1978. The Seventh Day Adventists (S.D.A.) in the protest politics of the Tonga plateau, Northern Rhodesia. *African Social Research,* 26: 453–467.

Domenichini-Ramiaramanana, B. 1999. *Sujétion royale et sujétion privée. Quelques aspects à Mananjary sous Ranavalona 1re.* Paper presented at the Colloque International sur "L'Esclavage et la traite sur la côte orientale de Madagascar." Tamatave, September 20–22, 1999.

Drouhard, M. E. 1926. Inscriptions relevées sur les rochers de l'île Nossi Mangabe, Baie d'Antongil. *Bulletin de l'Academie Malgache,* 91–96.

Ellis, S. 1985. *The Rising of the Red Shawls. A Revolt in Madagascar 1895–1899.* Cambridge: Cambridge University Press.

Ellis, W. 1848. *History of Madagascar,* volume 2. London, Paris: Fisher, Son & Co.

Ellis, S. & Randrianja, S. 2000. Les archives de la compagnie néerlandaise des Indes Orientales et l'histoire de Madagascar. L'expédition du navire de la V.O.C. le Schuylenberg, September 1752. In: I. Rakoto (ed.) *La route des esclaves. Système servile et traite dans l'est malgache.* Actes du Colloque International de Toamasina (September 20–22, 1999). Paris, Montréal, Budapest, Torino: L'Harmattan.

Emoff, R. 2002. *Recollecting from the Past. Musical Practice and Spirit Possession on the East Coast of Madagascar.* Middletown, Connecticut: Wesleyan University Press.

Engelke, M. 2003. The Book, the Church and the "Incomprehensible Paradox": Christianity in African History (Review Article). *Journal of Southern African Studies,* 29 (1): 297–306.

—— 2004. Text and performance in an African church: The Book, "live and direct." *Amercian Ethnologist,* 31 (1): 76–91.

Esoavelomandroso, F. 1993. Apogée de l'action missionnaire (1914–1939). In: B. Hübsch (ed.) *Madagascar et le christianisme.* Paris: Karthala, ACCT; Antananarivo: Editions Ambozontany.

Esoavelomandroso, M. 1979. *La province maritime orientale du "Royaume de Madagascar" à la fin du XIXe siècle (1882–1895).* Antananarivo: FTM.

Evans, M. E. 2000. Beyond Scopes. Why creationism is here to stay. In: K. S. Rosengren et al. (eds.) *Imagining the Impossible. Magical, Scientific, and Religious Thinking in Children*. Cambridge: Cambridge University Press.

Evans-Pritchard, E. E. 1937. *Witchcraft, Oracles, and Magic among the Azande*. Oxford: Clarendon Press.

Evers, S. 1999. The construction of history and culture in the southern high lands: tombs, slaves and ancestors. In: K. Middleton (ed.) *Ancestors, Power and History in Madagascar*. Leiden, Boston, Köln: Brill.

——— 2002. *Constructing History, Culture and Inequality: The Betsileo in the Extreme Southern Highlands of Madagascar*. Leiden, Boston, Köln: Brill.

Fanony, F. 1975. *Fasina. Dynamisme social et recours à la tradition*. Antananarivo: Musée d'Art et d'Archéologie de l'Université de Madagascar. Travaux et Documents XIV.

Feeley-Harnik, G. 1982. The King's men in Madagascar. Slavery, citizenship and Sakalava monarchy. *Africa*, 52 (2): 31–50.

——— 1984. The political economy of death: Communication and change in Malagasy colonial history. *American Ethnologist*, 11: 1–19.

——— 1991. *A Green Estate. Restoring Independence in Madagascar*. Washington and London: Smithsonian Institution Press.

Filliot, J.-H. 1974. *La traite des esclaves vers les Mascareignes au XVIIIe siècle*. Paris: ORSTOM (Mémoires ORSTOM No. 72).

Forman, C. W. 1990. Some next steps in the study of Pacific Island Christianity. In: J. Barker (ed.) *Christianity in Oceania. Ethnographic Perspectives*. ASAO Monograph no. 12. Lanham, New York, London: University Press of America.

Freeman, L. E. 2001. *Knowledge, Education and Social Differentiation amongst the Betsileo of Fisakana, Highland Madagascar*. Unpublished Ph.D. thesis, University of London.

Gerber, R. 1950. *Le mouvement Adventiste. Origines et développement*. Dammarie-lès-Lys: Editions Les Signes des Temps.

Gifford, P. 1994. Some recent developments in African Christianity. *African Affairs*, 93: 513–534.

——— 1998. *African Christianity. Its Public Role*. London: Hurst.

Gow, B. A. [n.d]. *The Attitude of the British Protestant Missionaries towards the Malagasy Peoples, 1861–1895*. Nairobi: East African Literature Bureau.

Graeber, D. 1995. Dancing with corpses reconsidered: An interpretation of *famadihana* (in Arivonimamo, Madagascar). *American Ethnologist*, 22 (2): 258–278.

——— 1997. Painful memories. *Journal of Religion in Africa*, 27 (4): 374–400.

——— 2001. *Towards an Anthropological Theory of Value*. New York and Houndmills: Palgrave.

Grandidier, A. 1903–1920. *Collection des ouvrages anciens concernant Madagascar*. Paris, Comité de Madagascar: Imprimerie Paul Brodard.

——— 1905. *Collection des ouvrages anciens concernant Madagascar*. Tome III. Paris, Comité de Madagascar: Imprimerie Paul Brodard.

Grandidier, A. 1907. *Collection des ouvrages anciens concernant Madagascar.* Tome V. Paris, Comité de Madagascar: Imprimerie Paul Brodard.

——— 1913. *Collection des ouvrages anciens concernant Madagascar.* Tome VIII. Paris, Comité de Madagascar: Imprimerie Paul Brodard.

Grandidier, G. 1898. *Histoire de la fondation du Royaume Betsimisaraka.* Extrait du Bulletin du Comité de Madagascar. Paris: Challamel.

Grey, C. 1933. *Pirates of the Eastern Seas (1618–1723). A Lurid Page of History.* London: Sampson Low, Marston & Co.

Harding, S. 1987. Convicted by the holy spirit: The rhetoric of fundamentalist Baptist conversion. *American Ethnologist,* 14 (1): 167–182.

——— 1991. Representing fundamentalism: The problem of the repugnant cultural other. *Social Research,* 58 (2): 375–393.

——— 1992. The gospel of giving: The narrative construction of a sacrificial economy. In: R. Wuthnow (ed.) *Vocabularies of Public Life. Empirical Essays in Symbolic Structure.* London, New York: Routledge.

——— 1994. Imagining the last days: The politics of apocalyptic language. In: M. E. Marty & R. S. Appleby (eds.) *Accounting for Fundamentalisms* (The Fundamentalism Project, volume 4). Chicago and London: The University of Chicago Press.

——— 2000. *The Book of Jerry Falwell. Fundamentalist Language and Politics.* Princeton and Oxford: Princeton University Press.

Hardyman, J. T. 1948. *Among the Betsimisaraka.* Antananarivo: LMS.

Hastings, A. 1990. Christianity in Africa. In: U. King (ed.) *Turning Points in Religious Studies: Essays in Honour of Geoffrey Parrinder.* Edinburgh: T & T Clark.

——— 2000. African Christian studies, 1967–1999: Reflections of an editor. *Journal of Religion in Africa,* 30 (1): 30–44.

Hefner, R. W. (ed.) 1993. *Conversion to Christianity. Historical and Anthropological Perspectives on a Great Transformation.* Berkeley, Los Angeles, Oxford: University of California Press.

Hefner, R. W. 1993a. World building and the rationality of conversion. In: R. W. Hefner (ed.) *Conversion to Christianity. Historical and Anthropological Perspectives on a Great Transformation.* Berkeley, Los Angeles, Oxford: University of California Press.

——— 1993b. Of faith and commitment: Christian conversion in Muslim Java. In: R. W. Hefner (ed.) *Conversion to Christianity. Historical and Anthropological Perspectives on a Great Transformation.* Berkeley, Los Angeles, Oxford: University of California Press.

Heirich, M. 1977. Change of heart: A test of some widely held theories about religious conversion. *American Journal of Sociology,* 83 (3): 653–680.

Hoekema, A. A. 1963. *The Four Major Cults. Christian Science, Jehovah's Witnesses, Mormonism, Seventh-day Adventism.* Grand Rapids, Michigan: William B. Eerdmans Publishing Company.

Höschele, S. 2004. *Christian Remnant—African Folk Church. The History of Seventh-day Adventism in Tanzania, 1903–1980.* Unpublished Ph.D. thesis, University of Malawi.

Holt, J. 1969. *How Children Fail.* Harmondsworth: Penguin.

Hübsch, B. (ed.) 1993. *Madagascar et le christianisme*. Paris: Karthala, ACCT; Antananarivo: Editions Ambozontany.

Hübsch, B. 1993a. Madagascar et le christianisme (vue d'ensemble). In: B. Hübsch (ed.) *Madagascar et le christianisme*. Paris: Karthala, ACCT; Antananarivo: Editions Ambozontany.

Jacquier Dubourdieu, L. 1997. *Le rôle des mouvements évangéliques dans le réaménagement des sociétés, des espaces et des pouvoirs urbains. Le cas de Tananarive*. Paper presented at SISR (Société Internationale de Sociologie des Religions), Toulouse, July 7–11, 1997.

——— 2002. De la guérison des corps à la guérison de la nation. Réveil et mouvements évangéliques à l'assaut de l'espace public. *Politique Africaine*, 86: 70–85.

Jebens, H. 1995. *Wege zum Himmel. Katholiken, Siebenten-Tags-Adventisten und der Einfluss der traditionellen Religion in Pairudu, Southern Highlands Province, Papua New Guinea*. Bonn: Holos.

Josephides, S. 1982. *The Perception of the Past and the Notion of "Business" in a Seventh Day Adventist Village in Madang, New Guinea*. Unpublished Ph.D. thesis, University of London.

Keenan, E. 1975. A sliding sense of obligatoriness. In: M. Bloch (ed.) *Political Language and Oratory in Traditional Society*. London, New York, San Francisco: Academic Press.

Kessler, J. B. A. 1967. *A Study of the Older Protestant Missions and Churches in Peru and Chile. With Special Reference to the Problems of Division, Nationalism and Native Ministry*. Ph.D. thesis, University of Utrecht. Goes: Oosterbaan and Le Cointre N. V.

Knight, G. R. 1993. *Millennial Fever and the End of the World: A Study of Millerite Adventism*. Boise, Idaho: Pacific Press.

Kopytoff, I. 1997 (1968). Ancestors as elders in Africa. In: R. R. Grinker & C. B. Steiner (eds.) *Perspectives on Africa. A Reader in Culture, History, and Representation*. Oxford: Blackwell.

Kottak, C. P. 1980. *The Past in the Present. History, Ecology, and Cultural Variation in Highland Madagascar*. Ann Arbor: The University of Michigan Press.

Kuhn, T. S. 1996 (1962). *The Structure of Scientific Revolutions*. Chicago: University of Chicago Press.

Lambek, M. 1981. *Human Spirits: A Cultural Account of Trance in Mayotte*. Cambridge: Cambridge University Press.

——— 1992a. Taboo as cultural practice among Malagasy speakers. *Man* (N.S.), 27: 245–266.

——— 1992b. Motherhood and other careers in Mayotte. In: V. Kerns & J. K. Brown (eds.) *In Her Prime: A New View of Middle-Aged Women*. Urbana: University of Illinois Press.

——— 1993. *Knowledge and Practice in Mayotte. Local Discourses of Islam, Sorcery, and Spirit Possession*. Toronto, Buffalo, London: University of Toronto Press.

——— 1995. Choking on the Quran. And other consuming parables from the western Indian Ocean front. In: W. James (ed.) *The Pursuit of*

Certainty. Religious and Cultural Formulations. London, New York: Routledge.

——— 2002. The Weight of the Past. Living with History in Mahajanga, Madagascar. New York and Houndmills: Palgrave macmillan.

Larson, E. J. 1997. Summer for the Gods. The Scopes Trial and America's Continuing Debate over Science and Religion. New York: Basic Books.

Larson, P. M. 2000a. The route of the slave from highland Madagascar to the Mascarenes: commercial organization, 1770–1820. In: I. Rakoto (ed.) La Route des Esclaves. Système Servile et Traite Dans l'est Malgache. Actes du Colloque International de Toamasina (September 20–22, 1999). Paris, Montréal, Budapest, Torino: L'Harmattan.

——— 2000b. History and Memory in the Age of Enslavement. Becoming Merina in Highland Madagascar, 1770–1822. Portsmouth, NH: Heinemann; Oxford: James Currey; Cape Town: David Philip.

Lave, J. 1988. Cognition in Practice. Cambridge: Cambridge University Press.

Lehmann, D. 1996. Struggle for the Spirit. Religious Transformation and Popular Culture in Brazil and Latin America. Cambridge: Polity Press.

——— 1998. Fundamentalism and globalism. Third World Quarterly, 19 (4): 607–634.

Lévi-Strauss, C. 1972. The Savage Mind. Oxford: Oxford University Press.

Levine, D. H. 1995. Protestants and Catholics in Latin America: A family portrait. In: M. E. Marty & R. S. Appleby (eds.) Fundamentalisms Comprehended (The Fundamentalism Project, volume 5). Chicago and London: The University of Chicago Press.

Lewellen, T. C. 1978. Peasants in Transition: The Changing Economy of the Peruvian Aymara: A General Systems Approach. Boulder: Westview Press.

——— 1979. Deviant religion and cultural evolution: The Aymara Case. Journal for the Scientific Study of Religion, 18 (3): 243–251.

LMS Reports 1876, 1881–1890, 1882, 1888, 1889, 1890, 1891, 1901–1910, 1911–1920, 1921–1930. Tananarive: LMS Press.

Lovett, R. 1899. The History of the London Missionary Society, 1795–1895. London: Henry Frowdl. Vol. 1, 673–802.

Lupo, P. 1985. Tamatave et la mission catholique à la fin du XIXè siècle. Omaly sy Anio, 21–22: 197–215.

——— 1997. Ancêtres et Christ. Un siècle d'évangélisation dans le sud-ouest de Madagascar, 1897–1997. Fianarantsoa: Ambozontany.

MAC (Meeting for African Collaboration) 1993. New Christian Movements in Africa and Madagascar. Catholic International, 4 (1): 28–36.

Mack, J. 1986. Madagascar: Island of the Ancestors. London: British Museum.

Malley, B. 2004. How the Bible Works. An Anthropological Study of Evangelical Biblicism. Walnut Creek, Lanham, New York, Toronto, Oxford: Altamira Press.

Mangalaza, E. R. 1994. La poule de Dieu. Essai d'anthropologie philosophique chez les Betsimisaraka (Madagascar). Bordeaux: Les Presses Universitaires de Bordeaux.

Martin, D. 1990. *Tongues of Fire: The Explosion of Protestantism in Latin America*. Oxford: Basil Blackwell.

Marty, M. 1992. Fundamentals of fundamentalism. In: L. Kaplan (ed.) *Fundamentalism in Comparative Perspective*. Amherst: The University of Massachusetts Press.

Marty, M. E. & Appleby, R. S. 1992. *The Glory and the Power. The Fundamentalist Challenge to the Modern World*. Boston: Beacon Press.

Marty, M. E. & Appleby, R. S. (eds.) 1991. *Fundamentalisms Observed* (The Fundamentalism Project, volume 1). Chicago and London: The University of Chicago Press.

—— 1993a. *Fundamentalisms and Society. Reclaiming the Sciences, the Family, and Education* (The Fundamentalism Project, volume 2). Chicago, London: The University of Chicago Press.

—— 1993b. *Fundamentalisms and the State. Remaking Politics, Economics, and Militance* (The Fundamentalism Project, volume 3). Chicago and London: The University of Chicago Press.

—— 1994. *Accounting for Fundamentalisms* (The Fundamentalism Project, volume 4). Chicago and London: The University of Chicago Press.

—— 1995. *Fundamentalisms Comprehended* (The Fundamentalism Project, volume 5). Chicago and London: The University of Chicago Press.

Maxwell, D. 1998a. Editorial. *Journal of Religion in Africa*, 28 (3): 255–257.

—— 1998b. "Delivered from the spirit of poverty?": Pentecostalism, prosperity and modernity in Zimbabwe. *Journal of Religion in Africa*, 28 (3): 350–373.

—— 2001. "Sacred history, social history": Traditions and texts in the making of a Southern African transnational religious movement. *Comparative Studies in Society and History*, 43 (3): 502–524.

Mendelsohn, E. 1993. Religious fundamentalism and the sciences. In: M. E. Marty & R. S. Appleby (eds.) *Fundamentalisms and Society. Reclaiming the Sciences, the Family, and Education*. Chicago and London: The University of Chicago Press.

Meyer, B. 1998. "Make a complete break with the past": Memory and postcolonial modernity in Ghanaian Pentecostalist discourse. *Journal of Religion in Africa*, 28 (3): 316–349.

—— 1999. *Translating the Devil. Religion and Modernity among the Ewe in Ghana*. International African Library 21. Edinburgh: Edinburgh University Press (for the International African Institute, London).

Middleton, K. 1999a. Introduction. In: K. Middleton (ed.) *Ancestors, Power and History in Madagascar*. Leiden, Boston, Köln: Brill.

—— 1999b. Introduction (Special Volume on Religion in Madagascar). *Journal of Religion in Africa*, 27 (3): 229–238.

Miyazaki, H. 2000. Faith and its fulfillment: Agency, exchange, and the Fijian aesthetics of completion. *American Ethnologist*, 27 (1): 31–51.

Moore, J. 1993. The creationist cosmos of Protestant fundamentalism. In: M. E. Marty & R. S. Appleby (eds.) *Fundamentalisms and Society*.

Reclaiming the Sciences, the Family, and Education. Chicago and London: The University of Chicago Press.

Mosca, L. 2000. La traite à Madagascar dans la seconde moitié du XVIIe siècle à la lumière de quelques documents anglo-américains. In: I. Rakoto (ed.) *La route des Esclaves. Système Servile et Traite Dans l'est Malgache.* Actes du Colloque International de Toamasina (September 20–22, 1999). Paris, Montréal, Budapest, Torino: L'Harmattan.

Munthe, L. 1982. *La tradition arabico-malgache, vue à travers de manuscript A-6 d'Oslo et d'autres manuscripts disponibles.* T.P.L.F.M.

Needham, R. 1972. *Belief, Language, and Experience.* Oxford: Blackwell.

Noll, M. A. 1994. *The Scandal of the Evangelical Mind.* Grand Rapids, Michigan: William B. Eerdmans Publishing Company.

Numbers, R. L. 1976. *Prophetess of Health: A Study of Ellen G. White.* New York: Harper and Row.

―――― 1992. *The Creationists.* New York: Alfred A. Knopf.

Nyaundi, N. M. 1997. *Seventh-Day Adventism in Gusii, Kenya.* Kendu Bay: Africa Herald Publishing House.

Ortner, S. 1984. Theory in anthropology since the sixties. *Comparative Studies in Society and History,* 26 (1): 126–166.

―――― 1995. Resistance and the problem of ethnographic refusal. *Comparative Studies in Society and History,* 7: 173–193.

Owusu-Mensa, K. 1993. *Saturday God and Adventism in Ghana.* Archives of International Adventist History. Frankfurt am Main: Peter Lang.

Parry, J. 1985. The Brahmanical tradition and the technology of the intellect. In: J. Overing (ed.) *Reason and Morality.* ASA monographs 24. London: Tavistock.

Peacock, J. L. & Pettyjohn, T. 1995. Fundamentalisms narrated: Muslim, Christian, and Mystical. In: M. E. Marty & R. S. Appleby (eds.) *Fundamentalisms Comprehended* (The Fundamentalism Project, volume 5). Chicago and London: The University of Chicago Press.

Percy, M. 1996. *Words, Wonders and Power. Understanding Contemporary Christian Fundamentalism and Revivalism.* London: Society for Promoting Christian Knowledge.

Petit, M. 1964. Un essai de colonisation dans la baie d'Antongil (1895–vers 1926). *Annales de l'Université de Madagascar,* 3: 33–56.

―――― 1966. *La plaine littorale de Maroantsetra. Étude Géographique.* Antananarivo.

―――― 1967. Les Zafirabay de la Baie D'Antongil. *Annales de l' Université de Madagascar.* Serie Lettres et Sciences Humaines, 7: 21–44.

Pfeiffer, B. E. 1985. *Seventh-day Adventist Contributions to East Africa, 1903–1983.* Frankfurt am Main: Peter Lang.

Poewe, K. O. 1978. Religion, Matriliny, and Change: Jehovah's Witnesses and Seventh-day Adventists in Luapala, Zambia. *American Ethnologist,* 5 (2): 303–321.

Poirier 1923. Chez les Betsimisaraka et les Tsimihety de Maroantsetra. *Bulletin Économique,* 1: 135–145.

Pont, M. 1930. Note sur les sépultures des Zafirabay d'Andranofotsy, Province de Maroantsetra. *Bulletin de l'Academie Malgache*, 13: 187–189.

Pouillon, J. 1982. Remarks on the verb "believe." In: M. Izard & P. Smith (eds.) *Between Belief and Transgression. Structuralist Essays in Religion, History, and Myth*. Chicago: University of Chicago Press.

Rabearimanana, L. 1993. D'un christianisme missionaire à un christianisme malgache (1940–1960). In: Hübsch, B. (ed.) *Madagascar et le christianisme*. Paris: Karthala, ACCT; Antananarivo: Editions Ambozontany.

———— 2000. L'esclavage et ses séquelles actuelles à Ambohimanga-Antsihanaka. In: I. Rakoto (ed.) *La Route des Esclaves. Système Servile et Traite Dans l'est Malgache*. Actes du Colloque International de Toamasina (September 20–22, 1999). Paris, Montréal, Budapest, Torino: L'Harmattan.

Rafael, V. L. 1993 (1988). *Contracting Colonialism. Translation and Christian Conversion in Tagalog Society under Early Spanish Rule*. Durham and London: Duke University Press.

Raison, F. 1974. L'acculturation par l'Ecriture Sainte à Madagascar (Imerina). Une religion de l'écriture dans une civilisation orale. In: J. Le Brun (ed.) *Histoire de texte. Recherche sur la place de livre dans le christianisme*. Paris: Université de Paris.

Raison-Jourde, F. 1991. *Bible et pouvoir à Madagascar au XIXe siècle. Invention d'une identité chrétienne et construction de l'État (1780–1880)*. Paris: Karthala.

———— 1995. The Madagascan churches in the political arena and their contribution to the change of regime 1990–1993. In: P. Gifford (ed.) *The Christian Churches and the Democratisation of Africa*. Studies of Religion in Africa, XII. Leiden, New York, Köln: E. J. Brill.

Rajaonarimanana, N. 1995. *Dictionnaire du Malgache Contemporain*. Paris: Karthala.

Rajaonarison, E. 1994. "Mamandraka," "graver le livre": Ecrit, histoire et pouvoir chez les Antemoro. *Omaly sy Anio*, 33–36: 133–145.

Rakotozafy, M. 1997. L'expérience des Mpiandry ches les FLM. In: *Madagascar, Églises Instituées et Nouveaux Groupements Religieux*. Institut Catholique de Madagascar. Antananarivo.

Rambo, L. R. 1993. *Understanding Religious Conversion*. New Haven, London: Yale University Press.

Ramino, P. 1993. Les églises chrétiennes après 1960 (1960–1990). In: B. Hübsch (ed.) *Madagascar et le christianisme*. Paris: Karthala, ACCT; Antananarivo: Editions Ambozontany.

Rasolofomanantsoa, O. 1997. L'ésclavage à Madagascar. Aspects historiques et résurgences contemporaines. *Actes du Colloque International sur l'Esclavage*. Antananarivo: Institut de Civilisations, Musée d'Art et d'Archéologie.

Razafiarivony, M. 1999. *Les missions britanniques et l'esclavage (sur la côte est)*. Paper presented at the Colloque International sur "L'Esclavage et la traite sur la côte orientale de Madagascar." Tamatave, September 20–22, 1999.

Razoharinoro-Randriamboavonjy 2000. Sources de l'histoire de la traite des esclaves sur la côte orientale de Madagascar. In: I. Rakoto (ed.) *La Route des Esclaves. Système Servile et Traite Dans l'est Malgache.* Actes du Colloque International de Toamasina (September 20–22, 1999). Paris, Montréal, Budapest, Torino: L'Harmattan.

Robbins, J. 1998. On reading "World News": Apocalyptic narrative, negative nationalism and transnational Christianity in a Papua New Guinea society. *Social Analysis,* 42 (2): 103–130.

——— 2001a. God is nothing but talk: modernity, language, and prayer in a Papua New Guinea Society. *American Anthropologist,* 103 (4): 901–912.

——— 2001b. Whatever became of Revival? From charismatic movement to charismatic church in a Papua New Guinea society. *Journal of Ritual Studies,* 15 (2): 79–90.

——— 2001c. Secrecy and the sense of an ending: narrative, time, and everyday millenarianism in Papua New Guinea and in Christian fundamentalism. *Comparative Studies in Society and History,* 43 (3): 525–551.

——— 2003a. What is a Christian? Notes toward an anthropology of Christianity. *Religion,* 33: 191–199.

——— 2003b. On the paradoxes of global Pentecostalism and the perils of continuity thinking. *Religion,* 33: 221–231.

——— 2004. *Becoming Sinners: Christianity and Moral Torment in a Papua New Guinean Society.* Berkeley, Los Angeles, London: University of California Press.

Robbins, T. & Palmer, S. J. 1997. Introduction. In: T. Robbins & S. J. Palmer (eds.) *Millennium, Messiahs, and Mayhem. Contemporary Apocalyptic Movements.* London, New York: Routledge.

Ross, H. M. 1978. Competition for Baegu souls: Mission rivalry on Malaita, Solomon Islands. In: J. A. Boutilier, D. T. Hughes, & S. W. Tiffany (eds.) *Mission, Church, and Sect in Oceania.* Ann Arbor: The University of Michigan Press.

Schoffeleers, M. 1985. *Pentecostalism and Neo-Traditionalism: The Religious Polarization of a Rural District in Southern Malawi.* Amsterdam: Free University Press.

Sharp, L. 1993. *The Possessed and the Dispossessed. Spirits, Identity, and Power in a Madagascar Migrant Town.* Berkeley, Los Angeles, London: University of California Press.

Shepherd G. 1980. The Comorians and the east African slave trade. In: J. Watson (ed.) *Asian and African Systems of Slavery.* Oxford: Blackwell.

Sicard, F. 1981. Benyowski. *Bulletin de l'Academie Malgache,* 59: 17–19.

Simpson, A. 1998. Memory and Becoming Chosen Other: Fundamentalist Elite-Making in a Zambian Catholic Mission School. In: R. Werbner (ed.) *Memory and the Postcolony. African Anthropology and the Critique of Power.* London, New York: Zed Books.

——— 2003. *"Half-London" in Zambia. Contested Identities in a Catholic Mission School.* Edinburgh: Edinburgh University Press (International African Library).

Simyan, J. 1933. Le passé Malgache. Le deuxième établissement tenté par le Comte de Benyowski à Madagascar. *La Revue de Madagascar*, 4: 77–92.

Snow, D. A. & Machalek, R. 1983. The convert as social type. In: R. Collins (ed.) *Sociological Theory*. San Francisco, Washington, London: Jossey-Bass Publishers.

Southall, A. 1986. Common themes in Malagasy culture. In: C. P. Kottak, J. A. Rakotoarisoa, A. Southall, & P. Vérin (eds.) *Madagascar. Society and History*. Durham: Carolina Academic Press.

Spuhler, J. N. 1985. Anthropology, evolution, and "scientific creationism." *Annual Review of Anthropology*, 14: 103–133.

Steley, D. 1990. *The Seventh-day Adventist Mission in the South Pacific, Excluding Papua New Guinea, 1886–1986*. Unpublished Ph.D. thesis, University of Auckland.

Stoll, D. 1990. *Is Latin America Turning Protestant? The Politics of Evangelical Growth*. Berkeley, Los Angeles, London: University of California Press.

———— 1994. "Jesus is Lord of Guatemala": Evangelical reform in a death-squad state. In: M. E. Marty & R. S. Appleby (eds.) *Accounting for Fundamentalisms* (The Fundamentalism Project, volume 4). Chicago and London: The University of Chicago Press.

Sundkler, B. 1961 (1948). *Bantu Prophets in South Africa*. London: Oxford University Press (for the International African Institute).

Swanson, T. D. 1994. Refusing to drink with the mountains: Traditional Andean meanings in evangelical practice. In: M. E. Marty & R. S. Appleby (eds.) *Accounting for Fundamentalisms* (The Fundamentalism Project, volume 4). Chicago and London: The University of Chicago Press.

Sylla, Y. 1985. Les Malata: Cohesion et disparité d'un "groupe." *Omaly sy Anio*, 21–22: 19–32.

Taussig, M. T. 1980. *The Devil and Commodity Fetishism in South America*. Chapel Hill: University of North Carolina Press.

Tibi, B. 1993. The worldview of Sunni Arab fundamentalists: Attitudes toward modern science and technology. In: M. E. Marty & R. S. Appleby (eds.) *Fundamentalisms and Society. Reclaiming the Sciences, the Family, and Education*. Chicago and London: The University of Chicago Press.

Tronchon, J. 1986 [1974]. *L'insurrection Malgache de 1947*. Fianarantsoa: Ambozontany, Paris: Karthala.

Urfer, S. 1993. Eglise et vie nationale. In: B. Hübsch (ed.) *Madagascar et le christianisme*. Paris: Karthala, ACCT; Antananarivo: Editions Ambozontany.

van Dijk, R. 1997. From camp to encompassment: discourses of transsubjectivity in the Ghanaian Pentecostal diaspora. *Journal of Religion in Africa*, 27 (2): 135–160.

———— 1998. Pentecostalism, cultural memory and the state: contested representations of time in Pentecostal Malawi. In: R. Werbner (ed.) *Memory and the Postcolony: African Anthropology and the Critique of Power*. London: Zed Books.

Vance, L. L. 1999. *Seventh-day Adventism in Crisis. Gender and Sectarian Change in an Emerging Religion.* Urbana and Chicago: University of Illinois Press.

Vérin, P. 1986. *The History of Civilisation in North Madagascar.* Rotterdam, Boston: A.A. Balkema.

Walsh, A. 2002. Preserving bodies, saving souls: Religious incongruity in a northern Malagasy mining town. *Journal of Religion in Africa,* 32 (3): 366–393.

Weber, M. 1920. Die protestantischen Sekten und der Geist des Kapitalismus. In: *Gesammelte Aufsaetze zur Religionssoziologie I.* Tuebingen: Mohr.

Westermark, G. 1987. Church law, court law: Competing forums in a highlands village. In: L. L. Langness & T. E. Hays (eds.) *Anthropology in the High Valleys. Essays on the New Guinean Highlands in Honor of Kenneth E. Read.* Novato (California): Chandler and Sharp.

———— 1998. History, opposition, and salvation in Agarabi Adventism. *Pacific Studies,* 21 (3): 51–71.

Wood, P. 1993. Afterword: Boundaries and horizons. In: R. W. Hefner (ed.) *Conversion to Christianity. Historical and Anthropological Perspectives on a Great Transformation.* Berkeley, Los Angeles, Oxford: University of California Press.

Woolley, O. 2002. *The Earth Shakers of Madagascar. An Anthropological Study of Authority, Fertility and Creation.* LSE monographs on Social Anthropology, volume 73. London, New York: Continuum.

Worsley, P. 1970 (1957). *The Trumpet Shall Sound.* London: Paladin.

Index

CPSIA information can be obtained at www.ICGtesting.com
Printed in the USA
242737LV00002B/3/P